Chinese Literature and Culture in the World

Series Editor
Ban Wang
Stanford University
Stanford, CA, USA

As China is becoming an important player on the world stage, Chinese literature is poised to change and reshape the overlapping, shared cultural landscapes in the world. This series publishes books that reconsider Chinese literature, culture, criticism, and aesthetics in national and international contexts. While seeking studies that place China in geopolitical tensions and historical barriers among nations, we encourage projects that engage in empathetic and learning dialogue with other national traditions. Imbued with a desire for mutual relevance and sympathy, this dialogue aspires to a modest prospect of world culture. We seek theoretically informed studies of Chinese literature, classical and modern—works capable of rendering China's classical heritage and modern accomplishments into a significant part of world culture. We promote works that cut across the modern and tradition divide and challenge the inequality and unevenness of the modern world by critiquing modernity. We look for projects that bring classical aesthetic notions to new interpretations of modern critical theory and its practice. We welcome works that register and analyze the vibrant contemporary scenes in the online forum, public sphere, and media. We encourage comparative studies that account for mutual parallels, contacts, influences, and inspirations.

More information about this series at
http://www.palgrave.com/gp/series/14891

Xiaoping Wang

Ideology and Utopia in China's New Wave Cinema

Globalization and Its Chinese Discontents

Xiaoping Wang
College of Chinese Language
  and Culture
Huaqiao University, Xiamen Campus
Xiamen, Fujian, China

Chinese Literature and Culture in the World
ISBN 978-3-319-91139-7   ISBN 978-3-319-91140-3   (eBook)
https://doi.org/10.1007/978-3-319-91140-3

Library of Congress Control Number: 2018943647

Cover credit: Alexander Ipfelkofer/Getty

Printed on acid-free paper

This Palgrave Macmillan imprint is published by the registered company Springer
International Publishing AG part of Springer Nature
The registered company address is: Gewerbestrasse 11, 6330 Cham, Switzerland

CONTENTS

LIST OF FIGURES

CHAPTER 1

Introduction: China's "New Wave Cinema" in the Era of Globalization

For several days in October 2015, many readers in China were enticed by an image on the cover of the new issue of a popular Chinese journal, *China Newsweek* (中国新闻周刊), which appeared on a multitude of newsstands. The picture shows the famed Chinese auteur Jia Zhangke 贾樟柯 (1970–) being hugged by his wife (also his favorite actress) Zhao Tao 赵涛 (1978–), looking self-assuredly at the camera and, implicitly, the readers. His face is the focal point of the image, highlighting the appeal of this national celebrity (but not that of his wife as a film starlet). In itself, this shows the fact that this former "underground" director has become a well-known member of the social elite of the country's cultural world. However, the more intriguing aspect lies in the contents of this special edition, which is not only dedicated to the director, but also to the group to which he once belonged and through which he honed his skills.

The caption under this cover picture reads "[Where there is] Jia Zhangke, there are old friends in the world" (贾樟柯/山河有故人), which has two levels of connotation. First, it refers to his most recent movie *Shanhe Guren* (*Mountains May Depart*, 山河故人) (2015), which literally means "the mountains, the rivers, and the old friends." Yet, its second level of meaning, "old friends in the world are vanishing," may be more significant, as it echoes the key feature article of the special edition of *China Newsweek*. Entitled "Jia Zhangke and the Disappearing Sixth-Generation," the last two paragraphs of this essay encapsulate the gist of its significance:

© The Author(s) 2018
X. Wang, *Ideology and Utopia in China's New Wave Cinema*, Chinese Literature and Culture in the World, https://doi.org/10.1007/978-3-319-91140-3_1

Jia Zhangke believes that the so-called "sixth generation" has disappeared. After the commercialization of Chinese film industry around 2004–2005, the mission of this generation has accomplished. In general, the populace's individualist concept has been awakened. "Their (the sixth-generation directors') efforts were to transform themselves to be individuals, but not a 'generation' or a group," he says.

The dispersal of the sixth-generation is not the disappearance of the spirit of a certain type of movie; but the directors who by chance had been included into that genealogy begin to seek the direction most fit for them. The collective group vanishes, and changes to be individuals experimenting [by] themselves. In reality, this is the more normal state of condition.[1]

Whether or not the generation has disappeared (or whether it ever existed) is moot. However, in this moment, at least we can ponder the following questions: In what circumstances did the group of auteurs emerge? What kind of social reality was transcribed, projected and articulated in their movies? The cinema that this generation created has been compared to Italian Neorealism and French New Wave; to a certain extent, it could be regarded as China's cinematic "new wave." What are the similarities and the differences between these different cinematic movements? And, finally, in what circumstances did China's "New Wave Cinema" more or less reluctantly disintegrate and disperse? This chapter begins our examination with a contextualization or better, historicization, of this idiosyncratic cinematic phenomenon.

GLOBALIZATION AND CHINA'S INTEGRATION INTO GLOBAL CAPITALISM

In his seminal paper "Notes on Globalization as a Philosophical Issue," Fredric Jameson affirms "the relationship between globalization and the world market," seeing it as "the ultimate horizon of capitalism." In other words, globalization is "an intrinsic feature" of the "multinational stage of capitalism."[2] In this stage, we witness:

the rapid assimilation of hitherto autonomous national markets and productive zones into a single sphere, the disappearance of national subsistence... the forced integration of countries all over the globe into precisely that new global division of labor...standardization on an unparalleled new scale...the worldwide Americanization or standardization of culture, the destruction of local differences, the massification of all the peoples on the planet.[3]

Indeed, globalization is the spreading of global (read 'Western') financial capital into other parts of the world, mostly the third world, and has been surging forward since the 1980s. China began to embrace this process only after the 1990s, when the state decided to welcome the Western market and import its economic model in order to reconstruct a market economy. Although the government refuses to acknowledge its adoption of Western neoliberal principles, its policies—such as large-scale privatization, massive deregulation and the neglect of rampant marketization—have brought about dire economic and social consequences. In light of this fact, critics argue that "from the perspective of post socialist states, the term globalization often appears to be simply a label for the rapid, technologically enabled spread of capitalism into areas it had not previously penetrated—or had previously been kicked out of."[4] With global capitalism as the major catalyst of the spread of financial capital, some scholars believe that Western Europe and America have lost their monopoly on global power and are seeing the weakening of their economic forces. In this way, globalization is taken as a process of decentralization, or bringing about the absence of a "center."[5] In this "epochal tide," the phenomena of "becoming cultural of the economic, and the becoming economic of the cultural" characterizes both globalization and postmodernity.[6] As Jameson aptly notes, "globalization essentially means unification and standardization."[7]

With its economic reform policies in the early 1980s, China joined the global market, despite lingering reservations due to its residual socialist principles. Since its beliefs regarding globalization in the early 1990s, the Chinese government has advanced a higher version of capitalist modernization, especially after Deng Xiaoping's southern tour in 1992. Calling for a thorough repudiation of taboos dividing socialism from capitalism, the advocates of market reform accepted many tenets of the neoliberal "Washington consensus," which violates the socialist doctrine. Since then, globalization has decisively engulfed China with the establishment of market-oriented institutions and the so-called "modern enterprise system." While, in the 1980s, to a great extent the Chinese government still abided by the socialist principles when designing its economic policies, since the 1990s it has often unabashedly followed the neoliberal principles to stimulate its economy, which involves illegal privatization of state-owned enterprises. Thus, while the period after the 1980s in China has generally been considered by scholars as the post-socialist era, we need to make a qualitative differentiation between the two distinct eras.

After three decades of "development," China now apparently has "risen up" to be the self-styled "strategic partner" of the singular super-power that is the United States. The new English neologism "Chimerica" was created towards the end of the 2010s to describe the new situation of economic symbiosis in international political-economic relations.[8] In terms of the domestic class structure, an almost total replacement of Maoist socialist politics has also been completed:

> If Mao had led the communist revolution in the first half of the twentieth century by mobilizing China's lower social classes and championing the cause of anti-imperialism, the CCP under Deng Xiaoping and his successor Jiang Zemin installed China's "digital revolution" from above by relying on the country's technocratic elites and rearticulating China's political economy with transnational capitalism, leading to the de facto formation of a hegemonic power bloc consisting of Chinese state officials, a rising domestic urban middle class, as well as transnational capitalists, foreign state managers and policy makers.[9]

From a leftist point of view, this "monopolization of China's basic political structure by capital and power is not at all a coincidence," because the two processes—the "fall of the workers' state and the legal and political changes produced by China's adaptation to market economics"—are "inextricably intertwined."[10] Therefore, the challenging situation that China now poses to scholars around the world is "a poor country that has managed to rise up in the global capitalist order while dramatically increasing domestic class inequalities, and a nation with staggering ethnic, gender, urban-rural, and regional divides."[11]

Regardless of how we understand the so-called "China miracle," there is no doubt that China's successful story depends on its reliance on, rather than severance from, the existing rules of the game. In this light, we could say that this process confirms nothing but a "singular modernity,"[12] which also brings out a relentless commodification or marketization of all social relations including culture, resulting in a striking cultural logic. Jason McGrath has succinctly summarized this point: "the apparently diverse and disconnected phenomena that appear in the new, pluralized cultural field are in fact all related in that they are manifestations of the logic of marketization; capitalism…thrives on its own occultation by virtue of becoming naturalized and invisible as a total system."[13]

Even so, we cannot simply take the commodification of society (including labor relations and the modes of cultural production) as the direct result of marketization, as this would confound capitalism with the mechanism of the market, or conflate capital with the market system. Rather, it is the principle of neoliberalism—the so-called "Washington Consensus"—that articulates the interests of the Capital that brings about the particular cultural-political dominant. This qualification will give us alternative vision and perception regarding a different world that could have existed in the past and may come into being in the future, if not already existing in the present.

One significant reason for this alternative is the existence of socialist ideas; these have not been officially repudiated by China's ruling party, whereas among ordinary people they still have tremendous influence. Left-wing intellectual Zhao Yuezhi therefore believes that "China's neo-liberal elite's inability to pursue wholesale neoliberalization in the past 30 years" is "due to the Chinese state's communist legacies."[14] In particular, she observes that:

> precisely because its political legitimacy is still based on its socialist preten-sions, and because class struggle over its direction is by no means settled despite the ascending power of the bureaucratic, capitalist, and manage-rial strata, there is the danger that the reforms are reversible, with "the masses" threatening to "seek a restoration of their own unique form of class power" (Harvey 2005: 151), compelling the leadership to rearticulate the state's hegemony in favor of the low social classes to "live up to its rev-olutionary mandate against foreign capitalists, private interests, and local authorities." (Harvey 2005: 150)[15]

Zhao points out that "this unfolding struggle over the terms of the CCP's hegemony, and the future direction of China's ongoing transfor-mation" has been witnessed in the "elite and popular communication politics in China since the early 2000s."[16]

It is in terms of this dialectical knowledge that the other dimension of the concept of "post-socialism" is instrumental in order for us to evaluate what has been and what is taking place. In addition to referring to "a neg-ative, dystopian cultural condition that prevails in late socialist societies"[17] generating "feelings of deprivation, disillusion, despair, disdain, and some-times even indignation and outrage,"[18] it also "comes as an imaginative and self-consciously risky experiment to critique the neoliberal embrace of capitalist globalization on the one hand and the residual assumptions of the Cold War and revolutionary legacy on the other;" as critic Ban Wang contends. Capitalist globalization then "strives to transcend the classical, received definitions of *capitalism* and *socialism*," and "gestures toward an understanding of an ill-articulated social formation, both grounded in Chinese reality and responsive to the global market."[19]

THE SIXTH GENERATION DIRECTORS AND THEIR VISIONS IN THE NEOLIBERAL AGE

It is within this global expansion of the neoliberal tide that China's film industry underwent a profound transformation, its institutional framework being completely overhauled, especially after its major turn in the middle of the 1990s. Since then, "China's mainstream visual culture has been implicated in the global expansion of capitalism and is becoming less and less concerned with understanding Chinese culture and history." Consequently, critics observe that despite "all its innovations, much of contemporary visual production may be at risk of eschewing realism and historical consciousness."[20]

But even before this new stage of reform had fully presented itself, a trend had arrived in the Chinese filmic world in the early 1990s, going by such names as films of the underground, the urban generation, the avant-garde, the "independent cinema;" or films made by the Sixth Generation auteurs.[21] Whatever the nature of the focus on this new cultural drive, film scholars hold the consensus that its emergence "signaled the arrival of a new kind of cinema in Chinese film history, one truly derived from individualized experience."[22] The idiosyncratic novelties of these works have been widely acknowledged:

> Aesthetically, they abandon the traditions of both Chinese melodrama and Hollywood commercialism and aspire to the status of innovative European art films ridden with existentialist crises. Ideologically, they forsake grand narratives and utopian ideas (national allegory, enlightenment, and revolution) and prefer marginalized people (rock musicians, alienated artists, mental patients, migrant workers, prostitutes, gays and lesbians) and their unconventional, uneventful, and un(der)represented lifestyles.[23]

What is most noteworthy of this new cinema is its realistic move. Fixed frames, long takes and fragments or gaps in narration are often used to minimize directorial intervention.

The term "China's New Cinema" was used to refer to Chinese films from the early reform era or those by the Fifth Generation directors; here, I would apply the term "China's New Wave Cinema" to describe the films by the Sixth Generation directors, known for their qualitatively different styles, content, grammar and narrative architectonics; albeit the filmic productions of the two generations generally share comparable realistic impulses. Indeed, depending on various shifting social-historical conditions, political circumstances and also artistic styles, realism is abundant in variety. When discussing the succession of various forms of literary realism, Jameson has ingeniously shown the dialectics between historical content and literary form:

> Each successive realism can also be said...to have been a modernism in its own right. Each realism is also by definition new: and aims at conquering a whole new area of content for its representation. Each wishes to annex what has not yet been represented, what has not yet ever been named or found its voice...This is to say not only that each realism arises out of dissatisfaction with the limits of the realisms that preceded it, but also and more fundamentally that realism itself in general shares precisely that dynamic of innovation we ascribed to modernism as its uniquely distinguishing feature.[24]

Cast in this light, what demands our special attention is the new socio-economic-political reality in the new historical conjuncture that was inscribed by the Sixth Generation directors into their films, which was taken by them to be "independent"—if not totally independent from the state facility then, at least, from the "state ideology" as the directors deem themselves to be.

Fans of world cinema would immediately recall Italian Neorealism and French New Wave when they watch these "independent films" by the Sixth Generation auteurs, which share many similar features with those two monumental film movements: the cinema itself thus could be taken as a peculiar "new wave" style. Many theorists of Italian Neorealism regard it as less of a consistent set of stylistic features and more as the relationship between film practice and the social reality of post-war Italy. For example, Millicent Marcus has elaborated on its lack of consistent film styles.[25] Likewise, China's New Wave cinema is created neither by an actual school, nor by a group of theoretically motivated and like-minded directors and scriptwriters; in actuality, it was a moment or trend within the Chinese film world. Both of the two cinemas explore the living conditions of the poor and the lower-working class, with characters' survival being their primary objective. Both cinemas portray the mundane activities of the disadvantaged devoid of self-consciousness, with non-professional actors and on-site performances. These similarities should be explored via their social-historical contexts. Italian Neorealist films originated in the 1940s from the post-World War II Italian society, when poverty, oppression, injustice and desperation prevailed; these difficult economic and moral conditions engulfed the populace, especially torturing the poor and the disenfranchised working class. Thus, the directors aimed to represent changes in the Italian psyche and conditions of everyday life. Similarly, China's New Wave cinema also marked more than a decade of cultural change and social transformation since the 1990s and thereafter, when globalization introduced the neoliberal credo to China. This resulted in the massive privatization of state-owned enterprises with millions of workers being laid off, whose living conditions became lamentable. But, simultaneously, we need to take note of the differences. Italian Neorealist films were often shot in the streets because the film studios suffered significant damage during the war; on the other hand, the directors of the early films of China's New Wave cinema could only shoot on location because they could not obtain support from the official studio. This occurred when the state still maintained its socialist system of production and distribution in the post-socialist era, before it fully participated in the tide of commercialization in order to benefit from globalization.

In this regard, it is also helpful for us to compare China's New Wave cinema to the French New Wave of the late 1950s and 1960s, which was subject to the influence of Italian Neorealism. It is acknowledged that the socio-economic forces after World War II greatly affected this cinematic movement. The French New Wave rebelled against popular art forms in pre-war traditions; classical French film employed a linear narrative, which was often adapted from traditional novelistic structures. Out of political necessity and financial difficulty during this time, France tended to fall back on this older formula; but the directors of French New Wave believed that these forms could precipitate the audience into submitting to a dictatorial plot-line. For this reason, the type of high-minded, literary period films held in esteem at domestic film festivals—the French "cinema of quality"—were especially among their targets for criticism. By the same token, although never a formally organized movement, China's New Wave cinema filmmakers were linked by their self-conscious rejection of the socialist realist movies which were "endorsed officially for decades as the primary, politically correct method of producing literature and art in China" and which had "become formulaic and prescriptive" and symbolized "an authoritarian tradition."[26] They also repudiated their predecessors—the Fifth Generation directors—who had orchestrated legendary, fake folk customs to place stress on the "cultural myths and national identity" of the Chinese nation as a response to the officially endorsed, dogmatic realism. Unfortunately, however, this gradually became elitist and formulaic within itself.[27] Consequently, with the spirit of iconoclastic youth, both French New Wave and China's New Wave cinema desired to film more current social issues on location, experimenting with various editing techniques, visual styles and narrative structures. For instance, they often used portable equipment that required little or no set-up time; thus, the films created had a documentary feel. In addition, fragmented, discontinuous editing and long takes were frequently used filming techniques; and the combination of objective realism and subjective realism created narrative ambiguity. In short, both the expression of the director's personal vision in the film's style and content were valued, as part of a general impulse to break with traditional and existing paradigms. Thus, most of the directors subscribe to the auteur theory, which holds that the director's personal signature should be visible from film to film.

But the more recent, if not the most relevant, area for comparison is the Taiwanese New Wave cinema. The first wave of this cinema unraveled at the start of the 1980s and ran through that decade, just before their contemporary Chinese auteurs emerged. Both China's New Wave films and the Taiwanese New Wave cinema won many major awards on the international film festival circuit for their efforts to "explore social tensions and problems in cinematically compelling and often original ways, blending social realism with modernist innovation."[28] Although Taiwan's New Wave can be discussed from the perspective of commercial competition with films from Hong Kong and home videos (because of which the Taiwanese government initiated a project to fund new, indigenous directors—a move markedly different from the situation in China), it is better placed within the cultural-political context of the island's economic success in the 1970s. This context displayed the rapidly changing ways of life and highlighted the dynamics between the rural and the urban, between the modern and the traditional, in a much more salient way than ever before. As the world was undergoing steady change, socially conscious art house films focused an undaunted eye on society and culture undergoing its painful metamorphosis, especially concerning the underprivileged and the weak. Just like China's New Wave a decade later, Taiwan's New Wave cinema "carries out a rebellion against previous genre cinema...and attempts to produce a socially critical and aesthetically innovative cycle of films appropriate to explore contemporary Taiwan society"; and meant to "explore the conflicts between tradition and modernity and...deal with the concerns of the present moment—a conjuncture fraught with problems and perils, but also possibilities."[29] In short, they are both cultural and political interventions in a critical moment of dramatic transformation, the most significant being the rampant marketization of culture, the swift erosion of the ruling ideology and the rapid commercialization of a once authoritative society. It is not unexpected that one of the most important figures in the Taiwanese New Wave, Hou Hsiao-Hsien 侯孝贤 (1947–), is the cultural hero and model for many of China's New Wave directors—the most representative member being Jia Zhangke, who has acknowledged his debt to Hou on numerous occasions. Hou's trademark is a simple cinematic style of long takes with minimal camera movement and naturalistic, understated ways of acting—a style that is the most frequently endorsed.

The Neorealist feature films of China's New Wave cinema have received enthusiastic recommendations from critics. Some even argue that these works could be more real than straightforward documentary because "inserting drama into documentary increases rather than decreases the impact of reality." Thus, they could be "more effective in revealing the ugly truth...[and] may infuse authenticity to the documentary, circumstantial traces" with "its narrative and psychic motivations."[30] It is recalled that, during Mao's era, directors attempted to show the historical truth through the ideology of class struggle. By contrast, this New Wave cinema shows the naked, ugly reality by stripping down ideological representations that distort it. In other words, the cinematic output does not try to critique mainstream ideology but, rather, to capture unembellished street life, in order to unmask ideology while documenting contemporary China. In this way, through "recording and witnessing the twisted mindset, the drift of life experience, the loss of meaning, and the disintegration of the social fabric, these filmmakers seek truth against commercial technique, melodrama, and simulacra."[31]

The directors, most of whom were born in the 1960s and graduated from college in the early 1990s, experienced their intellectually formative years during the 1980s, when the values of Enlightenment were culturally dominant. Embracing the precepts of Western individualism, they then took up the social obligations of representing unofficial memories and projecting their artistic vision onto society. Thus, these directors often use documentary styles such as improvisation, non-dramatic plot, fragmented narrative and images, natural settings and non-professional acting as alternative stylistic choices to support the truthfulness of their work; this is believed to exist particularly in the daily lives of marginalized subjects. But this New Wave cinema underwent gradual development. The first wave of the trend witnessed the urge for self-expression in self-styled "marginal" figures, such as performance artists and urban bohemians; in the second wave, the "vulnerable groups," in particular, and "the silent majority," in general, entered the frame, solely because, in reality, these disadvantageds groups obtrusively appeared as the casualties of the state's pro-neoliberal reform agenda. Thus, the truth for them has a particular focus: the "normal" citizen's life, which is shown in officially produced films, is taken as concealing the deeper, real social problems. Observing this change in focus, Zhang Zhen suggests that the distinction between "the disaffected but nonetheless haughty urban bohemians" in the early films of the cinema and "the 'artisans' (petty thieves or migrant amateur performers) in small towns" of the later productions can be construed as "a visible marker for a paradigmatic shift within the Urban Generation in the 1990s."[32] But although early productions by this "new wave cinema were banned and prohibited from entering the public distribution channels and were thus identified by Western critics as "independent," "underground" or "dissident" works. When the government extended its "olive branch" in the early part of the new millennium, most of the directors were willingly co-opted by the central authority and enticed to embrace commercialization. This study considers the cinematic productions before and after the co-option as a whole, for the reason that the ideology and utopia (and, to a certain extent, aesthetic style and innovation) as expressed and displayed in them has no fundamental difference.

Unlike the Chinese government broadcasting the bright future brought about by its integration with the world market, China's New Wave cinema was seemingly suspicious of this new "christening" of globalization. Additionally, its proponents were critical of the myth that globalism can be the ultimate solution to Chinese problems. For instance, in Jia Zhangke's cinematic works, ostensibly there are frequent messages of anti-globalist, anti-capitalistic themes. One of the discernible examples is the film *The World*, in which Chinese peasants travel to the city to become migrant workers to escape poverty, only resulting in a failure to see the so-called "fruits of globalism"—thus becoming even more lost and desolate, and even perishing, by following the "lies" of fortune and security. In this way, by "portraying...an underprivileged urban population," films such as this "debunk the myth of China as a success story of globalization."[33]

Yet, after stripping down the ideological underpinnings, which are now unfit for reality, what is the new ideology that China's New Wave cinema itself expresses or articulates? Could it be exempt from ideological "distortions"? If not, what is the "false consciousness" in terms of the classical Marxian definition of the ideology that it harbors? To answer this question, we need to ponder the particular circumstances in which the filmmakers emerged and developed. What is noteworthy is that "they are the first generation of Chinese filmmakers in the era of globalization."[34] The significance of this timing means that "globalization has imposed a radical break between them and their parents' generation in terms of working environment, lifestyle, and value system."[35] Therefore, inasmuch as their "life experiences are shaped by China's integration into the global market" and even "their films are often sponsored by overseas investors,"[36] their cultural-political vision regarding the unprecedented transformations taking place is also subject to the impingement of the historical sea-change—in particular, the onslaught of Western knowledge and ideology in this divergent and incongruent historical period.

IDEOLOGY AND UTOPIA IN CHINA'S NEW WAVE CINEMA

If, with the "intermediaries of the great, mostly American-based transnational or multinational corporations, a standard form of American material life, along with North American values and cultural forms, is being systematically transmitted to other cultures" including China,[37] and the directors themselves are of the generation that was termed as having "high culture fever" (namely, bombardment by various Western intellectual trends) in 1980s China, the question remains: are these young directors capable of resisting it?

No. Although globalization brought about the commercialization of Chinese society, in which the directors witnessed the "impersonal modern society undermining older families and clans, villages, 'organic' forms," and the logic of consumption "tears through what is so often metaphorized as the fabric of daily life,"[38] what they are discontent with is still much less the Western, bourgeois ideology coming hand-in-hand with globalization, than the domestic, residual socialist regime, which still appeared dogmatic at the time. In particular, the June Fourth Incident of 1989 for them did nothing but debunk the lies of the socialist utopia. Consequently, they neither show any interest in socialist ideals and practices, past or present, nor express any perceptive indignation over the state's violations of the principles of the workers' state and suppressions of the worker-peasants' protests.

Instead, these directors usually brandish the statement "My Camera does not lie," and Zhang Yingjin has remarked that this claim can be understood as a self-positioning of these filmmakers by showing "my impression," "my camera" and, finally, "my truth," which was surmised to articulate the viewpoint of ordinary people.[39] But whether the "truth content" of this era can be fully delivered by these filmic works without distortion is controversial. In order to be independent of official ideology (although not independent entirely of state institutions), in the later period the directors even avoided using direct realism, so as to (as they wished) present reality without a moral compass of sorts. Nevertheless, as it is some considerable time since socialist ideology was dominant, and any person living in society could not be thoroughly excluded from these ethical-moral values, we need to consider what their political, ethical and moral convictions were? In any case, we must ask what is the official or "dominant" ideology in China at the moment? The Marxist-Leninist-Maoist doctrines have been merely paid lip service on certain significant occasions, such as national party conferences which the party is obligated to hold. In reality, the party-state has no scruples about transgressing socialist principles when undertaking any activity believed to be instrumental to the stimulation of economic growth.

In this light, to say that China's New Wave cinema definitively avoids any moral compass is equivalent to saying that they are politically immune, which is nothing but declining an analysis of ideology. What should be brought to our attention is that, to convey its specific message, the directors now believe that absolute objectivity devoid of emotional attachment—the earliest objective of this group—is impossible. Thus, they can only claim relative objectivity or independent subjectivity—with which, they choose to distinguish their vision of the truth from the "pretenses" of the previous generation. Their commitment to "subjective" and "personal" perspectives on China includes subjective recollections of Chinese history and personal explanations of Chinese society. While the Fifth Generation was concerned with shaping a national identity from a collectivist point of view, the Sixth Generation now introduces a break from this style by using the term "personal filmmaking." Jia Zhangke once said, "The truth is not presented in front us so blatantly. The truth comes to us through the feelings and the understanding of one person towards another. Only this way we can grasp the truth. Truth or truthfulness does not lay bare in the life. You have to possess a certain degree of sensibility so as to straighten out the logic of emotion and disclose the buried truth."[40]

But what is the truth in this era; or, what is the "truth content" of this era? This new cinema has been defined "by its recurrent exploration of public spaces, and of the individuals within them."[41] The contradiction of this paradigm—or, rather, the discourse of "public space"—also brings out an arbitrary argument regarding the aesthetic characteristics of the cinema, which in my view is not always valid. The argument goes: "if independent Chinese film is engaged with a form of realist aesthetic, it can only be a realism of contingency, as argued by Luke Robinson, in which the primacy of *xianchang* dictates the progression and structure of the film."[42] It is known that one key figure in the Sixth Generation group, Wang Chao 王超 (1964–), often writes his scripts based on an a priori idea, and by which he designates the plots and narrative structure. Accordingly, the binary opposition between the public (space) and the private (space), which was once (and perhaps is still) a popular paradigm in studying contemporary Chinese society, is inadequate in this regard, if not totally irrelevant. However, the premise behind this Habermasian discourse of "public space" in this regardnamely, its assumption of certain "'shared humanity' or of an 'imagined community'...in which each individual is free to air an opinion on matters of public significance"[43]— still applies for these Sixth Generation filmmakers.

Nevertheless, for the directors to focus merely on the alleged universal "human condition" would not only take the risk of bypassing the inequitable political-economic issues of society, but also its predilection for sentimentality (which frequently verges on a sort of cheap, bourgeois moralism, no matter how "zero degree" it may seem on the surface) could easily be co-opted by the state, for both now reject the Marxian notion of class struggle and repudiate applying the Marxist methodology of class analysis.

It is in light of this fact, that we can go forward with discussing the ideology of the vision of "truth" held by this Sixth Generation group. As Jameson informs us, "ideology is not necessarily a matter of false consciousness, or of the incorrect or distorted representation of historical 'fact', but can rather be quite consistent with a 'realistic' faithfulness to the latter."[44] Nevertheless, "the displacement of political and historical analysis by ethical judgments and considerations," which is also witnessed in the works of China's New Wave cinema, is "generally the sign of an ideological maneuver and of the intent to mystify."[45]

Thus said, Jameson also urges us to realize the innate existence of utopian impulses in any contemporary works of art, either "those of high culture and modernism or of mass culture and commercial culture," "albeit in what is often distorted and repressed, unconscious form."[46] He confirms the fact that "genuine social and historical content must first be tapped and given some initial expression" in artistic works in order to let the content subsequently "be the object of successful manipulation and containment." Accordingly, he keenly reminds us:

> we cannot fully do justice to the ideological function of works...unless we are willing to concede the presence within them of a more positive function as well: of...their Utopian or transcendent potential—that dimension of even the most degraded type of mass culture which remains implicitly, and no matter how faintly, negative and critical of the social order from which, as a product and a commodity, it springs.[47]

In another article, he definitely uses this concept of "utopia" to designate "the demands of a collective life to come, and [to] identify social collectivity as the crucial center of any truly progressive and innovative political response to globalization,"[48] which is taken as "our deepest fantasies about the nature of social life, both as we live it now, and as we feel in our bones it ought rather to be lived."[49] This exploration is meaningful purely because:

> To reawaken, in the midst of a privatized and psychologizing society, obsessed with commodities and bombarded by the ideological slogans of big business, some sense of the ineradicable drive towards collectivity that can be detected, no matter how faintly and feebly, in the most degraded works of mass culture just as surely as in the classics of modernism—is surely an indispensable precondition for any meaningful Marxist intervention in contemporary culture."[50]

Indeed, ideology or reification (of certain concepts) and utopia are the two sides of the same coin in relation to China's New Wave cinema, which requires our dialectic inquiry, and thus also becomes the working hypothesis and methodology of the present study. It is under this strategy that we acknowledge the fact that it does not matter whether the director really upholds a particular scheme within his mind and expresses it in his work, for our interpretation "results from specific reading strategies that, whatever their validity in relation to the text (or fact) under scrutiny, depend heavily upon the context of reading itself."[51]

HISTORICITY OF THE FORM

When speaking of this double nature of artistic work, Jameson has further made a comparison between modernism and mass culture:

> Both modernism and mass culture entertain relations of repression with the fundamental social anxieties and concerns, hopes and blind spots, ideological antinomies and fantasies of disaster, which are their raw material; only where modernism tends to handle this material by producing compensatory structures of various kinds, mass culture represses them by the narrative construction of imaginary resolutions and by the projection of an optical illusion of social harmony.[52]

Judged by this contrast, what can be said about Chinese New Wave cinema? Although it is viewed by most critics to be an art of the elite, to take it as a phenomenon of elite culture (or mass culture) is misleading. Likewise, to label its works as realism, modernism or postmodernism would incur many controversies, as the films bear all the complexities of the genres/forms. This idiosyncratic feature points to its unique historical situation.

China's New Wave cinema's focusing on social outcasts does not simply mean it values the underprivileged who have not been included in the official version of realism until that particular time. The term *"diceng"* (lower- or under-class) was created as late as 2004, which itself confirms that the under-class is only a newly emerged social stratum that began taking shape in the 1990s, a consequence of the social-political-economic structural transformations. It is of little doubt that, in terms of critical consciousness, Chinese artists were earlier than Chinese scholars in discovering the gradually expanding social phenomenon. To be sure, they portrayed the dire and lamentable images of society's outcasts merely out of a humanistic spirit. However, the inclusion of these migrant rural workers living in urban areas (who currently compose the majority of China's industrial workforce) in the same class stratum as the "*diceng*," shows that what has appeared is not simply a marginal group. It is in terms of this new situation that we can argue that the birth of China's New Wave cinema itself contains a kind of epochal truth.

What this contention entails is that we should also heed to the historicity of the form of China's New Wave cinema itself. When discussing the historicity of modernism, Jameson has aptly noted that "the omnipresence of the commodity form determines a reactive stance, so that modernism conceives its formal vocation to be the resistance to commodity form, *not* to be a commodity, to devise an aesthetic language incapable of offering commodity satisfaction, and resistant to instrumentalization," which is "a symptom and a result of cultural crisis, rather than a new 'solution' in its own right;" rather, "the very terms of its solution – the conception of the modernist text as the production and the protest of an isolated individual, and the logic of its sign systems as so many private languages ('styles') and private religions – are contradictory and make the social or collective realization of its aesthetic project... an impossible one."[53]

This argument gives us inspirational thoughts regarding China's New Wave cinema, especially if we substitute it for the word "modernism." Certainly, China's New Wave cinema's reactivation against commercialization is merely half of the story; the other half is the challenging of the socialist realism of the past, which was incapable of fitting in with the new social content. Thus, China's New Wave cinema has a dual mission, which speaks of its nature as a product of post-socialist society. In this light, its aesthetic language, just like modernism, is also a "a symptom and a result of cultural crisis, rather than a new 'solution' in its own right;" which explains why "the social or collective realization of its aesthetic project" is impossible to reach by its "private languages" or styles,[54] although the nature of the cultural crisis is now much different.

But Jameson goes further into the historical conjuncture to analyze the transformation:

we must specify this development historically: the older pre-capitalist genres were signs of something like an aesthetic "contract" between a cultural producer and a certain homogeneous class or group public; they drew their vitality from the social and collective status…of the situation of aesthetic production and consumption, that is to say, from the fact that the relationship between artist and public was still in one way or another a social institution and a concrete social and interpersonal relationship with its own validation and specificity. With the coming of the market, this institutional status of artistic consumption and production vanishes: art becomes one more branch of commodity production, the artist loses all social status and faces the options of becoming a *poete maudit* or a journalist, the relationship to the public is problematized, and the latter becomes a virtual "public introuvable."[55]

Also, following this rationale, we might argue that what China's New Wave cinema faced when it emerged was the older socialist genres, such as works of socialist realism and other forms of mass culture. These older genres implied an aesthetic contract between the Maoist cultural producer and the "homogeneous class or group public," which was the masses of the socialist republic. This existing situation of "aesthetic production and consumption" was inexorably changed, since "the relationship between artist and public," being "a social institution…with its own validation and specificity," encountered its ultimate disintegration with the vehement encroachment of marketization throughout society. This was a consequence of the state's implementation of the pro-capitalist policies and deconstruction of residual socialist institutions. Therefore, it is not necessarily the case that the older artistic productions were nothing but lies (although they may be dogmatic), whilst the new cinema shows nothing but the "truth." Rather, it is the truth of a new era, which was destroying the existing social institutions and nullifying the previous social contract, that rendered the socialist cultural institutions old-fashioned and obsolete.

But Jameson perceptively notes that the modernism's aesthetic ideology of "making it new" has no "critical or theoretical value":

the strategic emphasis on innovation and novelty, the obligatory break with previous styles, the pressure—geometrically increasing with the ever swifter historicity of consumer society, with its yearly or quarterly style and fashion changes—to "make it new", to produce something which resists and breaks through the force of gravity of repetition as a universal feature of commodity equivalence. Such aesthetic ideologies have to be sure no critical or theoretical value—for one thing, they are purely formal and by abstracting some empty concept of innovation from the concrete content of stylistic change in any given period end up flattening out even the history of forms, let alone social history, and projecting a kind of cyclical view of change.[56]

Inspired by this teaching, we need to muse on the validity of the Chinese New Wave cinema's declaration of itself as "new" and its proclamation that "My camera doesn't lie" (which implies that it would be authentic or faithful to the reality). To be sure, there are differences between modernism and China's New Wave cinema, one of which being that, whereas modernism's "strategic emphasis on innovation and novelty" and its "obligatory break with previous styles" was against the pressure of commercial culture, China's New Wave cinema was mainly targeted against the rigescent yet disenfranchised political order and the "old-fashioned" aesthetics in the face of post-socialist reality. Nevertheless, this new cinema generally still followed the same path by "abstracting some empty concept of innovation from the concrete content of stylistic change," which resulted in "flattening out even the history of forms, let alone social history, and projecting a kind of cyclical view of change."[57] In accordance with this gesture, it also declines to reflect upon its own historicity and ideology, ignorant of (if not consciously denying) the existence of any false consciousness.

STRUCTURAL OUTLINE

The early works of China's New Wave cinema bear strong imprints of autobiographical narcissism; therefore, some critics suggest that they "betray the directors' collective psychological hangover from adolescent obsession with growing up."[58] Yet, even works with similar subjects could assume diversified facades which testify to the rich complexity of the group. As with other officially released movies of the same period, these films often "contain shots framing young break dancing alongside elderly people...in order to set up contrasts between modernity and tradition."[59] But this is a tradition that has a specific nature; that is, the socialist ethical/moral dogma, discipline and order, which was cast aside as outmoded. It is noted that the fashionable "rock 'n' roll music, by the late 1980s, had also become something that could not be separated in an artistic work delineating the life of the country's urban youth;" in essence, "Chinese rock music and the burgeoning youth culture interact actively in two aspects, i.e., rebellion and authenticity."[60]

Thus, in Chapter 2, "The Arrival of Post-Socialism: Silence, Sound and Fury," we witness in the first two films that the rock band and its music become the embodiment of the spirit of revolt and the expression of impassioned feelings. *Beijing Bastards* (1993) portrays the atmosphere of restlessness on the eve of the post-socialist era, whereas *Weekend Lover* (1995) narrates a fable of youthful indulgence and self-annihilation. Both of them record the chaotic and confusing nature of social life after the Tiananmen Incident in 1989, but decline a solemn reflection of the failure of the students' movement. Only about ten years later did the film *Summer Palace* (2006) appear, which presented a façade of recollection (if not reflection), reminiscing and ruminating on the pre-1989 feverish atmosphere. Upon careful scrutiny, however, this movie merely illumi-nates the birth of bourgeois subjectivity as the aftermath of the political crackdown in the wake of the rising market society. In the ruins of the historical trauma, the movie inexorably exposes (if not consciously high-lights) the epochal truth-content of the consequence of that political tur-moil and the emergence of a rampant market economy.

One of the most significant occurrences in the neoliberal era is the appearance of the so-called "new poor" in China—the migrant peasants and the alleged "white-collar workers" who could not fulfill their con-sumerist desires. Chapter 3 looks into the representations of these two groups within Chinese New Wave cinema by studying the film *Blind Shaft* (2003) vis-à-vis the "new poor" and *Pirated Copy* (2004) vis-à-vis white collar workers. These films explore the two key issues contained in the narratives: Should China's lower classes still pursue an endless mis-sion for enlightenment? In the age of global simulacra, what is the divid-ing line between the real and the fake, when sexual desire and violence, aroused and fed by the transnational digital media, are permeating every corner of urban China?

The development of the Chinese middle class, however vulnera-ble it is, has brought about worldwide attention. In Chapter 4, two films, *Green Tea* (2003) and *The Contract* (2006), are singled out to show their visual imagination of this new class. They represent the socio-cultural life of the new class—in particular, its taste, habitus and cultural distinctions. Meanwhile, the merits and weaknesses of this group are discussed vis-à-vis the cinematic texture and the social-historical sub-text, as well as the intertext of China's middle-class Western counterpart. In this way, its close ties to and concerns with the lower classes, and its symptoms of a historical amnesia (together with the ensuing shortage of a strong cultural-political willpower), will both be explored.

When China's New Wave cinema casts its camera into the most recent—and also, arguably, the most unfamiliar historical period (the Maoist era), we find noticeable differences from the mainstream renderings. In Chapter 5, two films serve as examples for us to analyze the various outlooks and scenarios. *In the Heat of the Sun* (1994) takes the Maoist era as one of "enlightenment," although a kind of incomplete enlightenment; *Eleven Flowers* (2012) treats it as an oppressive period that blurs the lines between fairness and injustice. Therefore, these two narratives embody the two representative point-of-views of the present era regarding Maoist society and its ideology—the radical and the conservative.

Is elitism or populism harbored by the auteurs of Chinese New Wave cinema? Through Chapters 2–4, we can observe that diversified tendencies and positions existed in this group of young directors. Since director Jia Zhangke is always taken to be the key figure in China's New Wave cinema, his works—notably those created after entering "mainstream film" and cooperating with the government—are worthy of inquiry. Thus, Chapter 6 makes an inquiry into three of his later productions, *The World* (2004), *24 City* (2008) and *A Touch of Sin* (2013). We will find that when Jia expands his horizons from the under-class to national history and expresses his idiosyncratic view of conflicts between social classes (for him, these conflicts are not considered as the so-called "class struggle") in contemporary China, the limitation of his perspective becomes evident.

Jia's weakness is generally shared by the directors of the New Wave cinema, which speaks of its peculiar historicity—that it is a transitional phenomenon occurring as China gradually assumes many neoliberal policies in order to profit from the material benefits of globalization. Therefore, in the Conclusion, I will discuss the politics of dignity, which is a popular theoretical topic in the contemporary academic world, and suggest that it exists at the core of this humanistic cinematography. The Chinese New Wave cinema offers a graphic example with which to explore the validity of this discourse (and the ensuing politics of recognition), because this discourse can be taken as the philosophy followed by these directors. Thus, when we bring the problematic of class analysis into our examination of this politics, the ideology of China's New Wave cinema can be clarified and its utopian desire elucidated.

NOTES

1. Jiahuan Wan, "Jia Zhangke he Xiaosan de 'Diliudai'."
2. Fredric Jameson, "Notes on Globalization as a Philosophical Issue," 34.
3. Ibid., 57.
4. Jason McGrath, *Postsocialist Modernity*, 14.
5. Tonglin Lu, "Trapped Freedom and Localized Globalism," 123.
6. Fredric Jameson, "Notes on Globalization as a Philosophical Issue," 3.
7. Ibid., 64.
8. This term was coined by historian Niall Ferguson and economist Moritz Schularick in late 2006. They suggest that the Chinese savings helped American overspending, bringing about a period of wealth creation leading to the financial crisis taking place in 2007–2008. See Niall Ferguson, "The Trillion Dollar Question: China or America?"
9. Yuezhi Zhao, "The Challenge of China," 565.
10. Hui Wang, "Two Kinds of New Poor and Their Future," 202.
11. Yuezhi Zhao, "The Challenge of China," 563.
12. Fredric Jameson, *A Singular Modernity*.
13. Jason McGrath, *Postsocialist Modernity*, 10.
14. Yuezhi Zhao, "The Challenge of China," 562.
15. Ibid.
16. Ibid.
17. Paul Pickowicz, "Huang Jianxin and the Notion of Postsocialism," 61–62.
18. Yingjin Zhang, "Rebel Without a Cause? China's New Urban Generation and Postsocialist Filmmaking," 54.
19. Ban Wang, "Studies of Modern Chinese Literature," 388.
20. Ban Wang, "In Search of Real Images in China: Realism in the Age of Spectacle," 497–498.
21. Based on Harry H. Kuoshu's study, Richard Letteri has succinctly summarized the features of the six generations, which is worthwhile quoting here. "The First Generation filmmakers produced films in the 1920s are considered 'pioneers' of Chinese film...both they and the Second Generation of the 1930s integrated melodrama with a social or critical realist style to create socially progressive films...Once in political control, the Communist party-state employed the Third Generation of filmmakers to create Communist propaganda films that celebrated the glories of the Communist revolution, its leader Mao Zedong and its heroically drawn soldiers and peasantry. The Fourth Generation filmmakers, who were trained in filmmaking in the 1960s under the Communist state, did not begin the process of reassessing the Communist Revolution and addressing the social concerns of the Chinese people until the post-Mao era (1979–1990). Graduated from the Beijing Film Academy in 1982, it

was the Fifth Generation filmmakers...who brought international fame to Chinese cinema with their rural allegories that subtly hid critiques of the Chinese patriarchal state and society...Finally, after graduating from the Beijing Film Academy in 1992...the Sixth Generation of filmmakers...began to experiment with a new realist style that focused on the economic and social conditions of everyday life in (mostly) urban China." See Richard Letteri, "History, Silence and Homelessness in Contemporary Chinese Cinema," 17–18. For detailed discussions of the various generations, see Harry H. Kuoshu, "Overview: The Filmmaking Generations."

22. Chen Mo and Zhiwei Xiao, "Chinese Underground Films: Critical Views from China," 148.
23. Yingjin Zhang, *Cinema, Space, and Polylocality in a Globalizing China*, 159.
24. Fredric Jameson, *A Singular Modernity*, 123.
25. Millicent Marcus, *Italian Film in the Light of Neorealism*.
26. Yingjin Zhang, "My Camera Doesn't Lie?" 27.
27. Ibid., 26.
28. Douglass Kellner, "New Taiwan Cinema in the 1980s."
29. Ibid.
30. Ban Wang, "In Search of Real Images in China: Realism in the Age of Spectacle," 503.
31. Ban Wang, "Epic Narrative, Authenticity, and the Memory of Realism," 211–212.
32. See Zhang Zhen, "Introduction," 16.
33. Tonglin Lu, "Trapped Freedom and Localized Globalism," 124.
34. Ibid., 125.
35. Ibid.
36. Ibid.
37. Fredric Jameson, "Notes on Globalization as a Philosophical Issue," 64.
38. Fredric Jameson, "Globalization and Political Strategy," 57.
39. Yingjin Zhang, "My Camera Doesn't Lie? Truth, Subjectivity, and Audience in Chinese Independent Film and Video," 40–41.
40. Lesley Yiping Qin and Jia Zhangke, "Look Back in Anger."
41. Sebastian Veg, "Introduction: Opening Public Spaces," 9.
42. Ibid., 10. *Xianchang* 现场 literally means "on the scene," referring both to the real scene "on the site" and the film set. Wang Chao thus would feel very surprised when he reads the following argument: "Reality is unpredictable, and only by capturing its randomness can the director be true to the individuals who populate it and whose stories he is telling." Ibid.
43. Ibid., 8.
44. Fredric Jameson, "Reification and Utopia in Mass Culture," 145.

45. Ibid., 146.
46. Ibid., 147–148.
47. Ibid., 144.
48. Fredric Jameson, "Globalization and Political Strategy," 68.
49. Fredric Jameson, "Reification and Utopia in Mass Culture," 147–148.
50. Ibid.
51. Ismail Xavier, "Historical Allegory," 341.
52. Fredric Jameson, "Reification and Utopia in Mass Culture," 141.
53. Ibid., 134–135.
54. Ibid.
55. Ibid., 136–137.
56. Ibid., 136.
57. Ibid.
58. Chen Mo and Zhiwei Xiao, "Chinese Underground Films: Critical Views from China," 153.
59. Xuelin Zhou, *Young Rebels in Contemporary Chinese Cinema*, 113.
60. Ibid.

References

Chen, Mo, and Zhiwei Xiao. "Chinese Underground Films: Critical Views from China." In Paul Pickowicz and Yingjin Zhang (eds.), *From Underground to Independent: Alternative Film Culture in Contemporary China*, pp. 143–160. Lanham, MD: Rowman & Littlefield, 2006.

Ferguson, Niall. "The Trillion Dollar Question: China or America?" *The Daily Telegraph*, June 1, 2009.

Harvey, David. *A Brief History of Neoliberalism*. New York: Oxford University Press, 2005.

Jameson, Fredric. "Reification and Utopia in Mass Culture." *Social Text* 1 (Winter) (1979): 130–148.

Jameson, Fredric. "Notes on Globalization as a Philosophical Issue." In Fredric Jameson and Masao Miyoshi (eds.), *The Cultures of Globalization*, pp. 54–80. Durham: Duke University Press, 1998.

Jameson, Fredric. "Globalization and Political Strategy." *New Left Review* 4 (2000): 49–68.

Jameson, Fredric. *A Singular Modernity*. London: Verso, 2013.

Kellner, Douglas. "New Taiwan Cinema in the 80s." *Jump Cut* 42 (1998): 101–115.

Kuoshu, Harry H. "Overview: The Filmmaking Generations." In Harry H. Kuoshu (ed.), *Celluloid China: Cinematic Encounters with Culture and Society*, pp. 1–20. Carbondale: Southern Illinois University Press, 2002.

Letteri, Richard. "History, Silence and Homelessness in Contemporary Chinese Cinema: Wang Xiaoshuai's *Shanghai Dreams*." *Asian Studies Review* 34 (March 2010): 3–18.

Lu, Tonglin. "Trapped Freedom and Localized Globalism." In Paul G. Pickowicz and Yingjin Zhang (eds.), *From Underground to Independent: Alternative Film Culture in Contemporary China*, pp. 123–141. Lanham: Rowman & Littlefield, 2006.

Marcus, Millicent. *Italian Film in the Light of Neorealism*. Princeton: Princeton University Press, 1987.

McGrath, Jason. *Postsocialist Modernity: Chinese Cinema, Literature, and Criticism in the Market Age*. Stanford, CA: Stanford University Press, 2008.

Pickowicz, Paul. "Huang Jianxin and the Notion of Postsocialism." In Nick Browne, Paul Pickowicz, Vivian Sobchack, and Esther Yau (eds.), *New Chinese Cinemas: Forms, Identities, Politics*, pp. 57–87. New York: Cambridge University Press, 1994.

Qin, Lesley Yiping, and Jia Zhangke. "Look Back in Anger—Interview with Jia Zhangke and Zhaotao on *A Touch of Sin*." http://www.asiancinevision.org/look-back-in-anger-interview-with-jia-zhangke-and-zhao-tao-on-a-touch-of-sin/. Accessed January 6, 2016.

Veg, Sebastian. "Introduction: Opening Public Spaces." *China Perspectives* 81 (2010): 4–10.

Wan, Jiahuan (万佳欢). "Jia Zhangke he Xiaosan de 'Diliudai'" 贾樟柯和消散的"第六代" [Jia Zhangke and the Disappearing Sixth-Generation]. *Zhongguo Xinwen zhoukan* 中国新闻周刊 [*China Newsweek*], 16 (39) (2015, October 26).

Wang, Ban. "In Search of Real Images in China: Realism in the Age of Spectacle." *Journal of Contemporary China* 17 (56) (2008): 497–512.

Wang, Ban. "Studies of Modern Chinese Literature." In Haihui Zhang, Zhaohui Xue, Shuyong Jiang and Gary Lance Lugar (eds.), *A Scholarly Review of Chinese Studies in North America*, pp. 377–389. Ann Arbor, MI: Association for Asian Studies, 2013.

Wang, Hui. "Two Kinds of New Poor and Their Future." In Saul Thomas (ed.), *China's Twentieth Century: Revolution, Retreat, and the Road to Equality*. London and New York: Verso, 2016.

Xavier, Ismail. "Historical Allegory." In Toby Miller and Robert Stam (eds.), *A Companion to Film Theory*, pp. 333–362. Oxford: Blackwell, 1999.

Zhang, Yingjin. "My Camera Doesn't Lie? Truth, Subjectivity, and Audience in Chinese Independent Film and Video." In Paul G. Pickowicz and Yingjin Zhang (eds.), *From Underground to Independent: Alternative Film Culture in Contemporary China*, pp. 23–46. Lanham, MD: Rowman & Littlefield, 2006.

Zhang, Yingjin. "Rebel Without a Cause? China's New Urban Generation and Postsocialist Filmmaking." In *Cinema, Space, and Polylocality in a Globalizaing China*, pp. 49–80. Honolulu: University of Hawaii Press, 2010a.

Zhang, Yingjin. *Cinema, Space, and Polylocality in a Globalizing China*. Honolulu: University of Hawaii Press, 2010b.

Zhao, Yuezhi. "The Challenge of China: Contribution to a Transcultural Political Economy of Communication for the Twenty-First Century." In Janet Wasko, Graham Murdock and Helena Sousa (eds.), *The Handbook of Political Economy of Communications*, pp. 562–563. Hoboken, NJ: Wiley-Blackwell, 2011.

Zhou, Xuelin. *Young Rebels in Contemporary Chinese Cinema*. Hong Kong: Hong Kong University Press, 2007.

CHAPTER 2

The Arrival of Chinese Post-socialism: Silence, Sound and Fury

The June Fourth Incident marked a turning point in the history of the Chinese Communist Party and the People's Republic, and unraveled a new decade of the party's reform and opening-up praxis. The aftermath was tumultuous: the "resulting disillusionment and cynicism among intellectuals and artists...led to an abandonment of high cultural ideals and an embrace of commercialism and the profit motive in the following decade."[1] The ensuing atmosphere of nihilism and hedonism, which is generally taken to be the salient symptom of post-socialist Chinese society, fully engulfed Chinese society. Critic Ban Wang gave an apt description of the new situation, "the watershed events of Tiananmen in 1989 and Deng Xiaoping's tour in southern China in 1992 ushered in a decade plagued by complexity and heterogeneity, competing visions, and perplexed reflections. Economic dynamism, political stagnation, and deepening social divisions made this period one of 'interesting times' that tried human's souls."[2] "Post-socialism" as a "label of historical periodization" usually refers to the post-Mao period. During this time, Deng's regime repudiated Mao's radical experiments with socialist concepts and institutions, and ushered in a pragmatic spirit in dealing with political-economic issues,[3] involving the formal implementation of market tenets without paying heed to socialist principles. It was in the 1990s that the curtains on a new era (which in China had been called the "post-New Period") were fully drawn back. This "new period"

© The Author(s) 2018
X. Wang, *Ideology and Utopia in China's New Wave Cinema*, Chinese Literature and Culture in the World, https://doi.org/10.1007/978-3-319-91140-3_2

witnessed a fundamental transformation of the social ethos, in which all the symptoms of post-socialism—nihilism, cynicism, hedonism, and "feelings of deprivation, disillusion, despair, disdain, and sometimes even indignation and outrage"[4]—began to dominate Chinese society.

Without exception, the first trend seen in China's New Wave cinema, portrayed this gloomy silence, as well as restless feelings of social repression. Scenes featuring rock 'n' roll, which is often considered the symbol of the youthful counter-culture of the West, can often be observed in these films. In this way, "rock music as an effective means for the articulation of dissent and resistance thus united in the early 1990s the rock musicians and the emergent Sixth Generation directors."[5] Common themes can be found in these films—non-conformity rebelliousness, hedonism, nihilism, cynicism, narcissism and pessimism. Three movies can be regarded as principle texts that exemplify the silence, sound and fury of the era. However, these three films also harbor fundamentally different connotations regarding respective cultural-political visions.

Beijing Bastards 北京杂种 (1993) is a portrayal of derelict youth. Focusing on the nostalgic Beijing youth, who are experiencing the conflicts between their dreams and reality, the film delivers a strong sense of confusion and apprehension. It is also a portrait of the callousness of social marginalization, seen through the casual eyes of roaming youths in a bustling yet spiritually devoid metropolis. Shot in a strikingly gritty style, using vulgar colloquial language, the story itself is not well-developed, appearing mostly fragmented and incomplete. Thus, it is often understood to be an unsuccessful work as it does not develop a narrative with which the viewer can identify. Yet, upon scrutiny, we can still find many nuances worthy of examination.

Two years later, another movie was released in China: *Weekend Lover* 周末情人 (1995), known for its noir style and tales of disaffected youth comparable to *Beijing Bastards*. It is also considered a defining film for the Chinese New Wave Cinema, particularly in its tone and subject matter, which focuses on modern urban life in China. While *Beijing Bastards* shows the silence of repressed life during the post-Tiananmen era, this movie displays the sights and sounds of the cultural scene during the same period. The topics covered in the film include rebellion, violence, sex, anti-authoritarianism, narcissism and self-indulgence. These are coupled with ambiguous images of female homosexuality, which can be viewed as the symbolic loss of masculinity. In the narration, the female protagonist can be thought of as the object of the male characters' affections; in other words, the incarnation of their desires. In the background, the city appears as a world full of bewilderment, loss and disappointment, as well as full of adventure and curiosity. It is against this setting that the dissatisfaction, emptiness and rebelliousness of the younger generations and their insoluble conflicts between reality and fantasy become the primary focal point. Life is suppressed and the indignation of the characters unrelieved; the solution for them becomes rock music and sexual lust, which subsequently becomes a kind of anesthesia and escape (together with violence and even murder). Similar to *Beijing Bastards*, the film does not illuminate or pinpoint the underlying causes of the younger generations' distress; only the surface themes of social alienation and cultural-political transformation were displayed. Incapable of evading the individualistic narcissism common to this generation, the film promotes a tale of indulgence and self-annihilation.

Summer Palace 颐和园 (2006), filmed ten years later, is concerned with related subjects which had been recognized as causing hype and staunch reactions from the Chinese viewership. The earliest—and only—film that touches upon the 1989 student movement and the Tiananmen Square Incident, it has been in the limelight at international film festivals. However, the director denies that he had any desire to narrate this event. The scriptwriter still claims that the film was merely an individual's personal feelings regarding this era. The presentation of the 1989 generation reminds the viewers of the students' self-affirmation and their justification of their desires during that time. Living within this new post-revolutionary, market-oriented economy, they are portrayed as being filled with melancholy reminiscences of the past which are buried within their own narcissism and self-pity. Despite being a film about individualism, the audience not only wonders how rational the love being displayed between the main characters is, but also whether the love story even follows the cultural-political logic of the period. All the characters depicted are reckless in love and show no spiritual values; all they wish is to fulfill their selfish desires, doing whatever it takes to make themselves happy. However, a more nuanced analysis suggests that, behind the unapologetic hedonism and melancholia in the film, there is a strong sense of fury that conceals the birth of a bourgeois identity among the ruins of this historical trauma.

Restlessness on the Eve of the Post-socialist Era

Beijing Bastards (1993) is the second film directed by Zhang Yuan (1963–), but is often considered the first "independent" film in China. This is perhaps, in part, due to the high level of publicity it received resulting from its censorship and denouncement by the Chinese government. Born in Jiangsu Province, Zhang Yuan began his love of film and art by learning to paint during his childhood. Having graduated from the Department of Directing at the Beijing Film Academy in 1989, he then started his career as a self-funded independent film director. His first "fictional documentary" *Mama* 妈妈, shot during the same year, won international recognition but received a cold reception domestically.[6] Finding himself wavering between subjective idealism and the reality of the Chinese film industry, and having witnessed many passionate young artists unfortunately being marginalized by society, he developed the concept of presenting his unique personal experiences on screen. After completion, this autobiographical wor—*Beijing Bastards*—won numerous international awards, as he had hoped it would; however, in China he was both ostracized and blacklisted (Fig. 2.1).

Fig. 2.1   A medium shot showing a street scene in *Beijing Bastards*

First, the title of the film is itself a highly derogatory, insulting and vulgar use of language. Furthermore, adding Beijing as its prefix easily causes possible political associations. The film presents the anxieties and losses of a group of young Chinese: a rock band, a pregnant young girl, an underground musician, a poor painter and college student, as well as including various other individuals living impoverished, dull and meaningless existences. Appearing highly fragmented, trivial and even barely intelligible at first, the movie actually has a narrative structure that comprises fragmented stories. However, it does not have a central theme; neither does it contain central characters as commonly would be featured in other films.

The young characters share a strong sense of solitariness arising from marginalization and confused interpersonal relations. Consequently, a suffocating feeling of emptiness prevails. I will probe into the narrative from three different perspectives: the restlessness of the post-revolutionary era, the generation gap between father and son, and characters' attitudes towards an uncertain future.

Being Discontented in the Post-revolutionary Era

Before the title appears, several tracking shots show a rainy evening, during which a young man, Kazi, and his girlfriend, Maomao, have a quarrel under a bridge when Kazi requests that Maomao has an abortion. Maomao refuses to do so and leaves in a fit of rage. This prelude demonstrates the moral deregulation and physiological indulgence of the younger generations (born in the 1960s) in the late 1980s, when the fading of Chinese revolutionary idealism caused the disintegration of asceticism.[7] Later on, Kazi dates a female college student in order to fill his spiritual and physical void; the subsequent banishment of the girl the next morning signifies his complete lack of emotional devotion and obvious narcissism. In hindsight, this kind of "sexual release" rampant in society at that time can be viewed metaphorically as the superficial means by which this generation of confused young people tried to establish their individuality and subjectivity, which nevertheless was evidence for their spiritual and moral emptiness.

Sex and rock music are witnessed throughout the film, which is the patented trademark of the emerging New Wave cinema. On the surface, these scenes are similar to the impulses of "sexual liberation" against society found in the whole "lost generation" in the West during the 1960s. As one critic noted, "because of the subversive, oppositional quality associated with rock music and the lifestyle it generates (sexual license; drug taking; 'creative' fashions and hairstyles), Western spectators have been understandably titillated to discover the existences of an underground rock culture in Beijing."[8] However, these two unique phenomena had different historical motivations. The emergence of Western rock music and the "sexual liberation" movement was a move against capitalist rule; it was thus an expression of the profound despair and hopelessness of the younger generation, who indulged in their desires and yearned for a release of their anxieties and political fears. As a contrast, the rock music and sexual indulgence in late 1980s China was the product of a post-revolutionary angst in which radical, revolutionary idealism was repudiated. Critic Andrew Jones aptly remarked that "the Chinese rock subculture has not reached the level of articulated *political* opposition, [but] the rock sensibility does hinge upon a clearly articulated, self-consciously held ideology of *cultural* opposition."[9] To be sure, the rock cultures in China and in the West also share similarities. To start with, they both harbor profound feelings of alienation (either arising from the commercialization of human labor and the exploitation of surplus values, or brought about by alienation in existing socialist societies in which people could not be the true masters of their own fortunes), which is witnessed as kind of omnipresent depression. People from both sides also felt that they were being hoodwinked: when the ordinary people in the West were affected by the global movements of anti-capitalism and anti-colonialism stimulated by Red China, they felt disgusted with bourgeois moral principles.[10] As a consequence of the complete repudiation of the Cultural Revolution by the Chinese authorities, the young Chinese deemed themselves betrayed and hence developed a sense of political weariness and cynicism. Accordingly, rock music on both sides contained a powerful liberating force: an idealist motive concealed deeply under the façade of decadence, shown as youthful restlessness and a quest for justice.

However, this liberating wave in China was, at the time, primarily expressed in a negative way due to a shortage of spiritual values. For example, the character Kazi indulges himself in promiscuous sexual relations while searching for liberation from these struggles. While looking for his missing pregnant girlfriend, he also becomes addicted to alcohol. In a series of montages, men and women are shown roaming aimlessly on the streets, the men trying to seduce women. In this way, the film pushes the audience to reflect on the phenomenon: is this what the so-called Chinese "lost generation" is really like?

The rock band, as a secondary "protagonist" in the movie, appears even before the couple shows up, and is intercut with the latter. Headed by leading singing star Cui Jian—a key figure of rock music in the 1980s and, here, playing himself—the band comes on the scene now and again throughout the film. Their experience delivers the message of a hostile society antagonistic towards their art. While practicing, they learn that their rented rehearsal venue must be taken back and are thus pressured to relocate numerous times—even forced to perform on construction sites. Such a self-solicited marginalization not only demonstrates their passion for their music, but also shows their youthful spirit of rebellion, breaking away from the established institutions. Obviously, their songs express their dissatisfaction with reality, their depression arising from their surplus but suppressed energies. Cui says to the worksite manager who comes to order them away, "From now on, you listen to me. We will absolutely perform here tonight. Do not dismantle it any more!" Such a paradoxical mix of conceit and self-contemptuousness is symbolic of their living conditions in the absence of power and authority. However, sometimes, these self-styled "cultural heroes" are also not portrayed in a positive light. There is a close shot of another rock band headed by Dou Wei (also a leading rock musician at the time) at the end of the film. When Dou's face is shown like that of a monster in the darkness, the scene cuts to a spectator, who scornfully remarks, "what a stupid band, like idiots, really!"

In other parts of the film, a "Gang of Three" often appears. A writer named Daqing[11] is cheated out of his money and has to seek assistance from a villain named Yuan Honghai, begging the latter to recover his lost money. During lunch, his friend Huang Yelu, a book peddler, appears. These guys are down and out but pretend to be in high-spirits. The film takes several shots to establish their personalities. After Huang is driven out of the restaurant following a quarrel with his friends, he turns his head to the spectators and yells: "You bastards! Are you laughing at me?" In another lunch scene, he feels ridiculed by Yuan and then begins to fight with him. Later, staggering ahead with Daqing, Huang tearfully says, "He looks down on me!" But, sometimes, he also admits, "I am absolutely an idiot." A scene showing Daqing urinating in the street implies that he lacks any kind of self-restraint (Fig. 2.2).

Fig. 2.2 A scene in the restaurant in *Beijing Bastards*

The film also gives us another minor character, Jin Ling, an art school student who has a love affair with Kazi. She intends to stay in Beijing but finds it extremely difficult—a situation shared by most college graduates at the time. So, she confides in Li Yu, the wife of a rocker, who is also living an unstable life. When Yuan comes to Zhou Ming, who only appears once in the film, he finds that Zhou has neither a reliable source of income, nor any decent job consequently, he has to stay with his wife (who is pregnant) all day long. Yuan mercilessly mocks him by saying that, "Having a kid is taking all your time?...Don't you have anything better to do?"

The lives of these underclass characters in the film are "representative," for they are the micro-landscape of the many urban youths during that era. There is a specially arranged shot of meta-language: in a close-up, turning his head to the camera, Daqing delivers a monolog, "We are those who do everything we want and never care about how others may think about it. We are all dissidents of the society." Feeling dissatisfied with reality, they are filled with a kind of spiritual void, and are anxious, restless, depressed and indignant. In another close-up, Cui Jian reads the lyrics of his song "Last Complaint" before singing, "We walk ahead against the winds, full of complaints. I don't know when

I was injured but I do feel pains." One can conclude that they are discontent with life in this post-socialist society. However, only from a historic vantage point can we account for their preternatural psyches and idiosyncratic behaviors.

The Effects of "Bastardization"?

It has been noted that the architecture in the film is "an unappetizing mixture of postindustrial Western functionality and third world squalor,"[12] a feature that is as "'bastardized' as the lives of the protagonists,"[13] who are "'bastardized' subjects treading uneasily between the claustrophobic, cramped quarters of the domestic sphere and the open, unpredictable spaces of the modern city."[14] These conditions can be viewed as one presenting a state that is "neither communist nor capitalist, neither eastern nor western."[15] The director also explains that his objective is to "reflect the state of mind of young people in contemporary China," which is described by him as "the global outcome of a bastardized contemporary culture."[16] Indeed, all the characters in the film appear very dispirited and awkward. For example, Daqing is shown demanding money from others but is also being pursued for outstanding debts; thus, he often has his broken leather shoes mended in the street (a metaphor for his dispirited life). Huang Yelu is unable to afford a taxi fare, eventually must dismiss the driver when the car arrives. This listless and apathetic condition is not unique to them. Other characters in the film, such as portrayed in a scene which shows several people sitting in a room playing Mahjong, can also be considered in the same light.

What is being shown here was the state of inertia in China after 1989 and before the beginning of a market-oriented economy in 1992. In the film, Cui Jian sings: "I am not recalling and I don't want to recall. But year after year the wind blows, changing its form but never going away; the injuries of so many people have been lauded as revolution." Berenice Reynaud suggests that the "bitterly cold, sweeping wind may be a metaphor for the brutal changes of Chinese society…or for the advent of the global market."[17] Indeed, Cui is expressing an intrinsic feeling of alienation, either that of an exhausted sense brought about by the clichés of "revolution after revolution," or of a sense of apathy towards the gospel of globalization, both of which being chanted and promoted by the regime which had brought about "the injuries of so many people."

Therefore, he feels that "I have only love inside my heart because it is not so painful. Oh, I can only trust myself." He goes on to proclaim, "I am not recalling and I don't want to recall. But the unclear past makes the winds even stronger." The audience is left to wonder what kind of a past prohibits them from recalling; what kind of a past is unclear to them? They feel frustrated by the misunderstanding of society. However, they also harm themselves by their failure to comprehend social changes. Both of these mindsets originate from the loss of idealism and political orientation. These inexperienced youths, facing the "changing winds" amidst the de-politicization process and full negation of the Cultural Revolution, are incapable of comprehending the political sea-change, and can only feel that "the injuries of so many people have been lauded as revolution." Consequently, for them, politics is a foreign concept; "I can only trust myself." Life in the political society only brings bitter memories; it is only "love inside my heart" that is "not so painful."

It is also out of this confusion that a state of bastardization of the indigenous culture takes place:

> Times are...changing, and globalization threatens the indigenous space of creativity, which, in turn, has to be renegotiated within rock culture itself...The bastardization of the space and that of the subject overlap, creating shifts in register between what is constructed as "the real" and what is experienced as "fantasy." A specific form of theatrical mise-en-scene is born out of such blurring of boundaries. Rock musicians are performance artists, and their concerts, as well as their lifestyle, are subject to elaborate forms of hybrid/bastardized staging...The "bastardization" of Chinese culture hinges on this hybrid form of theatricalization specific to the later stages of capitalism...in which every act, public and private, is commodified.[18]

In short, "by stressing blurring of boundaries between reality and fantasy, Zhang equates the process of (post-Debord) theatricalization with the situation of hybridization/bastardization in which he places his characters," Berenice Reynaud thus contends.[19]

Here, Reynaud stresses the elements of "fantasy" and "the curious/desiring gaze of the spectator, and how the subject is aware of this gaze,"[20] both terms being fashionable theoretical jargon coming from postmodern criticism. Differing from this critique, I prefer to point out the fact that what is being shown in the movie is still a realistic portrait of confusion, which is ultimately a result of the disappearance of socialist idealism, revealed by a lack of a father-figure in the lives of characters. In other words, the condition of post-socialism, described as a state of "bastardization," is actually a fatherless/rootless situation, being "neither communist nor capitalist, neither eastern nor western."[21] Thus, this can be considered a situation partially brought about by the new trend of globalization, which impinges upon the post-socialist Chinese society in the age of late capitalism.

In this regard, we can also conjure up the "bastardized" form of societal changes by the names of the characters. For instance, the Chinese name "Daqing" implies that he was born in the 1960s when the City of Daqing was the model of the socialist national industry. The name Huang Yelu indicates an intellectual who has embraced foreign culture (Yelu is equivalent to Yale in Chinese). Furthermore, the family name "Huang" in Chinese also refers to the color yellow, which carryies the connotation of "pornographic," which may allude to the personality of this penniless book peddler (it is worthwhile noting that booksellers at the time often sold pornographic works for profit due to the rampant trend of commercialization). Meanwhile, to some extent, the lifestyle of the characters similarly reflects the social, political and cultural transformations of China in the trend for mass commercialization. For instance, they spare no effort to win the favor of overseas patrons, shown in a scene in which an art professional advises Jin Ling that gaining the recognition of an overseas businessman is the only way out, revealing a pessimistic job market and the prevailing mindset of blindly worshiping and currying the favor of foreigners around the time of the late 1980s and early 1990s.

Another attribute worth special attention in the film is the background effects. A soundtrack of radios and TVs deliberately inserted into the diegetic space of the movie also signifies the advent of an era of globalization. During these scenes, we not only hear the announcements of the policies of national economic reforms, but also news about the intense battle between Vice President Aleksandr Rutskoi and President Boris Yeltsin for the direction of the national development of Russia (in the TV segments as shown, Rutskoi emphasizes his position as an officially elected vice president and therefore only the Russian people could dismiss him. He also vows to investigate the corruption of the Yeltsin administration). Such a fierce political situation in Russia after the disintegration of the former Soviet Union introduces the general state of the world in the post-socialist era. These significant changes in the former Soviet Union in wake of the June Fourth Incident, together with the other activities of politicians from various countries during the vehement changes in East Europe (delivered to the audience through the broadcast news in the sound track), constitute the backdrop to China's change of its foreign policies. A scene in which the television is broadcasting a piece of CCTV English news about President Jiang Zemin's daily activities when meeting his foreign counterparts is particularly revealing. The fact that the chairman of the CCP Central Committee packaged himself with the title of Western democratic institutions, in order to adapt to the trend of globalization, unwittingly demonstrates his lack of confidence in China's own political system. However, at that particular time it still took China a while before it was fully involved in the wave of globalization. Thus, scenes of elderly women wearing a red ribbon around their arm, reminiscent of the former Mao's times, also appear in the film from time to time.

However, deeper feelings associated with the loss of innocence and ideals by the young people cast an atmosphere of emptiness, which also transforms the ethical-moral customs in familial relations. Li Yu's grandma is shown complaining about being alone when Li returns home to retrieve her belongings. Her perceived ignorance of her grandma's complaints demonstrates that modernization and the improvement of living standards do not necessarily bring people the happiness that they expect. On the contrary, they bring a coldness into interpersonal relations. Critics thus generally believe that, in this movie, "nihilism has fully defeated the leading characters so that they become indulged in emptiness and could not pull themselves out, being unwilling to find the source of emptiness and unable to break away from it."[22] In fact, they are not unwilling to identify the source; they just do not have the ability to comprehend the changing political economy.

In addition, critics also believe that the spiritual emptiness originates from their refusal to follow the traditional patriarchal model: "the emptiness of Zhang Yuan and the diversified marginalized urban youngsters in his film comes from their decline to recognize the order of patriarchy; and it is the feeling of loss after breakaway from the traditional bondage."[23] To reach that conclusion, a comparison is further made between the films of the Sixth Generation directors and the directors of the Fifth Generation:

Directors of the 5th-generation changed from patricide to recognition of patriarchy and dithered between betrayal and loyalty. The 6th-generation directors were more callous as they did not acknowledge patriarchy from the very beginning. They were even contemptuous of patricide because it was based on the recognition of paternity in advance...Zhang Yuan and the characters in his film never wished to recognize such a rude cultural spokesman and token of order. They tenaciously expelled paternity... Therefore, no father is witnessed in his film and it is a carnival of the second generation. In particular, the recurring rock concerts become the symbol of their carnivals...The absence of father in such a small world of their own in the film renders them aimless and next to ineffectuality, and hence dissolves the subversive significance of rock music and launches themselves into a paradoxical situation. As a result, rock music seems to become a tool of seclusion to isolate them from the world where the patriarchy prevails.[24]

This critic continues to point out, "the narcissism of the director and the characters in his film and their refusal of patriarchy feed each other, which put them in a strange deadlock from which they find it hard to break through."[25]

Indeed, there is no central father figure throughout the movie. It can thus be inferred that this generation was without an intellectual mentor or supervisor—a traditional role played by a masculine father figure. Consequently, they live a self-indulgent life. For example, Kazi sleeps in late and wakes up late without a second thought; and his mother is cosseting her child, "I will make whatever it is you want to eat." However, digging deeper into the film, the role of father is not always completely absent. In the marketplace, we hear the song chanting "the golden sun for people of all ethnic groups," a revolutionary anthem for Chairman Mao, which vicariously shows the phenomenon of "Mao Zedong fever" in the early 1990s. Indeed, as the vehicle of patriarchy, politics is not fully bypassed in the film, although it is merely alluded to in an indirect manner, e.g. through the sound track broadcasting the news about the political battles in Russia, as well as through a flash of the Tiananmen Square in the rain. Such a euphemistic articulation signifies that the film must contain its barely concealed political information. Although the absence of the father in the film signifies estrangement from the previous generation in terms of ideals and experiences, the contemporary generation's repudiation of becoming a father (as shown in the beginning of the film by Kazi's insistence on abortion) also indicates their utter inexperience and complete immaturity.

Worse, as in the director's film *Sons* (儿子) (1996), the sons even "refuse to see their father for what he really is – an alcoholic with a heavy heredity (his own father was given to drinking, gambling, and philandering) and a hidden, tragic history."[26] When one character beats his father, a symbolic act of killing shared by many films at the time (started by the Fifth Generation directors, however), the implied message is clearly delivered: this new generation breaks Chinese traditional ethics of filial piety for the second time, following the first cultural patricide in the May Fourth movement of anti-traditionalism. The action itself is very significant: "after the father is put out of sight," the members of the new generation "leave their state of bohemian stasis and enter full speed into a concerted strategy of urban renewal. They become entrepreneurs"—a move welcomed by the incoming market-oriented society.[27]

Longing for the Happiness of the Future

As one critic has pointed out, the characters are, indeed, "tenaciously resisting the social order and culture that their father represents." However, it is a mistake to say that they are "willing to hide themselves in their extremely small world where they preserve their freedom and dignity."[28] Similarly, it is wrong to suggest that "their counterattack finally ends up in retreat and their pain into cowardliness to preserve their assumptive and self-deceiving satisfaction."[29] This is not merely because no individual can live in a vacuum state separate from society. Losing their sense of direction and feeling deeply alienated, what they try to attain is still to "return to the harmonious world of imaginary order and enjoy the ideal state of unity."[30] Consequently, rock music becomes their means of releasing their angst, indignation and dissatisfaction, although the singers do not consciously know the origination of the discontent. However, just like Cui Jian's rock song in the film shows, they have recognized the fact that:

(If) We want to find the roots of indignation; we can only march head against the wind…

(If) We want to end this last complaint; we can only march head against the wind.

The lyrics confirm that, in their minds, they have decided on their path: "I want to replace pain and harm with hope, but all I can do is march forward against the wind." Such a spirit of "marching against the wind" and such a constructive attitude of "ending the last complaint" and "replacing pain and harm with hope" signify clearly that they are not, as someone has commented, "fully in a spiritual quagmire beyond rescue."[31] Rather, their resolute attitude allows them to keep looking for ways out of their intellectual predicament. These lyrics are somewhat reminiscent of *The Military Song of the People's Liberation Army*, which was created and popularized within the period of the socialist revolution during their fathers' generation (which begins, "March ahead, march ahead, march ahead!"), which indicates that they have unwittingly inherited the "spirit" of their fathers. In this light, "I march ahead against the wind" could also be taken as the staunch vow of this new generation, which more or less maintained socialist ideals in the early days of reform. It is true that these confused, hurt and marginalized young people struggled in a society that they could not understand; yet, dialectically, they also have many cherished hopes and abide by their unbounded idealism.

Certainly, they may still be advocating individualistic feelings, which hold the tenet "I can only rely on myself," as expressed in the lyrics of the rock music. Additionally, they still remain in a general state of restlessness when they say "I don't know *why* we are so indignant but such indignation makes us feel good." However, society has accelerated the process of their reaching the state of maturity. At the end of the film, these once decadent and confused characters have become fathers (though reluctantly), thus having to shoulder their social responsibilities. The audience is also informed that Maomao chooses not to abort her baby and, instead, holds her child and returns to Kazi (who has just been released from jail). In the last scene of the movie, Kazi marches ahead in a with conviction amidst the cries of her baby and with Cui Jian's rock song being played in the background. The lyrics run like this: although "I sing and sing and still can't sing it away/the pains of the city;" yet "the pains make me believe/in the good times to come." The song goes on: "Suddenly, there's a mass movement in front of my eyes, changing my life like a revolution." Although it appears as though this is referring to the 1989 student movement, the lyrics suddenly change together with its implied implications, "A girl takes her love to me, and it's like wind and rain in my face," which humorously brings the audience into a very different situation. Prior to this scene, an image of innocent kids playing in the street has been presented, which aims to signify the memory of the (missing) innocent days, and implies a new quest for idealism (Fig. 2.3).

Overall, the film displays China during a major transitional stage. A scene of traffic flowing is shown at the beginning and end of the film to signify an accelerated state of modernization, as well as the chaos and alienation this brings about. It also implies a feeling of awe about it— Chinese people did not know how to deal with the complexity of the new consumer society right after the Mao era. What is commonly witnessed here are series of montages of dense and silent groups of buildings, the spacious yet empty Tiananmen Square, the East and West Chang'an Avenue in drizzling rain, nighttime neon lights, subway stairways, children playing games in the Hutongs, and even an operating table where babies are born. Although undergoing large-scale changes, the city of Beijing itself retains its grandiosity and silence. This, in some sense, demonstrates a kind of volatility of its natural history. Amidst the hustle and bustle, the younger generation is thus now growing up and beginning to walk into a brave new world.

Transcribing China in its revolutionary change through the youth of a particular artistic circle, the director shows the anxiety of his generation. Because the nature of the transition was still beyond the intellectual's recognition, according to Berenice Reynaud, "there are no grand vistas or master's gaze" here, the absence of which result in a "limited field of vision."[32] Still, the film maintains a reflective and critical attitude

Fig. 2.3 A rock 'n' roll scene featuring Cui Jian singing blasphemous lyrics

towards the youngsters by displaying their sexual indulgence. Even the lyrics contain self-criticism, such as "An unsteady will makes you feel/ even more painful." Cast in this light, the title *Beijing Bastards* does not fall short of the power of self-mockery and self-critique. Being estranged from their fathers, the youth of this generation were dissidents of an era of rapid de-politicization, who passionately expressed their dissatisfaction, indignation and confusion. But they still have cherished hopes for the future, looking for their new position and direction in a society when a post-revolutionary order was gradually taking shape.

A Fable of Indulgence and Self-Annihilation

Weekend Lover served as Lou Ye's (1965–) first feature-film since his graduation from the Beijing Film Academy in 1989. Shot and produced in 1993–1994, it was banned for two years in China. Finally, the ban was lifted, and the film was released internationally at the tail end of 1995,[33] winning the Rainer Werner Fassbinder Best Director Award of the 45th Mannheim-Heidelberg International Film Festival the following year. Unlike other movies produced by China's New Wave directors, it includes many elements of a commercial film, including brash music and coincidental events. Many coincidences taking place in the film also give the audience a feeling of destiny and story-making, hence undercutting the realistic effects of the movie.

Narrating a love triangle among three leading characters from Li Xin's perspective—Li Xin, her ex-boyfriend, A Xi, and her present sweetheart, Lala——the film shows their conflicts they experience, conflicts which eventually lead to violence and death. The theme of the cruelty of youth, together with the rebellious rock music running throughout, again epitomizes the dissatisfaction, indignation, emptiness and disobedience of the younger generation in late 1980s, and the audience can easily notice the shadow of despair, pain and death following these vulnerable lives. It seems that underlying Freudian themes and an urge for inexplicable dedication make up the bulk of the movie.

Indeed, what can be said about the characters in the film is that what they are looking for in love is nothing but their own self-image, demonstrating their egocentric and nihilistic attitude towards affection through violence and death, nevertheless, which betrays their inability to establish self-identity. This failure is closely related to their lack of faith and a lack of self-reflection. The title of the movie directly expresses the ambiguity and the motif of self-indulgence: the lovers meet each other during weekends in order to fulfill their superficial, physiological needs. Furthermore, although the "use of past tense in the voice-over" signifies "an attempt to reflect on the past from the perspective of the present," rather than engaging in genuine self-critique, it merely "testifies to that desire,"[34] which is typical of the "excessive dose of adolescent narcissism" existing in earlier films of the New Wave cinema.[35] Consequently, this film fails to give a comprehensive picture of the social over-determinations that bring about the final tragedy, and becomes once more a permissive release of juvenile impulses.

Strife Over Love and the Anxiety of Forging Identity

Since the relevant messages of the plotline are fragmented and scattered throughout the movie, it is difficult for the audience to pull them together in order to forge a complete picture of the narrative. But, as critics, we must strive to explain the story in chronological order. It begins as a flashback eight years previously, in 1985. A Xi and Li Xin were still high school classmates then, meeting at Li Xin's home each weekend while her parents were away. However, their love affair, which was taboo at a time when ascetic discipline was still very rigid and dogmatic, was reported by one of his class leaders. Out of anger, A Xi accidentally killed the cadre and was put in jail. Later, in 1993, where the story of the film starts, he has just been released. However, in a painful revelation, he discovers that his "sweetheart" Li Xin is now in love with Lala, an amateur musician. Failing to put an end to Lala's passion, he attempts to have an intimate relation with Li Xin out of despair, but she stabs him. Unwilling to accept such a tragic ending, he forces Li to have sex with him by threatening to spoil Lala's upcoming concert. Having noticed the pain on Li's face upon her late arrival at the concert, Lala realizes what has happened, rushes to A Xi's apartment and stabs him to death. At the time, A Xi is packing to leave for the countryside, which implies that only the simple and rustic countryside affords a haven, whereas the urban city is taken as an abyss of desire. While he is dying, a smile comes to his face, as if he is relieved (Fig. 2.4).

Undoubtedly, A Xi has strong affection for Li Xin, which is alluded to in some places. Something the audience may not notice is a cigarette lighter which appears throughout the film. In the first scene, Li Xin puts the lighter into A Xi's pocket while they are preparing to make love,

Fig. 2.4 A closeup shows A Xi enviously observing what is happening to his lover

implying her attempt to ignite his desire. Later, when A Xi is packing and preparing to return to the countryside, he raises his head to look at the lighter on the table; despite feeling somewhat sentimental, he puts it down, indicating that he realizes he has forfeited her love permanently and has decided to give it up. The last time we see the lighter is when he is dying and returns to his room, lighting the lighter and smoking his last cigarette.

As the rebel of the time, A Xi is wild and arrogant, an egocentric individualist who does not hesitate to take any action in order to fulfill his desires. For example, he dares to inflict injury on his classmate when the latter becomes an obstruction to his way of living. Also, after he is released from jail, he tries to win Li back through violence. For this, he eventually pays with his life. But his pain is not entirely unique: the pain is shared by an entire generation; the actor Jia Hongsheng (1967–2010) who played the role of A Xi found himself unable to escape adverse feelings in society and later committed suicide. In other words, egoism is the symptom of the times. When so-called altruistic socialist morality dies out, unabashed individualism is pursued in order to satiate personal desires at all costs, which nevertheless leads to self-destruction.

For the sake of love, A Xi takes all measures to satisfy his desires so as to locate the meaning of his existence. But he can never establish his self-assurance in this way. He is still under age (both physiologically and intellectually) when his life comes to an end.

The character who counteracts A Xi's arrogance in the film is Lala, who gets to know Li Xin only by chance. On the surface, Lala and A Xi diverge in many ways. Li once tells herself (and to the audience), "Even if A Xi had not been put in jail, I still may have ended up with Lala, because A Xi would not have loved me for a long time. But Lala will." The words imply that she believes A Xi is only fond of her beauty but that Lala loves her deeply. On the surface, Lala looks simpler; the movie implies that he has more professional ambitions. Consistently pursuing his dreams of a musical future, he establishes a band with himself as the lead vocalist. By contrast, A Xi seemingly has no plans for his future; rather, he cares more about money. It is due to him requesting Li to give a package to his business partner that Li accidentally meets Lala. A Xi is more selfish and aggressive. In certain places, the movie seems to allude that it is his Westernized lifestyle that makes him more nihilistic and empty-minded.[36] However, in actuality they are not different at all in nature: they both fight for their love with determination and persistence. They are both anxious due to the uncertainty of their future, and they both live for their desires. Their difference, if any, is that A Xi has greater desires (some of which are invisible and unarticulated) while Lala only focuses on Li Xin and rock music. What is more, Lala kills A Xi accidentally, just as A Xi had previously killed his classmate. In this sense, Lala is also immature. In fact, they are not only the two sides of the same coin, but also mirrors of each other, and also mirrors of a whole generation of young people. In this blind world of youthful innocence, there is no adult man and no reason. As Li confesses in her monologue when she reminisces the past years later, "we thought that others did not know us. But we were wrong. Everyone had undergone his youthful age."

Being the incarnation (and also the object) of desire, Li Xin always satisfies her own desires. After A Xi is put in jail, she starts to look for emotional (and physiological) satisfaction. Then, she meets Lala and accepts his advances regardless of her lover A Xi. Certainly, we could say that Li Xin and A Xi do not experience genuine love when they are together, but her betrayal is apparently unfair to A Xi. It is her callousness that throws A Xi into despair; and she is selfish enough not to inform Lala earlier about her relationship with A Xi. After these complicated love affairs, she is on the brink of collapse. Murmuring about her past in front of the camera, she looks pale under the dark lights; having cut her hair cut in a demure style, she looks simple and naive, but also a little mysterious. In this moment, she confesses to her bosom friend, "Actually, I have long been rotting away. I knew it when I was young…many parts of my body have been like this. But neither A Xi nor Lala have realized it;" "Do you know who has caused all of this? It is me. I destroyed my own life…I feel that I am too evil, too bad." Finally, she murmurs, "A Xi's ghost has been inside me. Are you scared?" The confession shows that she knows her problems. Like the two male characters, she has been exploring herself, too; however, her subjectivity—the "reasonable," self-controllable self—is never established.

Why the Lack of Identity?

Like *Beijing Bastards*, there is also no father figure in the film.[37] Rather than making the young people independent, this situation launches them into a state of confusion: they are empty-headed at this historic moment when an ideological guide, such as had been previously emphasized, is absent. Directionless, they attempt to seek warmth through contact with others; therefore, in numerous scenes, the audience witnesses the characters making calls in a telephone booth. Filmed in dark lighting, little dialogue is shown in these moments, though their facial expressions signify that they are disheartened. Feeling discontent with society, they are filled with vague aspirations; yet, they find it difficult to express their yearnings. They engage in smoking, drinking and sexual intercourse; but, despite the physiological release that accompanies their reckless behavior, they are incapable of attaining any understanding of their existence.

This was common for many young Chinese people following the repudiation of Mao's revolutionary radicalism, and when "to get rich is glorious" was touted as the new life principle. A particular scene specifically reflects this: when Lala is dating Li Xin, a long shot shows a wall with a publicity column on it in the distance. The information is barely visible as it is blocked by Lala; only some words can be seen—"through efforts." Apparently, the objective of such "efforts" has already become blurred. One can confer from this scene, that the ultimate goal of communism has already faded, giving way to the prevailing materialist environment. Consequently, despite their continuous physical growth, this generation of youth can be viewed as lacking spiritual cultivation.

During A Xi and Li Xin's final date, the camera turns towards the wall behind them twice. What is engraved on the wall signifies the height marks of A Xi's classmate Jianguo (the name literally means "state-building"), who is the owner of the house and who has accompanied A Xi to physically assault the class leader. This scene makes obvious reference to the physical growth of the character, whereas the implied message is that, although the People's Republic of China is already established and has been developing for thirty years, the younger generation has simply become a lost generation—and even "stunted"—following the repudiation of Maoist radicalism.

Through A Xi, Lala and Li Xin's love triangle, the movie attempts to illustrate the living conditions of urban Chinese youth, those born in the mid- to late 1960s, in the late 1980s. Throughout the decade, most of them were fans of Teresa Deng (1993–1995), a popular singer from Taiwan, and also came to idolize the Beatles and John Lennon, the heroes of Western rock music. However, during their intellectually formative years, they did neither participated nor comprehended the Chinese Cultural Revolution. They sometimes listened to Chinese model operas; however, they could not appreciate the historic connotations, as these had been rejected as ultra-leftist. Accordingly, they did not understand the past; neither could they recognize the ongoing changes in society. They now followed the tenets of liberal cosmopolitanism, but declined to be the successors of socialist traditions and ancient Chinese culture, both of which were taken to be feudalist ideas and praxis. Unlike others of the generation who were full of concern for the external world and earnestly looking for their new roles in society, these characters simply chose to imitate the sub-cultures of Western youth, taking this as a sign of modernity, but also feeling vexed by the isolation accompanying it. Simple imitation did not enable them to forge a new identity as, although Chinese society was itself undergoing a major reconstruction, Western ideology was not yet fully embraced by society and the social structure remained largely the same in nature.

During a voice-over in one scene, Li Xin reflects on her naivete, "I remember that I loved drinking because I thought I was the most painful person in the world; and I complained the society for being not understand me. But I gradually came to realize that it was not that the society did not understand us, but it is we that could not comprehend the society." Indeed, they feel a sense of strong repulsion from the outside world. Their juvenile angst is simply an imaginative cultural retaliation against society, which epitomizes their extreme spiritual narcissism and cultural apathy. This is particularly witnessed in the lyrics of their rock songs. Though they know "many people are callous in the world", they simply yell out some ambiguous petitions, "please offer us food, your majesty, so that our children can grow as they need; please remove spiritual walls, your majesty, so that our desires and fantasies can be fulfilled." To be sure, these yearnings could be understood as their appeal to authority; yet, at the same time, when they sing the lyrics "desires or despairs are around you, flying up and down," they simultaneously condemn it: "Nonsense, you are talking nonsense, you are spoiling people's habits." At one point, Li Xin admits in her monologue that, when the band members are crying out, "We feel that we are the owners of the city, as if everything could be permanent. But actually we don't know what the future will be like."

Inability of Making Reflections and the Continuation of Daydreams

In this monolog of reminiscence, Li Xin muses, "Life remains the same, but our attitude towards life has changed. We have learned to look back at ourselves and our past." Here, she seems to understand her juvenile superficiality. But does she really comprehend? At the very beginning, a sentence in large Chinese characters appear on the full screen claiming that the story to be unfolded is based on "real events" about a group of young people in the 1980s. This declaration demonstrates the director's desire to usurp the privilege of claiming truth or authenticity. Is that effective? Critics notice that the film is full of medium and close shots, featuring intricate and layered interior lighting, which is intended to show "the attitude of close watch and meticulous examination;" the director also emphasizes subjectivity and personality in his presentation of details.[38] Does this subjectivity deliver authentic messages from the era?

When A Xi commits his crime in 1985, China was still developing relatively smoothly along its path of economic reform and opening-up, but the process of secularization and de-politicization also accelerated, which is cued in the movie by the Teresa Deng's concert in the prelude and the frequent background music comprising songs from Hong Kong and Taiwan, as well as the cups of Coca-Cola. Secret love affairs and fights among high school students as shown in the film were also commonly witnessed in reality. However, the movie does not fully tap into the societal texture. Although the restless and rough lifestyle of these young people seemingly corresponds to the social mood of the time—the dissatisfaction of certain classes underneath the superficial prosperity—the movie does not reveal the cultural-political nature of their restlessness, partly because it never establishes organic links between the story and the historical and social subtexts.

Eight years later, in 1993, or the year after Deng Xiaoping's South China tour, the veil of the market-oriented economy was fully lifted; this was when A Xi is released from jail. The film shows that people are still watching imported, dubbed Western films (Li and Lala are bored with them in a theater) and playing video games; the radio talk-show discusses the troubles arising from extramarital affairs. In addition, Li is working in an American enterprise (a fast-food restaurant called "Californian Rainbow"), yet no explanation is made as to how she is Westernized and what is the relation between her behavior and the trend towards Westernization. The only thing related to the market society is the dissolution of a band.

This rock band is the one in which Lala is a member and it is tied to another storyline involving two lovers, Zhang Chi and Chen Chen, both being close friends of Lala and Li Xin. Zhang is a talented but marginalized musician. Chen who is about to separate from him is an employee of a Hong Kong music production company and busy with her job earning a living. By chance, the two couples come to know each other and Lala becomes the lead vocalist of Zhang's band. Zhang and other members of his band are also living in anxiety and perplexed. They are all steeped in their professional and emotional predicaments (Fig. 2.5).

But there are problems in portraying the couple. Why are they about to separate? Surely, it must be something related to Zhang's poverty (unlike a few rock players at the time, he has yet to become a popular and profitable pop star), but the movie does not deliver the message clearly. It presents an event showing Chen's boss from Hong Kong, but none of his characteristics are portrayed. Zhang's arbitrariness is shown (he forces others to give up seats and leave a store, which reminds us of a similar scene with Yuan Honghai in Beijing Bastards), but is this just revealing the egotism of an artist? Although his romantic imagining of the USA reveals part of his personality (he says, "A man like me should be born in America"), only his dedication to work is stressed: he intends to reestablish a band when the one he in is ready to dissolve due to every member having a new engagement, which is the only message in the

Fig. 2.5 Lala performs in the concert

diegetic space showing the diversification of characters in a market-oriented economy.

A particular gender-related message is worthy of note; it shows the secularization or diversification of society. After Chen Chen and Li Xin get to know each other, they avoid Lala and amuse themselves in the bathroom, which is a strange scene worthy of contemplation, possibly implying that they are lesbians. However, even so, it does not add any special message to the film. One possible interpretation might be that both have realized the need to conceal something from men (Chen Chen simply discovers the secret of Li Xin and A Xi's relationship). But this does not organically integrate into the plot-line of the film. In short, the film does not enhance our comprehension of society; neither does it help us to know more about the love triangle or its intended significance.

The film closes with an epilogue. This takes place one day in 1999 when and is a daydream. On the surface, this sceneis merely a copy of the typical scenario of Hollywood mafia movies, in which the "returning heroes" gather several years later to celebrate their success. However, this corresponds to the popular taste of the era: dreaming of getting rich overnight in an opportunistic market economy with the spirit of "entrepreneurship". During the scene, Lala has an expression of vigor, vitality and carelessness; he looks handsome in his red T-shirt, beige pants and sunglasses upon his release from jail. The members of his rock band, driving a black limousine (an emblem of fortune and upper-class identity of the era), welcome him back. When the door of the car opens, they come out one by one, standing in a line; Zhang Chi, wearing a business suit, a tie and a pair of sunglasses, looks just like a member of the Mafia. They appear in high spirits and their previous gloominess is gone, indicating that they have become the heroes of the new era.

Li Xin is sitting on the bonnet of the car, looking very charming with her backless skirt, heavy makeup and long hair. The classical limousine with a beautiful woman sitting on it is a landmark image of entrepreneurial success in the market era. There is no dialogue; everyone is smiling victoriously. Then Lala finds Chen Chen holding the hand of a small child, and looks up to Li Xin who grins at him in return. The caption shows:

Lala: "What is his name?"
Li Xin: "Lala!"

The imagination of the prospects of the next generation is often seen in the productions of the Sixth Generation directors. However, the scene here denotes something very different, for children here are the emblem of fortune and success, instead of the bearers of hope. These market heroes, who have become mafia-like figures, are carried away in their imaginative successes. These youngsters have been vexed by and have deeply indulged in sexual relations, but they finally "succeed" and no longer feel the pain of the 1990s when they were growing up. However, this does not necessarily mean that they have a real understanding of society. Instead, they have only adapted to society.

In the end, the camera rapidly rises up and a panorama of these men and women is presented; the following caption appears: "A Long time later, presumably in 1999, someone said he saw them in another city and that they were all very happy. This is a film about them." They are now "successful" and starting to create myths for themselves, taking their lost past of emptiness, depression, violence and death as legendary stories, which does nothing but show that they do not yet know the era.[39] The director's intended criticism, if any, is not realized as he might have wished. Indeed, here, "the lack of moral conviction" has "produced a sense of moral ambiguity."[40] The cruel story of youth is only narrated in a superficial way, just like the many long and static shots are used to signify the hastiness of youth.[41] Towards the end, amidst their daydreams, the young people do nothing but continue their perplexity, although they have seemingly come to realize their juvenile ignorance with the vicissitudes of time.

THE BIRTH OF BOURGEOIS SUBJECTIVITY IN MELANCHOLY

The diegetic story of *Summer Palace* starts from the mid-1980s and ends in 2003. Entering the 2006 Cannes International Film Festival as the only Chinese movie entry for the Golden Palm award without the government's approval, it reaped no awards; because of this, it was banned domestically and the director and producer were prohibited from producing films for five years.[42]

The film focuses on China's college students (who were generally taken to be elite intellectuals in Chinese society at the time), and on their emotional lives and confusion during the 1980s and 1990s, with the heroine, Yu Hong, taking the lead as the narrative voice. While critic Chris Chang takes the film to be a "sprawling, deeply moving epic,"[43] Jason Solomons finds it "stylish [and] atmospheric"[44] and David Denby praises its "use of jump cuts and a handheld camera, combined with Yu's solemnly lyrical and literary narration," which makes it "feel, at times, like a French New Wave film from 1967."[45] Other commentators often complain about the movie's excessive length (it lasts 140 minutes),[46] its "raw and unsettling" quality,[47] which makes it "occasionally involving but way over-stretched tapestry that plays like a French art movie in oriental dress."[48] They have been given to wonder why the director had "chosen to indulge in the enigmatic sign of melancholic female body, her whims and moods, her desire and crisis, to represent historical trauma as such?"[49] There are also opposing views. A.O. Scott, for one, is enchanted by the aesthetic features of the movie, "[despite] its 2-hour-20-minute length, 'Summer Palace' moves with the swiftness and syncopation of a pop song. Like Jean-Luc Godard in the 1960s, Mr. Lou favors breathless tracking shots and snappy jump cuts, and like Mr. Godard's, his camera is magnetized by female beauty."[50]

Why are there so many contradictory points of view? The key point lies in how we interpret the complex and intense erotic, love/hate relationship of the characters, played out against a volatile backdrop of political unrest.

Critic Derek Elley believes that it "shoots for metaphysical drama but ends up saying very little beneath all the poetic voiceovers, sexual encounters and political seasoning," despite the fact that it is "the first to feature…full frontal nudity by its male and female leads."[51] Since the extravagant indulgence in sexual promiscuity (and its ultimate failure) in an intense atmosphere of melancholia has caused uneasy feelings among the audience, critic Yiju Huang has also pondered the following issues: "what is the ultimate function of portraying this impasse of melancholia? Does it bear any political significance regarding the remembrance of the historical trauma? Is it a digression from historical truth or is it an attempted redemption of historical sickness?"[52] The result of her study is that this impasse becomes "a psychological constellation of rebellion against the coherence of the ego;"[53] and she suggests that "the representation of historical trauma in an unmediated form ultimately partakes in the violence of the dominant language that has caused the trauma in the first place" (Fig. 2.6).[54]

Although this explication touches upon the social-political correspondence (the historical trauma), ultimately, it merely resorts to a metaphysical speculation (on the "rebellion against the coherence of the ego") to undergird a seemingly historically specific but unfounded argument ("ultimately partakes in the violence"). I would suggest that, while "The youth's nude bodies and their promiscuities have become an

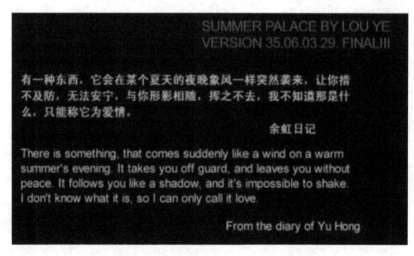

SUMMER PALACE BY LOU YE
VERSION 35.06.03.29. FINAL!!!

有一种东西，它会在某个夏天的夜晚象风一样突然袭来，让你措不及防，无法安宁，与你形影相随，挥之不去，我不知道那是什么，只能称它为爱情。

余虹日记

There is something, that comes suddenly like a wind on a warm summer's evening. It takes you off guard, and leaves you without peace. It follows you like a shadow, and it's impossible to shake. I don't know what it is, so I can only call it love.

From the diary of Yu Hong

Fig. 2.6 The opening shot of *Summer Palace*

allegorical site of excess,"[55] the symbolic and symptomatic significance of this excess reaches far beyond its direct consequence (that it "cannot [be] made into a coherent whole or generate meaning")[56]; therefore implicating more profound meanings. In short, while it "essentially resists transcending historical ruins and reinvesting the myth of history," what it articulates is more complicated than applying the "heroine's ego impoverishment" as "a counter power against the violence of the hegemonic regimes."[57] Rather, the relationship with the other is more nuanced than a simple, antagonistic way of dualism; in other words, it is a love-and-hate complex. This complex existing between the students/ intellectuals and the government went across the borderland of socialist/post-socialist boundary; nevertheless, the tie was ultimately severed, leading to the birth of a bourgeois subjectivity/identity.

Rampant Desire in a Restless Era

Throughout the film, critics have found that the movie "immersed in a dreamlike rhythm that escapes logic, refuses the control of language, and blindly follows the chaotic, repetitive pattern of Yu Hong's uncontainable desire."[58] Although it is not blindly doing so, upon close scrutiny the storyline, which seemingly comes from Yu's perspective and follows her life trajectory, renders the movie as though it is a "chick-flick." Before the story starts, a few lines with the signature "Yu Hong's diary" appear on the screen. Being Yu Hong's lifelong preoccupation as well as the source of her melancholy, her romantic experience unfolds with the entries of her diary, her voiceover as well as her numerous passionate love-making scenes stun the audience.

However, she is not the first character that shows up. The one who appears at the very start is an adolescent teenager; his smoking signifies a youthful rebelliousness. He is Yu Hong's lover, a postal carrier living in a northeastern, peripheral town. Yu Hong, then a girl in the last year of high school, is madly in love with him. This love affair is not a common situation for youngsters of that time, given China's highly acetic education and stern school discipline of the era. Finding that Yu's college acceptance letter has arrived, the carrier hurriedly sends it to her while she is taking care of her family's grocery store though, in reality, he is reluctant because he knows she will soon have to leave. After he protects Yu from being insulted by thugs, the two consummate their affections. The subtitle indicates that this takes place in 1987.

A high school student casually giving herself away cannot be understood simply by her instincts of impulsiveness. Rather, the behavior is closely tied to the epochal trend of the period, which promoted the idea of "liberation of human nature." After Yu enters Beiqing University (obviously a combination of China's top two Beijing universities— Beijing University and Qinghua University), she quickly takes to campus life like a fish to water. She drinks, smokes and hangs out in bars, doing everything she pleases, which quickly makes her a social butterfly. She also befriends her neighbor Li Ti; through Li's boyfriend, Ruogu, she meets the suave Zhou Wei and the two of them rapidly begin a passionate love affair.

But, despite strolling through the trees at the summer palace, floating on a small boat enjoying each other's company, and "having that special talk overnight," Yu still feels that there "exists a kind of impurity between us…(for) I just want my life to be more exciting." In that era, college students in China were considered the princes of society, and lived and enjoyed the privileges the state had to offer. However, idealizing sexual liberation as a kind of beautiful self-indulgence in the general tide of pursing a free-style life, they still did not want to commit themselves to love. Therefore, Zhou develops special relations with another woman, a female classmate. Yu takes revenge by having an affair with her tutor. However, even this act cannot heal her wounds and Yu feels miserable. When Zhou beats her in public, Yu endures the humiliation. This overly dramatic scene stirs up an uneasy feeling, revealing the magnitude of her emotions.

Although the two decide to call it quits, they do not separate for long. In the meantime, a quasi-homosexual relation develops between Yu Hong and Li Ti. At a school party, they wear the same outfits and dance with each another. The unusual part about this is that Li has simultaneously kept up her affair with Zhou all along. Yu standing before a mirror confesses to her relation with Li, "Gazing at the mirror, (I find that) this is not the face of a young girl anymore…When I stare at this face of mine, it looks like the face beside mine. I wish I could have both of these two faces in the same time." The words hint at the inseparability of the two sister-like characters and their compatibility. This sisterhood was fashionable in campus at the time, although homosexuality was a sensitive topic. With gestures of anti-establishment, the loose sexual life signifies a challenge to the ascetic society.

Incapable of keeping Zhou as her only love, Yu Hong begins to lead a self-destructive life of pleasure. She not only teaches her roommate, a well-behaved and traditional-minded girl, Dongdong, how to masturbate, but also takes two dubious, disheveled men to her dorm. Judging by the promiscuous and shameless behaviors, some audience member may agree with the accusation of a "decadent, bourgeois way of life" meted out by the authority at the time. Nevertheless, the movie tries to give credit to her carnal desires with the case of a cadre-like student who leads a boring and failed emotional life; also, we witness Yu Hong mercilessly goads her: "You are either jilted, or having nobody love you; or you must be a lesbian!" In addition, this cadre's act of stealing books is meant to confirm Yu's judgment that she is a hypocritical person. Yet, this verification is problematic. Vilifying an orthodox student for the purpose of self-glorification is merely an expression of weakness. What is more, how could a "good" student behave this way, apart from the possible fact that she is penniless? Thus, the plot of the episode itself shows its snobbish inclination: the "hypocrisy" of the woman originates from her destitution and her naive following of the school discipline (and, implicitly, socialist morality), which constitutes a sharp contrast to our heroine Yu Hong with her "noble," "honest," and free-thinking mind. To complicate the matter, for no obvious reason, Yu falls to the floor; the bird's-eye shot together with the melancholic music envelops her in an atmosphere of sadness and dreariness, giving the impression that she is a failed hero. Yet, could this be a sign that her reckless sexual activities have caused her to become pregnant?

When this chaotic game of love goes back and forth, the 1989 student demonstrations erupted. The film shows these students noisily climbing aboard trucks, just like rushing to a banquet. Within this exciting atmosphere, Yu is stirred up and joins them on their journey to the square. Intercutting back and forth, the film uses a documentary style to portray the scenes of student protest, the breaking and burning of military vehicles, the aim of which is to show the complexity and turbulence of the movement. In particular, a scene showing a soldier firing into the air to curb the students' recklessness deliberately exemplifies the restraint of the military force. Two things happen in this turbid environment; the first is that Zhou Wei and Li Ti sleep together one night and get caught by the school security (which implies that they would be immediately dismissed by the school). The second event is the post boy suddenly arriving to find Yu Hong in the mass hysteria of yelling and crying. Realizing what has happened, the dispirited postman, wearing his black sunglasses and with his disheveled head lowered, accompanies the disillusioned Yu, who now drops out of the school, back to their hometown (Fig. 2.7).

In the first half of the movie, Yu appears to be the leading character, despite Zhou's intermittent appearances. Until this point, all the male characters are just means for Yu to "discover herself." On a superficial level, there is a kind of transcendental quality about the woman and her love; yet her body and soul are not as united as the movie may try to suggest. As the critic Cui Weiping—she was the director's college tutor and also plays a minor role as a college tutor in the movie—tries to persuade us: "She (Yu) is not a woman without a soul; rather, she is a combination of both body and soul. Her body is in a way her soul, and she uses her body to activate her soul. When she makes love, she is actually building a relationship by means of an earthly way. She uses her body to measure up and discover others as well as this world."[59] It is worthy of note that indulgence in carnal pleasures does not necessarily mean having an elevated spirit and lordly soul. Yet, the following argument from Cui does reveal Yu's state of mind in the prevalent conditions:

Fig. 2.7 A medium-long shot shows Yu Hong's and Zhou Wei's youthful idealism

"Yu Hong, the character who lives by the passion of her own love, who indulges in the affairs of men and woman, is not only living by a kind of sentimental state of sorts, but rather is living her life entirely; this state of hers contains too many things she needs to set free inside, harbors too much impulsiveness, as well as too much fantasies. This was the idiosyncratic phenomenon of that time period...and was exactly the kind of social atmosphere during that decade."[60]

What exactly was that kind of social atmosphere? "Desire has gone rampant and circles around aimlessly in this youthful group of friends... Yu Hong and her fellow students are immersed in a frantic world fraught with sexual upheavals and emotional bewilderments beyond their own understandings."[61] All these have their social-political correspondences and over-determinations.[62] In the late 1980s, when China's economic reform had been taking place for a decade, the intellectual circle considered that socialist revolution and praxis was blind-minded, disastrous peasant revolts and feudalist dictatorship; nihilism and cynicism penetrated society. In addition, all sorts of Western bourgeois thoughts flooded into China and were regarded the symbol of modernity. The yearning for material goods and sexual liberation reached an unprecedented degree in this post-revolutionary world. It is in light of this condition that Cui's remarks could be appreciated fully, "It is almost Yu's body is filled with the devil that Faust has come across who does not know when his desire could be satiated. The turbulence of that era and her inside restlessness coincidently merge into one entity."[63] In accordance with this state, the "recurrent theme of sexual upheaval can be read as a most affective contemplation on the students' mass movement demanding freedom and democracy,"[64] and "the heroine's personal story, which seems self-involved and indifferent to the political upheavals surrounding her, is, in fact, an affective remembrance of the historical trauma."[65] On the other hand, however, although it is fair for the director to intend that "historical events are merely a background to the central relationships," the stake lies in the fact that "those relationships are far from extraordinary and are hardly enriched by the events;" therefore, "the essential lack of emotional content—beyond lovers bruised and divided by history"[66] also renders the organic ties between history or the societal, epochal truth-content and the students' "sexual experimentation" or promiscuity too slim to be observable (Fig. 2.8).

Fig. 2.8 A medium shot portraying the idealistic college students Yu Hong and Zhou Wei in *Summer Palace*

Melancholy and Confusion in the Market Society

The climax of the story occurs in the middle of the film, but it does not end at that point. After the high tide of the 1989 event ebbs, the characters begin physical migration and a spiritual drift. Their destinies develop along two distinct paths but intersect at certain points. Yet, the movie only portrays this rapid change, which spans almost a decade, in montages and with subtitles.[67] These montage sequences flash by with the pop song "Don't break my heart" sung by China's once famous rock band Black Panther, showing the fall of the Berlin Wall (1989), the disintegration of the U.S.S.R. (1991), the Asian Olympics Game held in Beijing (1991), Deng Xiaoping's Southern tour of the country (1992) and Hong Kong's return from British rule (1998). In short, these earth-shattering events are paralleled with the characters' diasporic experiences. This could show the inseparability of the characters' destinies with that of their country, and even the entire world; however, this narrative short-cut, which has little correlation, also exposes the film's inability to account for the organic ties between the two.

What happens to our heroes anyway? In 1991, Yu Hong again leaves her hometown. Given her elevated consciousness of her identity and class status, the intimate relations between her and the mail carrier can only be temporary. She first arrives in the prosperous overseas metropolis Shenzhen, the symbol of the success of China's reform and opening-up; but, four years later, she moves to the interior city Wuhan. As to why she undertakes this adventure and why she takes the migration further, the viewer does not discover. For a woman with high ambition and strong desire, Shenzhen, the famed port city, is an ideal place; yet, leaving there for Wuhan—an underdeveloped, inland city—is almost like self-abnegation. She finds a job as a clerical worker there, which apparently does not fit her with her idealistic personality. During this time, she meets an artist, a man of dubious character, who is already married at the time; the two allegedly find spiritual and bodily pleasure together. Her narrative is a continuous voice-over, "Today is Saturday, and other than going to find him, there is nothing else I could possibly do." She insists that, "a colleague who knows the law tells me, although this behavior is not illegal, it is immoral. But what is moral? Two people staying together, that is what I consider to be moral." In the meantime, she develops an intimate, abnormal affair with a mail worker named Wu Gang in her work unit. In a state of confusion, she is hit by a car and hospitalized. Although Wu vows to her that he does not care about her past, or even what is happening now, she rejects his proposal because his low income cannot support the expense of her. Her rejection was conveyed in a noble excuse, nevertheless: "It just like that you have a lighter, but you cannot make a flame on me." However, she also confesses that it is her luxurious material needs that do not allow her to be satisfied with a relatively well-off lifestyle. Her repayment for his love is to "let you know my good nature once and for all" by offering him her body. In fact, she does this to anyone she pleases; but she insists that, in her mind, she can maintain a sense of spiritual purity by "making love in a simple way," and in this way she can also remain faithful to Zhou Wei. We could suggest that these various excuses only expose the fact she has lost faith in love. She is living a life without any principle, or, in other words, the nihilistic principle of "no principle." As to what is right and wrong, this is purely defined and explained in her following the sort of pragmatism practiced by the political regime at the time. We could also argue that this principle is egocentrism, as she maintains the tenet of satisfying her bodily desires at all costs and the necessity of material enjoyment.

As for the hero Zhou Wei, he is the main character for the second half of the film. In this parallel storyline, Zhou makes it to Berlin with the assistance of Li Ti and her boyfriend. There, he appears aloof to the favor and affection he receives from the German women around him. Although he still has sexual relations with Li Ti, in his mind he cherishes his feelings for Yu Hong. When he finally decides to return to China in 1998, Li Ti, who is passionately in love with him, asks him, "What was happening with us that summer?" Zhou coldly responds, "Can you tell me what is going on with us now?" This retaliation confirms that Li is merely his sexual partner, but not his love. A close-up shot intends to convey the message: when the two are making love, Zhou closes his eyes and lays back, which is meant to signify that he is only submitting to her desires. Realizing the truth, Li leaves and unexpectedly kills herself by jumping off a tall building. It is obvious that she is emotionally tormented, because she never receives Zhou's love and because she might feel ashamed of betraying her husband Ruogu. However, this could only be inferred from the scene when she returns from Zhou's house and hugs Ruogu, burying her face in his back.

What is strange is that Ruogu does not get angry with Zhou for sleeping with his girlfriend. Instead, he facilitates Zhou's and Li's reunion while knowing that they will continue their affair. All we can surmise is that he loves Li so deeply that he tolerates anything she is doing. Yet, when Zhou inquires whether he has ever loved Li, all Ruogu answers is that he "possibly" loves her but "does not want others to love her out of fear that she would hurt them." Zhou refutes his reply, "You are wrong." It appears that Zhou understands Li much better than Ruogu and he still assumes that Ruogu knows nothing of their secrets. Nevertheless, it is better to say that the movie cannot find a satisfactory explanation for the kind of altruistic love Ruogu believes in all along.

After Zhou returns to China, he finds himself in a successful position at work and also finds a new girlfriend. An old classmate he happens to run into informs him that Yu Hong has already married a gas station worker (a situation that, again, falls short of explanation). After finding Yu, the two go to rent a room in a hotel at the well-known tourist resort of Beidaihe to rekindle their love. However, they realize that their old feelings have vanished once and for all.

The film almost reaches its end at this moment. However, there is an epilogue to come, which shows captions regarding their current lives. Yu Hong lives in a small city with her husband whom she met in

Chongqing, working at the service zone until the winter of 2003; and Zhou goes to Beidaihe for the last time in 2001. Following this, Zhou continues to live in Chongqing and never returns to Beijing. Judging by the fact that "their lives drift towards different trajectories," critic Huang Yiju believes that although they were "once passionate," however, they now "have become empty bodies devoid of souls."[68] Is this really the case?

My interpretation departs from a commonly held humanist understanding of the film. Although the protagonists' "delirium and restlessness escape the dominant discourse, disrupting its rhetoric of progression, and posing as an affective force to reveal the other scene of history – a historical trauma in its actuality,"[69] these achievements are merely the superficial effects that the film presents. The real darkness of the narration lies in its unconscious record of a historic origination of a new subjectivity, which emerges under this melancholy sorrow.

In "Mourning and Melancholia," Sigmund Freud (1856–1939) differentiated two concepts: mourning and melancholia, which are related yet disparate. They both originate from the loss of a loved object, in which "an object-loss was transformed into an ego-loss;"[70] yet, they depart when confronting existing reality. The subject can satisfactorily conquer the melancholic feeling by reinvesting its libido in a new object, thus, moving towards the future. In other words, the subject (re-)establishes its subjectivity after conquering its feeling of loss during the process of mourning. But the subject could also linger in its emotional indulgence with the missing object, and refuse to direct its energy away from the melancholic sentiment of loss in order to make a new life order. Zhou Wei and Yu Hong could be taken as examples that show the respective symptoms of mourning and melancholia.

Put in greater detail, "mourning is a social-political process that hails the subject and eventually binds historical losses into a stable meaning-system;" in this way, the subject is "reconstituted into the symbolic order through the process of mourning; the loss in historical trauma will eventually be transcended and integrated."[71] When the two protagonists finally break up, it is Zhou who chooses to leave without paying the slightest attention to Yu Hong, who is just bringing some groceries back for him that she has bought from the supermarket. This move is completely in accordance with his behavior all along, his having always been the domineering party in the relationship. When he finds that Yu has no more feelings for him, and is void of sexual passion outside her marriage, he decides to cut the ties. It is apparent that he does not hold onto the past; his self-centered ways push him to forget and forgo things that had gone before. Therefore, this last meeting is like an ultimate ritual mourning the fervor of youth that has passed. Being a successful businessman at home, he is now no longer willing to sink into the abyss of passion and melancholia.

On the other hand, in terms of melancholia, "the self refuses to be bound into the meaning-system of the Other and discerns the inevitable absence in it as well as in the self. The ruins from the historical trauma have become a permanent landscape for the self to dwell in and linger on."[72] This feature is saliently displayed in Yu Hong:

> Similar to Freud's patients of melancholia who present "an extraordinary diminution in self-regard" (Gay 1989: 584), Yu Hong's behavior is not ruled by morality and laws in any sense. Her very being evokes the sensation of a traumatic body that spills out and cannot be contained...She evokes an important characteristic of melancholia described by Freud – the incapability of any social achievement.[73]

Yet, the reason for her being "indifferent to moral obligations and social responsibilities" which "displays an impoverished ego that is confused, compulsive and discursive" could not be found in Freud's theory[74]; rather, it needs to be explored in the social-political atmosphere of the post-socialist China of the late 1980s, when hedonism, nihilism and anarchism prevailed after Mao's revolutionary idealism was rejected as being hypocritical rhetoric covering up a merciless power struggle. Consequently, Yu Hong's melancholia does not harbor "a vague hope of remedy against the historical sickness that has plagued everyone in its meaning system."[75] Rather, her abortion signifies the failure of this young generation who refused to reflect upon their own problem and the real origin of their bewilderment and nihilistic hedonism: "the viewer senses no shame, remorse, or vilification from Yu Hong; there is essentially no internalized gaze of conscience."[76] Instead, the young people like Yu Hong continuously glorify the amoral behaviors with moralized excuses, "While social norms will certainly see Yu Hong's promiscuity as a symptom of social failings, the repetitive indulgence in sex with different men in her diary, however, is accounted as redemptive in revealing her goodness and benevolence to the world."[77] Consequently, "The unborn child who cannot bear the name of the father directs the viewers' gaze away from the future and symbolizes the recurrent theme...the impasse of melancholia" (Fig. 2.9).[78]

When Love Fades Away: The Cultural Politics of Nostalgia and Recollection

What would Yu Hong have done after the winter of 2003? The subtitles do not provide any information. If she is not merely a simple replica of an archetype in real life, then all we can conclude is that the movie cannot figure out Yu's future life trajectory. This could be understood, as Yu herself is a hedonistic adventurer throughout; or better, she is a victim of materialistic society, even though she mistakenly believes that she is in control of herself. She never matures enough to be the true master of her reason. Like Zhou, she is a narcissistic, egocentric individualist. The difference lies in the fact that Zhou, being independent, is now a capitalist entrepreneur, who persistently conquers the world, including women. In comparison, Yu lacks any belief system and willpower in life apart from her self-consuming desire. Her melancholic sorrow is, in all actuality, the spiritual confusion running throughout her life.

When noting that Yu Hong's "lack of shame is an unmistaken symptom of melancholia that signifies the ego's impoverishment and social failings," critic Huang Yiju also finds that it is closely related to the social-historical experience—the director "has implicitly connected the lack of shame with the failure of the Other:"

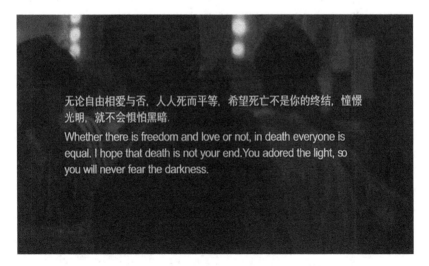

无论自由相爱与否，人人死而平等，希望死亡不是你的终结，憧憬光明，就不会惧怕黑暗.
Whether there is freedom and love or not, in death everyone is equal. I hope that death is not your end.You adored the light, so you will never fear the darkness.

Fig. 2.9 The closing scene of *Summer Palace*

> The disorder of the social political background of 1989 is allegorized in a series of personal, chaotic, and seemingly shameless events. The protagonists' flowing desires have particularly gone rampant just as their fellow students begin to demonstrate.[79]

But the director himself declares that he had tried to avoid touching upon the 1989 Tiananmen incident on screen; only later on did he reluctantly decide to include it from an individual's perspective (which is relatively limited), in order to create a way that he found acceptable.[80] Therefore, the movie ostensibly refrains from a third-person, omniscient perspective. But, as Cui Weiping aptly notes, although this is "a personal perspective," still "the person in and of itself is the product of a particular historical period."[81] Since the movie avoids correlation with the particular political affair, it falls short of presenting the socio-historical subtext. Consequently, the audience who have not experienced that era would feel that the degenerate and dispirited life of the characters is hard to understand.

But the 1989 incident being vicariously included is not a superficial one that could be excluded without undercutting its aesthetic significance. Cui has described the lifestyle of students at the time as a state of recklessness (*zaodong* 躁动), which is seconded by the director, who furthermore contends that it is similar to the rebellious impulsion of the 1989 movement.[82] The script writer Mei Feng also echoes this point:

> There is a certain coincidence here. That situation rarely happens in life: When two people are in love and their relationship develops into a feverous state of condition; suddenly they find that the environment in which they live in is also feverish. Conventionally, we say that love is a personal and intimate matter. But in the 80's and 90's, I feel that all our lives became lit up by our environment. In the period of June 4th, there had been lots of matrimonial ceremonies in the Square, and many unexpected love consummations. It seems that in that era, all these things were more than natural... The story of *Summer Palace* coincidentally happens in that period.[83]

Although he feels that the story merely "coincidentally happens in that period," I suggest that the way in which it happens and its origin is not entirely haphazard. The director himself confesses that, "People were also created by the sort of atmosphere... the atmosphere brought out these persons, which led to that kind of consequence."[84] However, although the film shows this atmosphere—laissez faire, hedonist and nihilistic, it could not reveal its origin and how this atmosphere brought out the consequence. Similarly, the roots of the protagonists' idiosyncratic personality were not delivered.

This is not entirely the fault of the director or the scriptwriter. In the past twenty years, as most of Chinese intellectuals involved in the movement, they did not feel the gigantic gaps and cracks between the elite group and the vast majority of the populace. But there are still a few scenes in the movie bearing social information unrelated to the primary plotline. In the bar, the college teacher, played by Cui Weiping, suddenly articulates a line: "Safeguarding [the rights of] the workers is the most honorable thing to do;" "Yes, [we need to] protect the [rights of] peasants." Apparently, she is discussing some social issues. During that time, bars were not popular in China, but college students in metropolitan cities often went to them, most being located in the area of foreign embassies, to enjoy free discussions of social-political issues. These bars thus served as a "public space." But, the director believes that "a two-hour movie" is "unable to enter many different systems...could not usher in the historical system and the political system;" thus, it "has to be self-constrained."[85] Consequently, the essential parts of the students-intellectuals' lives are left out. However, although Yu Hong may be uninterested in politics, Zhou must be the opposite. He is not spellbound by sexual lust in the same way as Yu Hong. Perhaps the director feels that, since the film is narrated from Yu's perspective, Zhou's multifaceted life need not be presented in full. However, the loose relationship between the characters and social-political matters (which is exactly where the epochal spirit was to be found) merely brings out a unilateral presentation that is incapable of revealing and explaining the multiple façade of the students and society. Although the director may deny this, Yu's idiosyncrasies can be viewed as a symptom of society; her drifting experience is a typical case of the "internal diaspora" of the era for elite intellectuals. But even though she is chosen to be the representative, without an organic correlation with the social-political elements, her unusual lifestyle falls short of what is considered "typical."

In this regard, the dialogue between the director and the scriptwriter confirms the close relations between the movement and the destinies of the protagonists. When discussing how the atmosphere created people and brought out certain unfortunate consequences, Lou Ye says that it is as though "the government and the student demonstrators had engaged in intercourse." He goes on to explain this unusual metaphor:

> It's just like an awkward feeling having intercourse. The government gave
> the student a punch and hit it too hard; the student fell down, blooding...
> The one who did it (the government) also felt that he had overdone...and
> so came back seeking redemption for this excessiveness out of impulsion...
> After the two broke up, they reminisced and reflected upon the previ-
> ous circumstances, declining the truth, avoiding each other, maintaining
> silence, and practicing self-forgetfulness, something like this.[86]

If we ponder upon this stunning metaphor by reflecting upon the emotional lives of the protagonists, we can conclude that the manipulative
personality of the authoritative figure Zhou Wei and the absolute trust
Yu Hong confers upon him, as well as the love-hate complex, are analogous to the relationship between the party-state and the students.[87] In
this light, while Yu's unapologetic promiscuity after her breakup with
Zhou is seemingly enigmatic (or a gesture of degeneration), it is but
"driven by a melancholic nostalgia for the lost object of her love;"[88] for
the "object of love," whether Zhou Wei or authority, had been found to
be imperfect.[89] Thus, "What is really at issue here is the disillusion with
the Other."[90] To be sure, here, the Other—the government—was the
one that, for the most part, still maintained its socialist ideals and policies
at the time, which facilitated its way of keeping honest dialogues with the
students and the populace in general.

From this perspective, Yu Hong is still symbolic of a certain type of
student. Her willfulness, casual ways, indulgence in carnal dissipation
in the name of love, keeping a distance from politics without any political ideals but reluctantly being involved, as well as her use of a diary
to try to rationalize her behavior albeit to no avail, as well as her way
of maintaining an idealized form of "reflection" are all symptoms of an
ultra-egocentric individualist and confirmation of her inability to bring
about an effective self-critique.

Towards the end of the movie, Yu Hong defends her selfishness,
believing herself to be a virtuous human being: "Right now, either in
work or in life, I am full of impecuniosity. For the sake of my innate
nature of desires and romance, I have paid my dues. But no matter how difficult life can be, I never lose my courage to continue living
on. People like me are born with this kind of destiny." What she articulates is nothing more than insisting on her narcissism and self-jus-
tification, which places her unchecked and irrational desires under
the label of "human nature," rejecting any socialized explication.

Moreover, this declaration calls for those people who "like me" or who "share my destiny" to glorify her self-image. All these gestures show her (and, to a great extent, the movie's) persistent move to idealize and romanticize her undisciplined lifestyle, as well as her inability to see through the illusion and undertake genuine, poignant reflection.

Consequently, what we witness in Yu Hong's life is a vicious cycle. "The tripartite structure of time, i.e., the past, present, and future, has in fact collapsed in this hypnotizing rhythm of repetition."[91] What the characters are unable to reflect upon is not only their narcissistic inclinations, but also the fact that their melancholy still relies upon a superficial sense of self-pity, and their inability to diagnose society and the origin of their egocentric individualism. In this light, the "illusion and disillusion of youths portrayed...is symbolically an allegory of historical illness."[92] As the director and scriptwriter have admitted, Yu Hong has surrendered to the "fantasy of her own body," which includes "the illusion of self-consolation and the illusion of homosexuality."[93] But the so-called "Yu Hongs" and the film producers of today still live within the straitjacket of this fantasy and are unable to break away from it, hence the existence of this omnipresent sorrow and melancholy. In other words, preoccupation with expressing this melancholy and creating an atmosphere of sorrow does nothing but confirm that the generation has yet to shed the gown of vanity and engage in poignant reflection upon this particular form of consciousness, which just goes to show the immaturity of this underdeveloped new generation of youth.

Circumstantial evidence is found in the portrayal of the character Ruogu. The movie is unable to account for his love, taking his altruistic attitude as a case of cowardice, hypocracy and ignorance (or not being "manly enough," hence the Chinese name *Ruogu*, literally meaning "like the ancients"). By contrast, the movie is keen to show the narcissistic, egotistical ways of Yu Hong and Li Ti, as well as Zhou Wei's strong urge to manipulate and dominate. All these facts substantiate the hollowness of their desires, which are created from the perspective of the social elites. In this new era of the Chinese market economy, the characters still become trapped in the fantasy of sexual emancipation brought about by post-revolutionary secularization and are unable to see through the market logic of commodity transaction, which disguises itself as "free" and, thus, begin using their bodies to exchange happiness and fulfill their desires. On the other hand, they feel emptiness and even agony because their idealized dream of "sexual liberation" has been widely implemented in this rampant market society, where sexual extravagance has become normalized following the principle of commodity exchange.

Because of this, the whereabouts of Ruogu are unknown at the end of the movie (the subtitles tell the audience that "Ruoguo leaves for Berlin the second year after Li Ti dies, and nobody knows where he goes"); whereas the audience is informed that an epitaph is engraved on Li Ti's gravestone: "Whether there is freedom and love or not, in death everyone is equal. I hope that death is not your end. You adored the light, so you will never fear the darkness." The characters no longer pursue the ideal of "Everyone being equal at birth," which is a socialist notion (without doubt, it is also the bourgeois ideal) seeking universal justice against the class hierarchy and discrimination that the students once sought. Rather, they are now satisfied by the hypocritical consolation that proclaims "In death everyone is equal." They glorify themselves by arguing that they are not afraid of the dark, but that they are just longing for the light of a kind of sexual utopia, which does nothing but show their innate shallowness. Without understanding their Chinese political past, when the characters see people on Berlin's street raising Marxist-Leninist flags, they pass by without seeming to care. They may feel that they saw too much of this in bygone Maoist days, and they feel that these people are still falling for a leftist illusion; or, they may believe that only in Germany is the socialist flag still meaningful. They had held a socialist mindset which Maoist teaching had conferred upon them; thus, they had concerned themselves with social-political affairs and intervened with the reality. But, after the brutal suppression, they found that they could no longer hold with these ideals any longer. However, while the movie "refuses to integrate the loss, forget the historical wreckages, and move on with the compelling force of history,"[94] it not only shies away from the idealism of this group of people that had attempted to fight for more democratic governance, but in its empathetic portrayal of the narcissistic individualists, it cannot break out the myth of indulgent melancholy to undertake poignant reflection and make a genuine critique.

While these students (and the movie) "refuse to be reconstituted and reintegrated into the social political meaning system after the traumatic rupture,"[95] most of them could not figure out the direction of the future. Neither do they realize that a particular subjectivity has been formed after the severance with the past. While Yu Hong continues her hedonistic philosophy, ignorant of political affairs and indifferent to any moral obligation—which is itself a particular form of life popular among the Chinese bourgeois community, Zhou Wei, the "spoiled child" in the new market economy, has grown up to be a hard-willed, merciless entrepreneur used to taking everything into his control. No longer is anything sentimental to him; no political belief is firm in his mind, his iron principle being nothing but pragmatism—which is also analogous to the government after it abandoned its commitment to socialist principles.

In a nutshell, when read against post-socialist social-political circumstances, the political significance of unapologetic indulgence, the inexorable sentiment of melancholia and the omnipresent sense of mourning, together with the relentless bitter feelings of resentment running throughout the movie, will yield to the inspiration of knowledge. In the acquisition of that knowledge, we witness the compelling yet imperceptible birth of an alien, egocentric subjectivity, behind which looms the shadow of a marvelous identity rarely seen in the history of the People's Republic.

NOTES

1. Jason McGrath, *Postsocialist Modernity*, 3.
2. Ban Wang, "Studies of Modern Chinese Literature," 386.
3. Yingjin Zhang has noted four ways of using the concepts of postsocialism: "postsocialism as a label of historical periodization; postsocialism as a structure of feelings, postsocialism as a set of aesthetic practices; and postsocialism as a regime of political economy." For details, see Yingjin Zhang, "Rebel Without a Cause?" 50.
4. Ibid., 54.
5. Ibid., 61.
6. The film depicts a young mother who was abandoned by her husband and has to bring up her mentally disabled 13-year-old son. Her efforts cause trouble for her colleagues and her lovers as well as her ex-husband, which further entraps her in considerable emotional conflict. The humanistic concern for the socially vulnerable and marginalized, and the unique narrative style of the film, has aroused attention within the international film arena. After 1991, *Mama* was invited to participate in up to 100 international film festivals, winning a series of prestigious awards. These honors made Zhang Yuan world-famous as a director.
7. The trend for abortion as a popular choice at the time was deemed emblematic of "bourgeois liberalization."
8. Berenice Reynaud, "Zhang Yuan's Imaginary Cities and the Theatricalization of the Chinese 'Bastards'," 269.

9. Andrew Jones, *Like a Knife*, 117.

10. The Cultural Revolution prevailed in China in the 1960s and profoundly influenced the student movement in France and Italy. In the USA, rock music spread during a time when America was deeply mired in the Vietnam War. This was the first golden era of rock music, during which many outstanding bands and musicians emerged.

11. His occupation is known only from the Internet. But his appearance in the film as a scholarly person wearing a pair of glasses symbolizes him as an intellectual.

12. Berenice Reynaud, "Zhang Yuan's Imaginary Cities and the Theatricalization of the Chinese 'Bastards'," 269.

13. Tony Rayns, *Catalogue for the Vancouver International Film Festival*, 26.

14. Berenice Reynaud, "Zhang Yuan's Imaginary Cities and the Theatricalization of the Chinese 'Bastards'," 284.

15. Tony Rayns, *Catalogue for the Vancouver International Film Festival*, 26.

16. Zhang Yuan, *Catalogue for the Locarno International Film Festival*, 43. He also says, "I think China is in the middle of a big change. After thirty or forty years of communist idealism Chinese society is slowly becoming pluralistic...through these people we can understand what sort of a society we are really living in today." Chris Berry, "Zhang Yuan, Thriving in the Face of Adversity," 42.

17. Berenice Reynaud, "Zhang Yuan's Imaginary Cities and the Theatricalization of the Chinese 'Bastards'," 270.

18. Ibid.

19. Ibid., 271.

20. Ibid.

21. Rayns, *Catalogue for the Vancouver International Film Festival*, 26.

22. Yigeren de tiankong, "Zhangyuan de Beijing zazhong: Yiciwulide xuanxie."

23. Ibid.

24. Ibid.

25. Ibid. The critic goes on further to argue that the indulgence "turns *Beijing Bastards* into a meaningless struggle and a pure discharge of feelings. Such bare narcissism and prevailing emptiness only causes a deep abhorrence among the spectators. Their fragmented painful experiences can hardly arouse any response from people. Instead, it only arouses a sense of numbness after a 90-minute long bombardment of the fragmented, roughly-patched visual images." Ibid.

26. Berenice Reynaud, "Zhang Yuan's Imaginary Cities and the Theatricalization of the Chinese 'Bastards'," 273.

27. Ibid., 275.

28. Yigeren de tiankong, "Zhangyuan de Beijing zazhong: Yiciwulide xuanxie."

29. Ibid.
30. Ibid.
31. Ibid.
32. Berenice Reynaud, "Zhang Yuan's Imaginary Cities and the Theatricalization of the Chinese 'Bastards'," 268.
33. Jonathon Watts, "Interview: Lou Ye, Camera Obscured."
34. Chen Mo and Zhiwei Xiao, "Chinese Underground Films: Critical Views from China," 153.
35. Jinhua Dai, *Wuzhong fengjing*, 380–416. Quoted from Chen Mo and Zhiwei Xiao, "Chinese Underground Films: Critical Views from China," 152.
36. He drinks Lipton tea; smokes the famed American cigarette brand Marlboro; and drinks Coca-Cola.
37. Parents of the characters are only mentioned during the beginning of the film when Li Xin's voice-over says that, since her parents are not at home during the weekend—possibly to live their own life, she can only spend the day reading picture-story books, which implies her lack of close familial relations.
38. Critics notice that "the camera with its mismatched sound-picture follows the footsteps of A Xi in the beginning of the film; and the sound track is a mixture of rock songs and the radio voice broadcasting a hotline program; both of which demonstrate the psychological state of the urbanites and their yearning for emotional discharge." Li Xuebing, "Lou Ye de Chengshi," 158.
39. From this perspective, I do not support the view that the movie "adds a final disclaimer announcing that all of transgressive acts...took place years before and that the characters have changed since then" is merely to "clear censorship." See Yingjin Zhang, "Rebel Without a Cause?" 64. Rather, it is more complicated. Indeed, the characters have not fundamentally undergone any change, but have more skillfully adapted to the newly transformed society in order to be "successful." They do not comprehend the significance of the epochal transformation deeply enough, although the film's narration takes the form of a reflexive recollection.
40. Chen Mo and Zhiwei Xiao, "Chinese Underground Films: Critical Views from China," 155.
41. For instance, the long shot shows A Xi fleeing hastily after the crime, and the track shot of the dilapidated elevator when Li Xin comes to A Xi's residence.
42. Variety Staff, "China Gives 'Palace' Pair 5-Year Bans."
43. Chris Chang, "Distributor Wanted: *Summer Palace*."
44. Jason Solomons, "Give Pedro the Prize."
45. David Denby, "Moral Landscapes."

46. For instance, Derek Elley of *Variety* has claimed that the film was "half an hour too long and poorly organized on a dramatic level;" Derek Elley, "Review: 'Summer Palace'." *The Daily Telegraph* also suggests that it is "thirty minutes too long." Sukhdev Sandhu, "Cannes 2006: Love in Paris and Hatred in Ireland." *The Guardian* also criticizes it for being "over-long and meandering." Jason Solomons, "Give Pedro the Prize."

47. Sukhdev Sandhu, "Cannes 2006: Love in Paris and Hatred in Ireland."

48. Derek Elley, "Review: 'Summer Palace'."

49. Huang Yiju, "By Way of Melancholia," 165.

50. A.O. Scott, "Summer Palace—Movie Review."

51. Derek Elley, "Review: 'Summer Palace'."

52. Ibid., 167.

53. Ibid.

54. Ibid., 165.

55. Ibid., 167.

56. Ibid.

57. Ibid., 177.

58. Ibid., 167.

59. See Jianghe Ouyang, *Zhongguo duli dianying fangtanlu*, 108.

60. Ibid.

61. Huang Yiju, "By Way of Melancholia," 166.

62. "This chaotic world echoes strongly with the Tiananmen Square Incident," Huang Yiju argues. Ibid.

63. Jianghe Ouyang, *Zhongguo duli dianying fangtanlu*, 125.

64. Huang Yiju, "By Way of Melancholia," 167, 177.

65. Ibid.

66. Derek Elley, "Review: 'Summer Palace'."

67. They run in the following order: "Autumn 1989, College Student Military Training"; "1989, Ruogu leaves Beijing for Berlin"; "1989, Yu Hong and Xiao Jun leave Beijing for Tumen"; "1989, Zhou Wei and Li Ti await a visa to Germany in Beijing"; "Beijing in 1990"; "Berlin in 1989"; "Beijing in 1990"; "1991 Yu Hong once again leaves Tumen for Shenzhen"; "Moscow in 1991"; "Shenzhen in 1992"; "1994 Zhoue Wei and Li Ti arrive in Berlin with the help of Ruogu"; "1995 Yu Hong and her friend Wang Bo from Shenzhen arrive in Wuhan"; "Hong Kong 1997."

68. Huang Yiju, "By Way of Melancholia," 167.

69. Ibid.

70. Peter Gay ed., *The Freud Reader*, 582.

71. Huang Yiju, "By Way of Melancholia," 168. Volume 21, Issue 1, Cover Date: 2010. By Way of Melancholia: Remembrance of Tiananmen Square Incident in Summer Palace.

72. Ibid., 168.

73. Ibid.
74. Ibid.
75. Ibid.
76. Ibid., 170.
77. Ibid.
78. Ibid., 168.
79. Ibid., 171.
80. Lou Ye said: "First and foremost, I wanted to shoot a love film. Unfortunately, this love story coincidentally touches upon something everyone wants to avoid talking about. I think this is rather a pity. I really didn't want to do something like this, and I definitely didn't plan to touch upon this." See Jianghe Ouyang, *Zhongguo duli dianying fangtanlu*, 120.
81. Ibid., 121
82. Ibid., 125.
83. Ibid.
84. Ibid.
85. Ibid.
86. Ibid., 125–127.
87. Critic Huang Yiju also maintains that "the self-involved love story of a melancholic young woman can be read as an allegory of the historical trauma of the Tiananmen Square Incident. What occurred in the summer of 1989 was indeed an ambiguous love relation that the youths have engaged passionately with their homeland. It was simultaneously euphoric and excruciating, haunting and baffling. The love was so traumatic that it has flooded the mental apparatus and shattered the coherence of the ego, literally in the historical context and figuratively in *Summer Palace*." Huang Yiju, "By Way of Melancholia," 173. It is notable that, in terms of the object of love or the Other, she displaces the government with the homeland.
88. Ibid., 173.
89. Huang Yiju aptly remarks that "through her relationship with Zhou Wei, Yu Hong has significantly perceived...the lack in the Other albeit its shimmering façade that constantly allures and hails the self...What is really at issue here is the disillusion with the Other." Ibid., 174. Yet, Huang does not take the figure of Zhou Wei as an embodiment or incarnation of an authoritative Chinese government.
90. Ibid., 174.
91. Ibid.
92. Ibid., 167.
93. Jianghe Ouyang, *Zhongguo duli dianying fangtanlu*, 102.
94. Ibid., 174.
95. Huang Yiju, "By Way of Melancholia," 177.

REFERENCES

Chang, Chris. "Distributor Wanted: *Summer Palace*." *Film Comment*, January/February, 2007.

Chen, Mo and Zhiwei Xiao. "Chinese Underground Films: Critical Views from China." In Paul Pickowicz and Yingjin Zhang (eds.), *From Underground to Independent: Alternative Film Culture in Contemporary China*, pp. 143–160. Lanham, MD: Rowman & Littlefield, 2006.

Dai, Jinhua (戴锦华). *Wuzhong fengjing* (雾中风景) [*A Scene in the Fog*]. Beijing: Beijing daxue chubanshe, 2000.

Denby, David. "Moral Landscapes." *The New Yorker*, January 21, 2008.

Elley, Derek. "Review: 'Summer Palace'." *Variety*, May 18, 2006.

Gay, Peter, ed. *The Freud Reader*. New York: W. W. Norton, 1989.

Jones, Andrew F. *Like a Knife: Ideology and Genre in Contemporary Chinese Popular Music*. Ithaca, NY: East Asia Program, Cornell University Press, 1992.

Li, Xuebing (李学兵). "Lou Ye de Chengshi" (娄烨的城市) [The City of Lou Ye]. *Beijing dianying xueyuan xuebao* (北京电影学院学报) [*Journal of Beijing Film Academy*] 1 (1995): 157–159.

McGrath, Jason. *Postsocialist Modernity: Chinese Cinema, Literature, and Criticism in the Market Age*. Stanford, CA: Stanford University Press, 2008.

Ouyang, Jianghe (欧阳江河). *Zhongguo duli dianying fangtanlu* (中国独立电影访谈录) [*On the Edge: Chinese Independent Cinema*]. Hong Kong: Oxford University Press, 2007.

Rayns, Tony. *Catalogue for the Vancouver International Film Festival*. Vancouver: Vancouver International Film Festival, 1992.

Reynaud, Berenice. "Zhang Yuan's Imaginary Cities and the Theatricalization of the Chinese 'Bastards'." In Zhang Zhen (ed.), *The Urban Generation: Chinese Cinema and Society at the Turn of the Twenty-First Century*, pp. 264–294. Durham: Duke University Press, 2007.

Sandhu, Sukhdev. "Cannes 2006: Love in Paris and Hatred in Ireland." *The Daily Telegraph*, May 19, 2006.

Scott, A.O. "Summer Palace—Movie Review." *New York Times*, January 18, 2008.

Solomons, Jason. "Give Pedro the Prize." *The Guardian*. May 21, 2006.

Variety Staff. "China Gives 'Palace' Pair 5-Year Bans." *Variety* (2006, September 4). http://variety.com/2006/film/news/china-gives-palace-pair-5-year-bans-1117949488/. Accessed February 20, 2016.

Wang, Ban. "Studies of Modern Chinese Literature." In Haihui Zhang, Zhaohui Xue, Shuyong Jiang and Gary Lance Lugar (eds.), *A Scholarly Review of Chinese Studies in North America*, pp. 377–389. Ann Arbor, MI: Association for Asian Studies, 2013.

Watts, Jonathon. "Interview: Lou Ye, Camera Obscured." *The Guardian* (2006, September 9). http://www.theguardian.com/commentisfree/2006/sep/09/comment.china. Accessed November 11, 2015.

Yigeren de tiankong 一个人的天空. "Zhang Yuan de Beijing zazhong: Yiciwulide xuanxie" 张元的《北京杂种》：一次无力的宣泄 [Zhang Yuan's *Beijing Bastards*: A Powerless Catharsis]. http://blog.sina.com.cn/s/blog_541949290100fj98.html. Accessed December 12, 2015.

Huang, Yiju. "By Way of Melancholia: Remembrance of Tiananmen Square Incident in *Summer Palace*." *Asian Cinema* 21 (1) (2010): 165–178.

Zhang, Yingjin. "Rebel Without a Cause? China's New Urban Generation and Postsocialist Filmmaking." In *Cinema, Space, and Polylocality in a Globalizing China*, pp. 49–80. Honolulu: University of Hawaii Press, 2010.

CHAPTER 3

The Fate and Fantasy of China's "New Poor"

In his most recent work, *China's Twentieth Century*, Wang Hui has noted the appearance of two idiosyncratic groups in China since the 1990s. He names these as the "new poor" and explains the origin:

> After the Cold War, a change has occurred in this idea of the poor. The most important factors propelling this change are those taking place under the direction of financial globalization: the new processes of industrialization and the development of information technology influencing the entire world, and the collapse of workers' states and the concurrent and related development of a new international division of labor.[1]

The largest section of the new poor in China refers to the migrant peasants working in the urban areas who have few citizen's rights and little hope of returning to their rural origins. This is "the product of shifts in the relations between classes and the growing opposition and polarization between the cities and the rural areas during China's transformation into capitalism's world factory."[2] The second type of new poor consists of "a group with a certain level of education, dreams of advancement and unfulfilled consumer desires."[3] Their income is similar to that of blue-collar workers, which renders them incapable of meeting the consumptive demands stimulated by consumer culture. In other words, they are those who desire to ascend to the status of middle class, yet are relentlessly left behind by the current Chinese political-economic

X. Wang, *Ideology and Utopia in China's New Wave Cinema*, Chinese Literature and Culture in the World, https://doi.org/10.1007/978-3-319-91140-3_3

structure, which consolidates the existing class hierarchy. Thus, in terms of their shortage of economic power, political rights and scarcity of cultural resources, the two communities share similar discontents. Yet. Wang also notes the lack of interaction between the two populations after he analyzes their cultural particularity, especially with reference to the communicational capability of the "pseudo-middle class":

> similar to the situation in Europe and the United States, this group actively participates in new forms of media, and displays a much stronger consciousness regarding political participation and ability to mobilize its members than the new workers. From the micro-blogging platform Weibo to every other form of Internet media, the "new poor" are exceedingly active, and whatever topics they discuss reach all levels of society. But until today, the mobilizing ability and political demands of this group have had little to do with the newly ascendant working class or the fate of rural migrant workers...they have given very little consideration to the connections between their own fate and that of the other stratum of new poor.[4]

In terms of this newly emerged situation, two New Wave movies, *Blind Shaft* and *The Pirated Copy*, suffice to provide us a typical picture of the new poor. The issues brought up by these films are the difficulties faced by the lower classes, commercialization and its effects on the lower classes, economic disparity, moral depravity, the illusion of cosmopolitanism, materialism and so on. The failures, suffering, and even the eventual deaths of characters in the cinematic world can be taken symbolically as the failure of society to provide for the lower classes. In this light, one could argue that the directors have a bleak and pessimistic view of society and its current political/economic system, although they have expressed it in an indirect way.

The crimes portrayed in *Blind Shaft* often appear and are highlighted in domestic news, which shows the frequency of the macabre acts taking place in China. Thus, the film "aims to invite the audience to take a long, hard look at the impoverished survival of the workers, at the wretched of the earth, at the lingering breath of moral conscience on the verge of being swept away by the logic of capital;" in particular, "the figuration of the human body registers how the logic of capital accumulation...has penetrated into the traditional human relations in China, reducing the human person into a thing."[5] Intending to make a representative piece of critical realism, the director brilliantly accomplishes his task. To a certain extent, he also attempts to employ a fable to account for the moral distortion of the younger generation. However, his critique does not extend beyond culture, and has no way of shedding light on the depths of politics and economics, which is out of his engagement with human nature only to show the "the tensions and contradictions as the worker tries to hold on to the last remnants of humanity."[6] When he exposes the lifestyle of the miners, it also carries anxiety regarding the legitimacy of representing the others or the lower classes.

In the second movie, the everyday activities of a salesman selling pirated DVDs bring together people from society's underbelly who want to buy his wares, including a female college instructor, a prostitute, a jobless couple, an HIV carrier, two fake cops, the owner of a small store and some peddlers that sell pirated DVDs. They all "have been left behind by China's bolting economy and are struggling to make a living."[7] Though they live in the same city, these people have no direct connection with each other, which attests to the typical situation of the "new poor," as mentioned. However, their fortunes, which, sometimes overlap to a certain extent, make up the main narrative of the film. Thus, the movie is also a "look at the lives of people cut off from the Chinese economic miracle who use film as their means of connecting to life."[8] The film displays an "edgy style" consisting of "prowling cameras and shaky lensing,"[9] but the overly dramatic yet also insufficiently dramatized plotline turns it into a "light-weight" film of a postmodern pastiche. While the portrait of society seems facetious, it does not delve into the heart of the darkness—namely by attempting to undertake a political-economic analysis of the tragedy. As such, it merely presents an outsider's view of the life of the underprivileged. Consequently, the reality that it presents is still unbalanced, even though it feels like an incisive, realistic critique.

THE LIFE OF "NEW WORKERS" AND THE FATE OF ENLIGHTENMENT

Upon returning to China after having lived in Germany for 14 years from 1988 to 2002, Li Yang (1959–) was taken aback by the incredible changes that had occurred in his mother country. Reportedly, "he was impressed by the rapid pace of economic growth but dismayed by what he saw as China's increasing inhumanity."[10] After having read hundreds of books about contemporary Chinese society, he decided to produce a movie that would show real life in China.[11] As his first feature film, *Blind Shaft* (*Mangjing* 盲井) has the appearance of a documentary. Critics thus praise it by saying that, "Infusing into this film documentary images and aesthetics, Li deployed several familiar documentary and neo-realist devices, weaving a seamless interface between documentary and feature film."[12] This helped the film win numerous awards in the West and also helped garner attention for the director himself. To be sure, in modern Chinese literature, some writers were still able to portray in vivid details the everyday lives of average miners despite not having grown up as a miner; Lu Ling (1923–1994) being a well-known exponent of this. But *Blind Shaft* still has its outstanding elements. It was adapted from the novel *Sacred Wood* (*Shen Mu* 神木) written by Liu Qingbang (刘庆邦) (1951–), which won the distinguished Laoshe Literary Awards in 2002. Liu's novel tells a story in which several criminals kill other miners at work, making their deaths seem like accidents, then pressure the foreman to pay them "hush money," a way to earn quick money in China in recent years.

The not-so-complicated plotline looks like a psychological thriller. When Song Jinming and Tang Chaoyang, two criminals from the rural areas who pretend to be miners, first show their faces they are underground inside a mine. After a short conversation with a co-worker, they kill him with a pickaxe. The characters then proceed to ask for compensation from the mine's foreman knowing that most mine owners and foremen wish to avoid attracting police attention. Everything goes smoothly and their plan succeeds. After this incident, they throw away the ashes of their victim and swagger off.

This scene is just a prologue. As for how they met the young co-worker, Mr. Yuan, whom they have just murdered, as well as how they were able to convince him to let them pretend to be his uncles when they went to find a job at the mine, these details are left unexplained. However, another similar scheme soon fully materializes while they are busy looking for the next target. This time, the two are at the train station; Tang spots and focuses on an immature and confused-looking rural 16-year-old, Yuan Fengming, who is standing amidst the men crowded on the side of the road looking for work.

Song Jinming, however, is extremely uneasy about this new potential crime as the boy reminds him of his own children back home, who are waiting for him to earn money so they can go to school. So, he asks the lad whether he is playing truant or if his family fails to provide the tuition fees. When he hears from the boy that his father has not returned home for six months and, due to this, Yuan is forced to go out and find work to pay for his younger sister's education, he is even more opposed to tricking and harming the boy. But Tang persists: "(If) you don't have money, wouldn't your kid go out and look for job like him? You feel empathetic on him, but who pities on you?" In this society of Social Darwinism which provides no protection or concern for the weak, everyone faces danger, and the best you can hope for is self-preservation (Fig. 3.1).

The three of them then go to a small coal mine and begin working as miners. The story afterwards revolves around the subtle relationship among them. Out of compassion, Song buys shoes and a helmet for this "orphan" and explains to him, "When you go down into the mine, be sure to wear it." This prompts Tang's observation, "If you have to spend 100 kuai, nothing beats buying things for your own child." In the mine, Song behaves very rudely to Yuan just in order to protect him; Tang, however, is very gentle but, in reality, very sinister, "Who isn't scared in

Fig. 3.1 A medium shot of the protagonists Song and Tang captures the lamentable living conditions of Chinese mineworkers

their first time going down to mine?" When Song finds Yuan still reading his textbook before going to bed, he feels regretful, "You have gone out of school, it's impossible for you to return back!" When he sees Yuan's family picture, he finally informs Tang of the misgiving that has been bothering him—he thinks that this boy could be the son of the man they just killed; if this were true, their "lineage would come to an end."

Yuan's diligence, naivety, earnestness and concern for others all remind Song of his own child, who is now in school. At the busy market, when Yuan sees a beggar who professes to have been accepted into high school but forced to skip class due to poverty, he borrows money from Song to help him out. Moved by Yuan's request, Song starts to feel compassionate as well. Being hesitant and unable to follow through with their plan, he continuously puts off perpetrating Tang's murderous plan. In the name of the "guild regulations," he finds Yuan a prostitute in order to complete his "life circle," and invites him to a farewell dinner. This makes the conflict between Tang and Song more pronounced.

The decisive moment finally arrives when Tang makes the first move by killing a miner who cautions them against the danger of having an accident, since it interrupts their plan. In response to Song's protest, Tang inexorably argues, "Whoever gets in the way will himself be killed!" He then strikes Song to gain the upper hand, leaving Yuan startled and in shock. When Tang steps closer and closer to Yuan, Song, who has just regained consciousness, attacks Tang from behind just before he falls to the ground in exhaustion.

Morality and Ethics in the Era of Neoliberal Reform

This is an example of an "underworld" in China, both in reference to the nature of the characters' work and also in a more metaphorical sense. The movie begins with a long tracking shot showing a deepening darkness during the gradual descent into the mine; the faces of the miners are covered in coal dust, and the lights on their helmets flicker on and off in the smoke. Next, we hear the metallic clinking of mining operations further down. The lift is carrying several miners who are lowering themselves down using a rope pulley. Up above, a tiny circle of daylight grows smaller and smaller, which symbolizes their ever-increasing distance from the light and that they are walking into the heart of darkness. The series of shots is apparently full of symbolic significance: "The descent into the 'hell' down the shaft is visceral and symbolic. The stark Ozu-like shots turn miners into prisoners entrapped in a bare, vast, hostile landscape."[13] If we say that a coal mine is just like a deep well, then in the 1986 movie "Old Well," we see the earnest zeal with which the male lead (played by the famed fifth-generation director Zhang Yimou, who was still himself an actor and cameraman) digs a life-giving well for the betterment of his community, which shows the passion to fight for progress in the "New Era" of the 1980s. By contrast, in this movie these workers risk their lives to earn a living in a world dominated by the Capital. It has been noted that the movie's most "compelling insight" lies in the fact that "the two miners as protagonists work the reifying logic of capital to its grotesque extreme."[14]

In terms of the arduous lives of miners, we need to know that in modern China it has long been the symbol of the hardship suffered by the working class. A few cardinal party leaders of the CCP (including Chairman Mao) thus made their names early on by organizing large-scale mining strikes, in particular in Anyuan, a well-known coalmine in south China. Around 50 years after the founding of the People's Republic, the large casualties faced by Chinese miners under the government's neoliberal policies again hit the international spotlight. The miners, who in the Maoist era were representative of China's "leading class," now come to play the role of an underprivileged group. This transformation should be understood in the changing social-political context. Known as "black gold," many coal deposits in China have been privatized since the 1990s, providing overnight wealth for their owners and attracting migrant peasant-workers from all over the countryside. In this light, the fact that the phenomenon of murdering fellow miners for compensation money did not happen until after the 1990s itself signifies the rampant materialism and the degradation of social ethics in the neoliberal age. The director himself has acknowledged that it "struck him as an ideal metaphor for what he viewed as the loss of values in today's China": "Some people now have mafia values…They can't find a normal way to make money. Violence pays."[15] It is also in light of this fact that critics confirm the merit of the movie: It "offers an unleavened look at the underside of Chinese-style capitalism that was previously available only in print."[16]

Yet, what kinds of value get lost in the epochal change? If we were to assume that these two criminals have no sense of right and wrong, it would not explain their differences. It is not difficult to find that the movie presents nuanced details in order to make a comparison. Song is always thinking fondly about his wife and child. This is in sharp contrast with Tang. While talking on the phone in the street, Song repeatedly warns his son to study well. Tang, on the other hand, feels any further conversation unnecessary. Song's unintentional affection toward Yuan comes from the fact that Yuan reminds him of his own family, as well as his own adherence to a sense of "moral duty" or "heavenly principle" (for example, he worries about terminating the boy's lineage). This thus shows that he has retained a simple sense of folk ethics; additionally, this "moral compass" can also be considered as being closely related to his ingrained concept of a "guild regulation." He constantly reminds Tang, "You can't break the code," "Do you still want to play in the field?" "Do you know the code?," and "Do you still follow the rule?" These are "folk morals," which see tricking and killing underage children as a sort of unspoken taboo. But this simple "folk moral compass" has faced a great number of challenges in recent decades and has almost been entirely rejected: the murder of the two men at each other's hands at the end of the film embodies this point. China's daily news presents countless examples of neighbors and fellow-townsmen swindling and tormenting each other. In this "new" Chinese society governed by pragmatism, which has sparked the re-emergence of a kind of social Darwinism, this social phenomenon is increasingly prevalent. However, Tang, who does not respect this kind of "folk ethics" or "natural morals," is portrayed as the "greedy clown." A subtle scene shows that he is literally made to look like a fool after he loses a game of cards in which a beard is glued to his chin.

What is worth pointing out is that this moral compass can no longer be seen as a set of universal values passed down from through time because, like anything else, it has been subjected to the impingement of changing social-political institutions and concepts. As such, it has been mixed with the concepts of good and fairness of the bygone socialist era, though the director does not necessarily understand this. This is most apparent in the scene that takes place within the bar. Song pokes fun at Tang, saying he cannot sing, while Tang retorts that he stood in the front row when the production brigade (a common unit of labor in the Maoist era) held a singing competition (then a form of popular entertainment), and even picks out the song "Socialism Is Good." He still remembers the lyrics clearly; however, he is laughed at by the girl behind the bar. Calling him an "old hillbilly," the girl makes fun of him, saying "What era are you from by singing such an outdated song?" (Fig. 3.2).

Fig. 3.2 Song and Tang sing the "red song" in the bar

What era is this? The next scene gives us a clue. When they have dinner at a small street-side restaurant, the television broadcasts a news report about an embezzler who was caught after embezzling millions of RMB. Tang remarks that "he would not feel sorry even if he would be executed," which shows that he has already lost any sense of principle and cares only about profit. Song, on the other hand, comments that "he's just like our party secretary back home," which indicates the pervasiveness of corruption, as well as his moral sense of justice. He claims that he wants to "gather all the money he needs to put his kid through school, and does not waste even penny," which explains his acts of desperation as the result of the changes brought about by the marketization of education, which forces ordinary people to spend their lifetime setting aside money and carefully planning expenditures just to provide their children with an education. Also, he continues to articulate the complaint that "At that time I didn't have any money, otherwise how would I have done this evil thing with you?!," thus confirming the fact that he believes himself to be forced into this lifestyle. The "mutton stew" that they want is now called "tonic mutton soup"—also a reflection of the deepening commodification of society that happens together with the industrialization of the sex-trade under the market economy. This rampant pragmatism that is oblivious to any principle makes them exclaim "Now everything is fake apart from the mother of our child;" "Even the mother of the child could be fake!"

The encroachment of traditional folk morality and the disintegration of socialist ethics due to ubiquitous materialism and the corruption of the bureaucratic capitalist class no room to survive even in the capitalist regulations. This is precisely the mindset behind the mine owner's decision of "settling things privately." The manager blatantly says to the workers seeking employment, "If you eat you have to move your bowels; if you go into the mine, you might die…Are you scared? If you're scared, then don't come! There will always be more people willing to join." For the sake of earning more profit, the bosses similar to him prefer to bribe the authorities, rather than buy the necessary safety devices.

What causes these rampant degradations? When being questioned by an interviewer, "Do you think that the problem of people becoming increasingly selfish is brought about by modern socio-economic forces like capitalism? Do people from rural society have that many desires?" The director denies the answer, and instead attributes the crux of the issue to the "desire" itself:

> A rural society has these problems as well. The problem with modern society is that people are becoming increasingly selfish, and have no restraints. Ours is a society in transformation; moralities of the past no longer have a hold on you, and there has yet to emerge a complete set of new ethics. The reason people want to have moral standards is that they want something to restrain you, to make you live a more civilized life. However, we Chinese people now only value our desires. In "Blind Shaft", they kill other people to better their lives. They often say, "If you pity others, then who will pity you?", and they use this rhetoric in order to justify these murders. However, they grew up singing "Socialism Is Good"; thus, the question remains: how did they end up this way? This is because there are officials who have educated them have made millions out of corruption. This can be seen as a thorough collapse of the values system. It's just like the case: The parents tell their children you have to do this, you have to do that, and suddenly the child finds out that the parents whom they admire do not even follow their own words. How is the child supposed to respond to this?[17]

Elsewhere in the interview, he admits that in the film he only "wanted to portray how human nature degenerates under the attraction of money, and the good side of humanity in this transitional period— how good confronts evil."[18] Apparently, he does not hold that the political-economic sea-change, in particular the neoliberal policy, has had a hand in the transformation of social ethics and folk morality. Nevertheless, even though non-historical "desires" have been singled out to be the culprit, the director still unconsciously takes a historical stance by posing the question "Why did they become this way?" He also points out that this is a thorough disintegration caused by a top-down collapse because the officials betray their ideals and principles; and he notes the lamentable societal impact of this shameless dishonesty.

Enlightenment or Not?

However, the focus of the director is still on the moral defects of the outcasts themselves, rather than society at large. He demonstrates the fact that they lack dignity when the driver of a private car yells at them to get away simply because he takes them to be hindering his progress, which shows the relentless divide between the rich and the poor. Despised, they go on to look for the cheapest prostitutes they can find so as to release their sexual desires, and squander their money for personal pleasure. As to the other miners, the movie shows that they drink, play cards, bathe and play pranks—images that exemplify their exuberance and vitality. This calls to mind Lu Ling's novel of the 1940s portraying miners' lives. It is as though we are taken back to that era.

Yet, being a leftist writer, Lu Ling had the urge to expose the merciless oppression of the ruling class and the exploitation of the capitalists; Li Yang, the director, has no such desire. He explained his directorial intentions in an interview with Liu Hui. When Liu compares his movie to Lu Xun's works, and argues that "those Enlightenment thinkers in our modern literature, such as Lu Xun, would regard the characters in *Blind Shaft* as living a callous and ignorant life, from which they need to be awakened; [therefore,] they need to be made to feel pain and only in this way can society be changed," noting that, in Li's film, "even though the overall tune is dark and cold," he can "still feel the tenacity and optimism of these miners," Li replies that:

> The idea that the intellectuals need to enlighten the lower class is actually a top-down way of thinking. Before I started filming, I also looked at them through colored glasses. I wanted to express their bitter feelings; however, when I interacted with them, it was I who gained a learning experience. They can, in some sense, be regarded as being oppressed by their situations. The vast majority of them decide to go into the mines in order to

pay for their children's school and give them a better future. You could say that their lives are just for today and have no future prospects. There are a lot of challenges in life, however, we must continue living so there's no need to complain. Their outlook on life would really stun many of us as "elitist" city-dwellers.[19]

He then expresses his admiration of the "tenacity" and "optimism" of the poor workers' "life philosophy":

They go on living with such tenacity; whatever happens, they just suck it up and keep on living...So I did not show how miserable their lives are; instead, I showed things like washing and poker to deliver their happiness. Facing adversity, they are optimistic, and they are philosophic about life. In respect to the troubles in their lives, there is nothing they can do. They can only hope for their children and grandchildren—that they can get the education they need to change their fate.[20]

Truly, they are left without recourse and they can only place their hopes in the younger generations. It is to the the credit of the director that he realizes portraying them as apathetic men would be unfair to them; and he is, indeed, moved by their strong sense of purpose, which allows him to see through the biased views and one-sided opinions of the enlightenment thinkers, who just enforce their high-brow ideals on the "benighted" underclass. However, the complete repudiation of the praxis of enlightenment is debatable; furthermore, it is not the enlightenment itself that is dubious but, rather, what needs to be enlightened and in what ways. In this regard, to a certain extent, the director has gone beyond the stage of holding misgivings about the question "Could the Subaltern Speak?" by allowing the exuberance of the underclass to be shown. However, he stops before this move, or he takes the opposite perspective by eulogizing their tenacity and persistence. However, what he does not do, which nevertheless sets him apart from the socialist cultural-workers of the past, is to explore the class resentment and the possible class consciousness that may be forming in these underclass characters. In other words, he still keeps a distance from the underprivileged without trying to integrate himself with them or to articulate their class awareness, although he assumes that he has delved into their lives and minds. Yet, being intellectuals, we must think about these issues: What has caused their plight? How can they be released from it?

Otherwise, even if we deny the principles behind the Enlightenment, and although this "objective description" may facilitate people knowing the life of these people, at most it delivers the spirit of humanism and humanitarianism, but does little to change the situation. For instance, it is this humanistic concern that propels the director to focus on Song, who keeps his sense of compassion until the very end, which allows him constantly to discover his own conscience, and thereby the whole story is revealed. But the destiny of the victim could never be transformed.

Certainly, there are some inspirational elements within the cinematic text, which nevertheless, regretfully, are not fully developed. The revised lyrics the girl at the bar is singing are adapted from the renowned revolutionary song "Socialism Is Good," which was popular during the Maoist era and even in the early period of economic reform. The amended lyrics are, "The reactionaries are not overthrown; capitalism returns back with U.S. dollars in its arms; the Chinese people are liberated, raising the tide of socialist sexual carnival," which apparently delivers a bit of black humor, exposing the dire consequence of political corruption and of blindly following materialism. But, although the scene subtly conveys the discontent of the masses with the resurgence of capitalism, this popular discontent is not fully represented in the film. This is not totally the fault of the director, to be fair, for, with respect to the restoration of bureaucratic capitalism and the reappearance of class oppression, the masses have yet to form a clear political consciousness and are unsure how to deal with it. The working class is still a class by itself, but not a class for itself. It is also because of this situation that cultural elites like the director assume that the Chinese lower classes cannot speak out and need the elite such as him to speak for them. What is more, he himself follows the government's rhetoric to account for the cause of the tragedy:

After the economic reform begins, countless privatized coalmines begin popping up across China. Originally, this was a good thing. However, it eventually turns into a nightmare for many of the miners. The safety measures taken at these coalmines are not up to the safety standards set up by the government. The mine owners do not want to spend money for the necessary safety equipment and instead use the money to bribe officials. This leaves no room for the consideration of the lives of the miners other than profits. The miners work in extremely dangerous conditions...There is no modern facility whatsoever; and no measures set aside for the preservation of life.[21]

His judgment—that the privatization of state-owned coalmines was originally a good thing—comes from the superstitions of neoliberal principles. However, the uncontrollable frequency of mining disasters caused by such privatization caused the government to "lose face" internationally. This therefore left the government no alternative but to take the coal mining industry back within its control. As a result, the frequency of mining disasters dropped drastically.

The Weakness of Humanistic Perspective and Moralist Critique

While the film questions the price of progress, the director does not even attempt to explain the social-political changes from the political-economic perspective. Instead, he chooses to explain this transformation from the perspective of Chinese people's decline in morality and the resurgence of their desires. In answering the interviewer's inquiry about his opinions regarding the changes that China has undergone, Li believes that "it [the lamentable consequence] cannot be helped," because:

> China needs to develop, which nevertheless will result in its own set of problems. For example, the increasing numbers of vehicles bring us increasing levels of convenience and comfort. However, this also brings along issues of pollution and energy resource management…[In other words, I believe] the lower the cost of development the better… The masses need to be restrained and should not be allowed to make money through killing and looting. It is normal that people have desires. However, it would be abnormal should these not be constrained.[22]

At another point, he maintains his belief in the ideology of "progress" while calling for the regaining of "spiritual values": I feel that the current stage of development is pretty good…But that's not to say that there are no problems. The problems come when you neglect the spiritual side of human development, the essence of humanity, the problems of good and evil. When you have so many bureaucrats and human beings corrupted by money, the problems pile up. When the economy develops up to a point, human beings need to return to developing themselves.[23] However, what is worth noting is that he does not believe in the socialist concept of values. When Liu asks him whether he feels that "the changing morality among Chinese citizens in the last decade has shown that the socialist values that used to be so widely publicized—such as 'one for all' and 'make selfless contributions to society'—are fundamentally weak and frail?," Li confirms the proposition:

> In my opinion, any set of values is very frail. This goes for China as well as other countries. I believe this because I think morals and values are something we as humans establish for ourselves, whereas the [Chinese concept of] "seven emotions and six desires", our greed, selfishness, and desire for food and drink, are all with us from birth.[24]

On the surface, value systems and moralities are man-made; nevertheless, what Li does not recognize is that they are the result of a process of socialization in which people learn to live together in society. Accordingly, it is society, rather than people themselves, that provides the necessary ground for the formation of certain ethical-moral concepts. Furthermore, a society's mainstream ideology is the ideology of the ruling class, which has an enormous effect on the morality of the masses. Therefore, the moral degradation of these people can be traced back to the deterioration of the political conception of the ruling class. However, here again, the director attributes this to a "universal" situation: Economic disparity is a common problem of all humanity. Man's desire for money and other attractions is boundless and this is how he loses his humanity. My film is set in China but the story could have occurred in Germany, the US or in Australia. I made it in China simply because I am Chinese and familiar with the country. The basic theme is universal.[25]

On the other hand, even though the director feels this way about human desire, and even human nature in general, he still tries to apply certain myths to present his "philosophical thinking" to the viewer. For example, the names of the main characters, Tang and Song, are the names of famous Chinese dynasties. The Tang Dynasty (618–907), which was established by minorities, and the Song dynasty (960–1279) have certain implications in the film. For example, the two characters eventually take each other to the grave, which may symbolize the corruption and decline of Chinese tradition, which then calls for a new force to revitalize and reawaken it. Yuan (1271–1368), another Chinese dynasty that was founded by invading foreigners, harbors additional connotations. The Chinese word itself signifies initial intent and vitality. Also, the boy's name "Fengming" (which literally means the "call of the phoenix") is reminiscent of a classical Chinese tale in which the Phoenix cries at Mt. Qi when King Wu appears, signifying that a sainted monarch has finally arrived to undo injustice in the world. The movie seems to use this as a way of enforcing hope in the Chinese society.[26] However, one must ask whether Fengming really can give people such hope?

First, is he really the son of the former co-worker that Tang and Song previously murdered? The film does not make it clear. However, it does give us a few hints. Tang and Song have argued over their leather shoes and, eventually, Yuan Fengming stares at the leather shoes of one of the men being put into the cremation oven. His facial expression is very uneasy (at this moment, the camera pans to the black smoke coming from the oven's chimney, which makes us think of the smoke coming out of the Nazi concentration camps). If we pardon Yuan for failing to save Song, who sacrificed himself to save Yuan,[27] the fact that Yuan falsely claims the financial settlement for both men and does not make their families come to take care of matters cannot be explained by his initial panic (even though the director sets aside time for a mother-figure, who is a close friend of Yuan's, to accompany Yuan at the mining site while he collects the money. Here, she almost acts as his guardian and urges him to accept the mine owner's terms so as to reduce his culpability. In essence, when accepting the compensation, Yuan is putting himself in the same position as the two men, if not worse, for his actions are obviously unworthy of Song's sacrifice. And his reluctant glance at the cremation ovens shows us that he is struggling with his conscience about this.

Though we are not told whether he will use this money to go back to school, he apparently is no longer the same pure child that he was before. His coming–of-age story is not completed when Tang and Song arrange for the prostitute in the film to take his virginity. It is this merciless society that eventually turns him into someone he does not want to become. If we assume that he is really mourning the loss of his innocence when he cries "I'm a bad person" after leaving the massage parlor, then when he looks at the crematorium, he is already speechless. This fatherless person (his father had been gone working for six months, and was very likely murdered) has again lost a father, albeit a surrogate. When he witnesses Song's true motives, his value system could be expected to become severely distorted. The sense of alienation that is caused by society is the most grievous. The innocence and naivete of the 16-year-old Yuan Fengming can be considered as polluted and eventually becomes something else entirely.

This is a very poignant revelation and critique. However, it should be pointed out that the director only looks at this series of events from a humanistic perspective. Yet, this non-historic "reflection" ostensibly holds a historical stance, such as when Yuan Fengming is filmed reading history textbooks. However, the ugliness of present society cannot be traced back to some common human trait. If we look at this problem from the perspective of the social and political change of past decades, we can come up with a more valid analysis for the cause of the alienation.

But the implications delivered by the lyrics are very powerful, even though they may be inserted without much political or aesthetic consciousness. The opening and developing of this critique must wait for the further maturation of the directors. To be sure, this also depends on the further capitalization of society, when the society can recognize itself for what it is and not make itself out to be something else.

Sex, Violence and Piracy in the Age of Global Simulacra

"A Murder Case Caused by A Steamed Bun," a short satirical movie made by a cinema fan, Hu Ge (胡歌) (1974–), took the internet by storm in 2006. It aimed at satirizing the absurdities of the plot-line of the film *The Promise* (2005), a "fantasy epic" written and directed by the well-known Fifth Generation director Chen Kaige (陈凯歌) (1952–). Hu's short film caused a social uproar, which is a sharp contrast to a film by He Jianjun (何建军) (1961–) from the previous year, *Pirated Copy*, which can be taken as a story of "a murder case caused by a pirated DVD." This full-length feature film has not been released in China and is only available on the internet, thus, there have been few social or political repercussions. Being shot completely in DV (Sonypd-150) video format and using a detached microphone that utilized a DAT audio format for the sound, it is filled with dramatic tension. Additionally, there is a decided lack of dramatic conflict in the film. Thus, critic Jay Weissberg feels that it is too "roughly hewn for average art-house tastes."[28] However, how can this be the case? And why does the director intend it to be this way by creating "a very funny, ironic sense of humor"?[29]

In the film, we witness the pervasive presence of sexuality and violence in contemporary China, and we see the despair that spreads through its lower echelons. The director applies the skill of Western postmodern parody and pastiche to present the hopeless lives of these people of the "new poor." This technique does a good job of revealing certain social networks, but the director's avoidance of the other aspects of society make it impossible to become a more cogent cognitive mapping.

Widely-Spread Despair: Sex and Violence in China

Very few works of the Sixth Generation directors document the lives of college students. Apart from Lou Ye's film *Summer Palace*, which portrays the rebellious students from the late 1980s, there are almost no other Chinese films touching on this subject. This unfortunate fact signifies that the uniformity of college life in China has far surpassed people's expectations; either that, or the lifestyle of the ivory-tower college students has been utterly severed from society. In *Pirated Copy*, we see a college student, but actually he is merely a drop-out and is now self-employed as a pirated-DVD vendor. Looking every bit the young, naive intellectual, he name is Shen Ming. We hear his story very late in the movie, when he introduces himself to a female instructor from a local university. As it turns out, a few years previously he was forced to quit school after it was discovered that he and his girlfriend slept together in the dorm, which even now is a disciplinary taboo in Chinese universities. Shuttling back and forth between the bar, the pedestrian bridge and various colleges, he is providing professors, students and even prostitutes, a kind of prohibited "spiritual food." He appears very professional in his job, patiently testing each DVD to make sure it works. He also offers a timely delivery service to his clients, acknowledging that he enjoys socializing with strangers. However, his carefree manner is just a façade; he was forced into this lifestyle, a fact that brings to him to a state of inexorable gloominess. In this regard, we need to note that, although the status of Chinese college students in the 1980s as "the pride of heaven" has steadily declined since the 1990s, when everything turned to the market economy, students still retain a certain amount of privilege thanks to the government's efforts to maintain social stability, whereby they are still granted certain special treatment such as receiving food allowances, medical subsidies and preemptive opportunities in the job market. Therefore, the vendor actually goes from being a student with a relatively high social standing to being a jobless vagrant with no social protections whatsoever, taking a risky job that could land him in jail at any moment. In this respect, he has become one of the lowest classes in the city.

But his job is the last link in the burgeoning (albeit illegal) chain of "cultural industry" that has swept through China since the 1990s. They sell not only pirated art films, but also pornographiv movies from the West, in response to the cultural demands of the masses. But, after China joined the World Trade Organization in 2000, the West used their technical advantages to increase pressure on China to fight piracy and protect intellectual property in order to ensure profit. This, in itself,reflects the inequality between first- and third-world countries in the age of globalization. However, the markets for pirated goods continues to spring up and flourish in China despite the government's strong prohibition, the reason being that it follows the same logic of capital accumulation. Because pirated copies are simple and convenient to make while bringing outrageous profits, it becomes a way to make big money for the producers. However, the actual sellers such as Shen Ming fall into the lowest class of society, making the smallest profits with which to support themselves. In this light, the industry and career also become symbolic of China situated at the bottom of the chain of global production and circulation.

The strangers that Shen Ming deals with indirectly show us the fact that sexual dissipation and violence have pervaded Chinese society, which is conveyed through two narrative threads. The first thread concerns Mei Xiaojing, a teacher at an art institute; the other one involves a middle-aged married couple who have recently lost their jobs.

When Mei visits Shen's small shack, Shen is watching a pornographic movie. When he sees this beautiful young woman through the peephole, he pauses the film, lets her in, and tells her that the person from whom she used to buy copies has been detained by the police. However, he then informs her that he can continue to supply the films she needs for college teaching. In an obvious attempt to lure her in, he unpauses the video and lets it replay, making her quite uneasy. But he goes on answering her questions, informing her that he has enjoyed watching movies since he was a child and that, even though he has his own DVD shop, he would rather stay home and watch DVDs all day than be in the shop—this is apparently intended to give her the impression that he is a connoisseur and a collector, rather than just a lowly salesman. As expected, he immediately finds the art video Ms. Mei needs and, on her way back home, Ms. Mei, who has already been physically aroused by Shen, attempts to sexually harass a young man on the subway.

Later on, she uses the DVD she has bought to comfort herself in the dorm and to talk about Pedro Almodóvar Caballero's film *Tie Me Up! Tie Me Down!* in her class. The last time that we see her is at the end of the film, when she and her students watch this movie together. When Shen delivers the DVD she wants to her classroom, she leaves the class and chases him down. The scene suddenly goes red as they make love in a classroom. After they finish, she tells Shen that her husband is homosexual. The emptiness, frustration and confusion shared by the couple become the emotional tie that binds them together. At the end of the film, when Shen is pursued by the police in the street, the college instructor drops the basket of tangerines she is carrying and joyously chases after him (Fig. 3.3).

However, Shen does not share her desire for sex, as he simultaneously maintains contact with a bargirl. The first time we see her is in the bar. She has dyed hair; dressed in a robe, she is smoking—the image is reminiscent of the lonely girl in Wong Kar-Wai's art-film *Chungking Express* (1994). She walks forward, directly facing Shen Ming and asking for the VCD she had requested, which is *In the Mood for Love* (2000), a movie also directed by Wong Kar-Wai. After the next scene, in which Ms. Mei is pleasuring herself, the film cuts to Shen and this bargirl making love to the music of *In the Mood for Love*, which is screening in the background.

I was wondering why it was so deserted.

Fig. 3.3 A close-up scene shows College teacher Mei harboring an irresistible desire for Shen

After finished, Shen seems to develop feelings for her, and asks for her name and address. But she just exhales a puff of smoke, assuming a worldly manner, and "enlightens" the inexperienced lad that he should not be so childish—a behaviour she emulates from the movie.

Through Shen's introduction, we learn that middle-aged Chinese men nowadays often buy pornographic movies to "cultivate a good taste in life," which reflects the sexual frustrations caused by the growing exposure to the lifestyles as portrayed in Western films in the age of globalization; but it also implies the emotional deficiencies of the populace in the materialistic age. Meanwhile, life still imitates art in China's "postmodern" society. The comments and explications that the female instructor has for these Western films when she is teaching come from her own life experience; the bargirl leans more toward imitating the characters in Wong Kar-Wai's films in order to create and validate her sense of identity. When the old values that bind society are lost, the imagination and simulacra existent in overseas postmodern films come to mold people's lifestyles and the structure of feelings.

While these people lead a grey life, the unemployed couple is the most hopeless. The first time we see the husband is in a montage at the beginning of the film, when men of all ranks and files are busy buying DVDs. We learn that he is buying *Pulp Fiction*, which has the effect of foreshadowing his later behavior. Disempowered notwithstanding, he searches for fake forms of self-empowerment in violent movies. However, in reality, he has completely run out of options. A worker having just lost his job, he needs to provide his children with school tuition and to support his family; so, he and his wife discuss the possibility of robbery. In the night, armed with a gun and trying to carry this out, they unexpectedly run into two fake cops who are in the act of kidnapping a prostitute with the intent of raping and robbing her. Repeating Samuel Jackson's line from *Pulp Fiction*, the laid-off couple shoot the fake police officer and his accomplice. Afterwards, they go to a small restaurant and drink to help get over the shock. But they do not have any money to pay the bill, so they prepare to rob the restaurant. However, when they come face to face with the equally destitute, disabled owner, they decide to kill themselves instead. Being so enthralled by Samuel L. Jackson's character in *Pulp Fiction*, who would read a verse from the bible before he killed someone, the man thus reenacts it in real life. In the era of global simulacra, popular forms of Western postmodern culture greatly impinge on the mentality and behavior of the Chinese (Fig. 3.4).

我跟你说 卖毛片是要判刑的
we could send you to prison.

Fig. 3.4 The police officer is interrogating a female peddler in the background when the male peddler is questioned in the foreground

Chinese Form of "Postmodernism"

This cultural influence exemplifies the Chinese form of postmodernism. The other episodes, together with the cinematic techniques used in the movie, also display this idiosyncratic way of life. In the prologue, we hear the raucous vendor yelling in various accents, "Hollywood movies! European art-films! Soft-porn Hong Kong movies!" At first, we only hear the voice of the people and see the high branches of a tangerine tree. Afterwards, there is a tracking shot and a close-up presenting the bustling market of pirated goods. A middle-aged woman selling pornographic videos is pushing a bike with a child on the back seat. She exchanges a few words with a man who negotiates the price with her, during which neither of the two persons' faces are shown; only close-up shots of hands exchanging goods accompanied by the sounds of haggling voices are portrayed. When one vendor is caught, in the police cell he argues that *L'Empire des Sens* is an art film, not pornography. Behind him, a mother with her child is also being questioned. These vendors, who are mostly women, are left behind to take care of things while their men, the migrant peasant-workers, leave early in the morning and come home late after a long day's work.

This form of montage runs throughout the movie. It revolves around the ins and outs of the daily lives of a group of people, making the film look like a Chinese form of postmodern pastiche. In the parallel narrative structure, we also witness the stories of some minor characters. A drummer who contracted HIV after receiving a tainted blood transfusion due to a medical mishap is also an art-film connoisseur and collects pirated DVDs. He has never seen the ocean but, after watching *A River Runs Through It*, he rushed to the beach to fulfill his dream of seeing the ocean just before he dies. Between the soft and loud percussive beats of the drum, the music begins to fade out. The ocean mist swirling about him, he experiences the boundless nature of fate. This scene is reminscent of a similar setting in Wang Chao's movie *The Orphan of Anyang* (2001). However, the scene here is not a reference to traditional conversion, as in *The Orphan of Anyang*, but an emphasis on death as a part of life. In addition to the run-down underground production factory making the pirated DVDs, the film also portrays the gold-digging behaviour of the prostitute, as well as the daily violence, revealing the reality of urban life. This idiosyncratic form of pastiche—which, in essence, is the microcosm of post-socialism—has a sort of consonance with Western postmodern art.

But, even though the film has these parallels with its counterparts in world cinema, the director tries to use simple techniques to show his understanding of contemporary China. From the first long tracking shot with the portable camera to the epilogue, in which the camera frantically follows Shen as he flees the police, the movie gives us a tangible sense of the real. Close-up shots of the characters are used numerous times in the movie, along with certain scenic shots, and impose on the audience a vivid sense of the pressures in the characters' lives. Just as Western postmodernism came after the feeling of powerlessness brought about by the alienation of the post-industrial era, Hong Kong's postmodern art of "nonsensical humor" is a reaction to the sense of helplessness of the local people in the face of the two superpowers (Britain and the PRC), the defining characteristic of mainland China's "postmodernism" appears in the mélange of lifestyles and "piracy" that arise out of a lack of morals. Piracy itself signifies the shortage of confidence in creativity, the sense of aimlessness in societal disorder and the day-to-day monotony of prosy living. Additionally, it also implies a disdain and transgression of Western, bourgeois morals and rules. All these go to show that the disorganized chaos of post-socialist Chinese society is as vibrant as ever.

In the first few scenes of the closing sequences, Shen is haggling with a customer over the price of his DVDs on the street; at the same time, he is careful to be on watchful and avoid the pursuit of the police. When the police finally arrive there is a four-minute chase sequence; there is no dialogue or music, only Shen's non-stop sprinting and the sound of his belabored breathing. This becomes a freeze frame that includes the teacher Mei chasing after him with a delighted expression on her face. This ending takes considerable inspiration from classic films of world cinema, such as *The 400 Blows* (1959) and *Children of Heaven* (1997). In *The 400 Blows* (1959), the running of the student being punished symbolizes their chasing of freedom. In *Children of Heaven* (1997), Ali runs in pursuit of achieving third place in order to get his dream prize, which is a nice looking pair of running shoes. But the running here, in *Pirated Copy*, symbolizes the pursuit of one's dreams in a state of hopelessness.

The Unknowable Other Side

However, it is also within this very scene that the film's major weakness is exposed. Even though the film portrays the omnipresent phenomena of sexual extravagance and violence in contemporary China, it is unable to show the link between the pirated movie industry and its operational logic—the new capitalist logic of profit. Furthermore, it merely orchestrates an overly dramatic deduction—"the pervasive influence those enticing discs have on the average Joe and Jane in Beijing,"[30] as Jay Weissberg succinctly summarizes—which is what renders it absurd and farcical. Even though the pirated movie industry can impinge on people's lives, there are other forces behind it, however imperceptible they may be.

Shen, the ex-student here, has no familial relationships (at least, this is not mentioned in the film). Therefore, we must ask, how would his family, whose hopes hang on him, be affected when they find out that he has cut short his professional career and makes a living by selling pirated DVDs? We are informed that all the other characters in desparate situations have previously had respectable jobs. For example, the vendor that gets caught reveals at the police station that he used to work in a restaurant, but he earned too little and was unable to support his family, so he was forced into this unpleasant trade. And the bargirl tells Shen that she used to be a server but felt too exhausted to continue with that work. These details give the audience an impression that these lower-class characters are a kind of social parasite that only wishes to earn fast and easy money. However, in reality, the main body of these pirated DVD vendors consists of those migrants unable to find work; and the majority of prostitutes in China are forced into this activity. Not only does the director not show the social gaps in society between the so-called "haves and have-nots," but, for whatever reason, his intention is to reveal that these people are lazy, and possibly even unworthy of our pity. For instance, it is almost as though he saying that they should be considered responsible for the widespread pornography problems that pervade society. The bargirl leads the leisurely life of a petite bourgeoisie and is unfazed by neighborhood hoodlums and rogues. Apart from Shen, of her clients we only witness a middle-aged gentleman. This prostitute claims that "I don't do this often" and that "in her spare time" she watches art-films, listens to music, and drinks and smokes in bars. She has been doing this for only two years and was clearly not forced into it. She does not collect any money from Shen after they make love, instead taking 50 discs from Shen's tightly packed shelf to enrich her personal collection of nearly 1000 DVDs. This shows that she is not under any kind of financial strain and that she is only concerned about elegance and hobbies. She also meets a man who wants to marry her after knowing her for only a few days. This is simply a much better (and unimaginable) situation for a prostitute than you would find in the pornographic novels from the late Qing.

Similarly, in terms of the violence being presented, the film portrays the problem as a social illness brought about by these lower-class people. For example, the man who has been laid off is naturally inclined toward violence and, as a result, when he is buying DVDs, he does not pay any attention to romantic films, only paying attention to action movies. At home, he and his wife put on masks and imitate the dialogue and scenes they see in the movies, using guns to simulate a shoot-out together. Even though they are laid-off and their financial situation incurs the sympathy of the audience, the film shows that, being deeply influenced by *Pulp Fiction*, they intend to get rich quick by robbing a bank. There is dialogue between the husband and a factory official; it implies that his dismissal was a result of the factory being inefficient, but he simply wishes to get his own back on the factory. His heroic actions do not receive any foreshadowing, making the audience feel that he is rash, hot-headed and crude, appearing as a caricature of the average Chinese worker. Even his suicide is spontaneous and unnecessary; as a result, he is incapable of gaining further sympathy. There is also a scene in which he is repeating the subtitle shown in a Western movie that he is watching, "People should be able to adapt to their environment. In unfair environments, those that become selfish and cruel are demons even though they have a kind heart." This seemingly works to indicate that he has been becoming a very "selfish and cruel demon" while being placed in this so-called "unfair environment." Before he kills the men raping a woman, he shouts to his victim, "Have you read Ezekiel 25:17? I'm trying really hard to be the shepherd." He continues "And I will strike down upon thee with great vengeance and furious anger those who attempt to poison and destroy my brothers." The ludicrous yet violent scene gives out a sense of absurdity; and there is absolutely no way for it to give the character either a greater sense of justice or a greater sense of inevitability. Rather, it merely shows a man falling into paranoia. In this way, the narrative takes the origin of the violence of the laid-off worker back to the influence of Western films, which turns him into a deranged psychopath, rather than it being the other way round—that his desperation forces him down the road to insanity. This is an inaccurate portrayal of the laboring class, or a very distorted representation of it (Fig. 3.5).

The flaws show that this film presents an examination of social sickness from the perspective of an outsider; consequently, it is unable to explore the real, underlying forces that are the cause of the tragic "spectacles" in a meaningful and profound way. Furthermore, this postmodern pastiche is presented in a somewhat shallow and superficial manner, which further negates its critical elements. Therefore, it is not necessarily that postmodern China has been so fragmented that it denies

我想大的银行人太多了 不好抢

Fig. 3.5 The impoverished laid-off couple considers robbing a bank

the cognitive mapping of its totality. Rather, what it shows is that the film is incapable of revealing the various forces that over-determine the lives of these lower urbanites, as well as the peculiar Chinese form of post-socialism.

NOTES

1. Hui Wang, "Two Kinds of New Poor and Their Future," 184–185.
2. Ibid., 187.
3. Ibid., 193.
4. Ibid., 189.
5. Ban Wang, "In Search of Real Images in China: Realism in the Age of Spectacle," 504.
6. Ban Wang points out that, "the dramatic part of the film presents human agency and desire in tension with the naked logic of capital...Documentary may lay bare a dark reality dominated by the logic of capital, but the light that illuminates the darkness comes from the lingering desire to be a human being, entitled to dignity, education, and community." Ibid., 506.
7. Jay Weissberg, "Review: 'Pirated Copy'."
8. Ibid.
9. Ibid.
10. Joseph Kahn, "Filming the Dark Side of Capitalism in China."
11. See Liu Hui and Li Yang, "Fantan: Dianying de Yiyi."
12. Ban Wang, "In Search of Real Images in China: Realism in the Age of Spectacle," 504.
13. Ibid., 505.
14. Ibid., 504.
15. Joseph Kahn, "Filming the Dark Side of Capitalism in China."
16. Ibid.
17. See Liu Hui and Li Yang, "Fantan: Dianying de Yiyi."
18. Stephen Teo, "'There Is No Sixth Generation!' Director Li Yang on *Blind Shaft* and His Place in Chinese Cinema."
19. See Liu Hui and Li Yang, "Fantan: Dianying de Yiyi."
20. Ibid.
21. Ibid.
22. Ibid.
23. Stephen Teo, "'There Is No Sixth Generation!' Director Li Yang on *Blind Shaft* and His Place in Chinese Cinema."
24. Liu Hui and Li Yang, "Fangtan: Dianying de Yiyi."
25. John Chan, "Sydney Film Festival: Blind Shaft Director Speaks About Filmmaking in China. Part 2."

26. Throughout the film, the background is almost ubiquitously grey, while the scenes in the mines are all pitch black. However, when Fengming goes down into the mines to work, he wears deep red clothing, a color that clearly signifies hope.
27. Yuan is overly alarmed and panicked at the time. But when he runs out of the mine, he does not respond to the guard's inquiry as to whether anyone is left inside—which, in fact, indirectly kills Song, since we are not sure whether Song was actually dead when he fell to the ground.
28. Jay Weissberg, "Review: 'Pirated Copy'."
29. Ibid.
30. Ibid.

References

Chan, John. "Sydney Film Festival: *Blind Shaft* Director Speaks About Filmmaking in China. Part 2." *World Socialist Web Site* (2003, July 18). http://www.wsws.org/en/articles/2003/07/sff2-j18.html. Accessed October 22, 2017.

Kahn, Joseph. "Filming the Dark Side of Capitalism in China." (2003, May 7). http://www.nytimes.com/2003/05/07/movies/07YANG.html?ex-=1052884800&en=9676e0be188f15f2&ei=5062. Accessed April 13, 2016.

Liu, Hui (刘晖), and Li Yang (李杨). "Fantan: Dianying de Yiyi" (访谈:电影的意义) [Interview: The Significance of Movie]. *Beijing Zhoubao* (北京周报) [*Beijing Weekly*]. (2010, March 17).

Teo, Stephen. "'There Is No Sixth Generation!' Director Li Yang on *Blind Shaft* and His Place in Chinese Cinema." *Sense of Cinema* 27 (2003). http://sensesofcinema.com/2003/feature-articles/li_yang/. Accessed October 22, 2017.

Wang, Ban. "In Search of Real Images in China: Realism in the Age of Spectacle." *Journal of Contemporary China* 17 (56) (2008): 497–512.

Wang, Hui. "Two Kinds of New Poor and Their Future." In Saul Thomas (ed.), *China's Twentieth. Century: Revolution, Retreat, and the Road to Equality.* London and New York: Verso, 2016.

Weissberg, Jay. "Review: Pirated Copy." *Variety* (2004, February 16). http://variety.com/2004/film/reviews/pirated-copy-1200536353/. Accessed December 12, 2015.

CHAPTER 4

The Taste and Tragedy of China's "Middle Class"

The birth and development of the "middle class" in China since the 1990s is a phenomenon that attracts worldwide attention. Although in terms of its size and proportion, this group of people is still relatively small and "represent[s] a minority of the national population and remain[s] mainly located in first-tier cities of the eastern part of the country"[1]; its growth is nevertheless endowed with much hope by Western politicians for the transformation of China into a "democratic" country. How to analyze and make a fair judgment of this new class therefore becomes a controversial issue. Since the end of the Cultural Revolution, China's political and cultural elites have repudiated the Marxist theory (and Mao's practice) of class struggle; in the 1990s, they ushered in the discourse of "social strata" from the West and have:

> dedicated themselves to the formation of "the middle class," making its growth "a national project that signifies China's membership in the developed world" (Anagnost 2008, 499). Within this discourse, the middle class—whose size and exact constitution remains fuzzy; ranging between 5 to 15 percent of the population—becomes a prized political and cultural trope, a force for social stability and perhaps even the agents of Chinese democracy. Under this neoliberal mode of citizenship, "citizen-subjects were no longer defined as equal members of a collective political body but by the degree of their individual progress towards middle class status." (Anagnost 2008, 499)[2]

© The Author(s) 2018
X. Wang, *Ideology and Utopia in China's New Wave
Cinema*, Chinese Literature and Culture in the World,
https://doi.org/10.1007/978-3-319-91140-3_4

In Chinese public media, the life of the Chinese middle class is always tied in with such discourses as "taste" (品味) and "inner quality" (素质), which show a class distinction and elite mindset. Since the mainstream media often "join commercial enterprises in promoting the triumphant prospects of development, prosperity, and middle-class, consumerist life-style,"[3] like their counterpart in the West, in China "the cloistral comforts of the middle class living room" are inevitably "equipped with the latest digital multimedia and soft drinks."[4] Indeed, critics find that members of Chinese middle class "often seek to show their new class status through their living standards and consumption practices...enjoy their new status, relation to time and opportunities for leisure, vacations and entertainment products with enthusiasm."[5]

In terms of their political attitude, however, political scientists are quite disappointed. According to Alice Ekman, "contrary to a widespread hypothesis, China's middle class is not the population group most inclined to change or question the current political order. Instead, a large part of this population appears rather conservative, in favor of the prevalence of the current political order."[6] In addition to their vulnerable social status and this "feeling of instability,"[7] the historical nightmare of the Cultural Revolution—partly a truth, and partly a myth created and bolstered by the ruling party—also contributes to their rejection of any radical thinking, especially "among the older generation of the middle class," in which "the trauma of the Cultural Revolution and the related fear of 'chaos', led to a form of aversion to political change that might lead to 'chaos' again, or to any form of large-scale division within the national population."[8]

In the Chinese filmic world, it has been observed that there is "nothing particularly surprising about the advent of the bourgeois cultural distinctions in Chinese cinema since the economic hierarchies currently in play have a certain inevitability about them when it comes to class markers under capitalism."[9] Two movies about the newly emergent class are worthy of particular attention. Although they are all produced by Sixth Generation directors, they have been publicly released. By examining their narrative contents, we can get a glimpse of the living conditions of this class and their idiosyncratic mannerisms, as well as their differences from the Western bourgeoisie.

The stylish photography of *Green Tea* (2002) gives it the appearance of a doxology of modernity represented by capital or wealth, to the extent that it becomes an extended commentary on the ever-increasing spiritual emptiness of middle-class life in Chinese market society. Generally speaking, the space that the middle class in the film occupies is "a world hermetically sealed by Doyle's cinematography and...will not allow the modern Chinese city to emerge beyond the smooth surfaces of its private interiors."[10] But what is the reality underneath this gaudy, illusory surface? Upon examination, it is none other than a kind of macabre historical nightmare which still haunts contemporary Chinese people (in particular, the middle class). The historical amnesia (in effect, the symptom of unaccountability) of the social-political experience of the Cultural Revolution remains a cause for this social trauma (leading to schizophrenia in the film); its tragedy and the resultant epochal transformation rarely enters into the conscious mind of the younger generations. Even when it is mentioned, it is merely dispelled as an unreasonable, terrifying dream, one that is suppressed within the collective unconscious. Living in the illusion of an affluent middle-class society brought about by global capitalism (which is represented by the life of urban hippies in the film),[11] the historic amnesia of Western postmodernism is replaced by a similar phenomenon caused by China's post-socialism.[12] When the Chinese youth who experienced their childhood during the Cultural Revolution finally grow up, they are incapable of understanding the historical experiences of that period, which contributes to their inability to understand the relationship between the past and the present.

How does the Chinese middle class exist within contemporary Chinese society? And how does it interact with other classes? The film *The Contract* (also known as *Lease Wife*), which was directed by Lu Xuechang (1964–2014) in 2006, is the first digital film from mainland China that features a prostitute as one of its main characters. Its plotline reminds us of the American romantic comedy *Pretty Woman* (1990) starring Richard Gere, which narrates the story of how a millionaire falls in love with a prostitute and impels her to undergo a self-transformation in order to become a refined, bourgeois woman. Whether or not *The Contract* shares this thematic subject awaits further discussion; however, the divergence between the two films tells us the truth of the contemporary Chinese "middle class society," as well as speaks of its structure and consciousness.

Taste of China's "Middle Class" and Its Historical Amnesia

With the urgent needs of Chinese urbanites for emotional fulfillment amidst the rampant quests for money and commodities in an aging society, online marriage agencies and blind date TV programs have been highly popular in recent years in China. *Green Tea*, a film produced and adapted by Zhang Yuan from Jin Renshun's novella *Adiliya by the Waterside* in 2002, is generally believed to be a common urban love story about a blind date between an older man and young woman in a metropolitan city. However, it has been found that it is also a "self-consciously art-house fare that itself has a Janus-faced relationship to the popular."[13] Differing from ordinary love stories, it mainly focuses on the search and confirmation of the identity of a woman. From this perspective, it is also comparable to the storyline of the classic, Krzysztof Kieslowski's *The Double Life of Veronique* (1991). One critic notes that, "Mainland cinema already has a small sub-genre of such movies (of phantom sisters)…though 'Green Tea' doesn't spend time on the mechanics of solving the mystery."[14] Yet, a reporter from China contends that the movie is "more like a thriller and suspense film that has as its clue the disclosure of Wu Fang and Langlang's (two female characters in the movie) identity."[15] The director Zhang Yuan himself insists that it is simply a love story. Usually taken to be a "romance thriller," it "did considerably well at the market but critically flopped for lapses in narrative construction and characterization."[16] But how exactly can this be the case? And what social and cultural significance can the film be expected to deliver?

Another particularity of this film is that it unveils the truth of the social-cultural life of the Chinese middle class. The title of the original novel comes from a piece of piano music; this is used as the background music in the hotel lobby where Langlang, the heroine of the film, works as the pianist to entertain guests. It is notable that hotel lobbies are "a space that has a particular resonance in Chinese modernity of the Dengist period" and "the greater part of the story takes place in this type of high-grade space which is distant from the urban poor."[17] Such high-profile places in the movie also include teahouses and metropolitan cafes. Moreover, the film is "determined not just to suspend all reference to Beijing but to anything that might signify something less than the pristine in urban representation." As a result, it has been found that "the world is so closed off from the hustle and bustle that is the Chinese city that it has the feel of a strictly studio film rather than a series of location shoots."[18] Other than this selection of spaces, the shots are also arranged ingeniously and creatively, seemingly to display in full the most extravagant part of the living space of China's emerging middle class. The most distinctive example is the scenes "shooting through semi-translucent material, in this case glass with writing, frosted glass, and plastic curtains."[19] However, the appreciating this fascinating façade is not sufficient. While "the interiors resolutely underscore the extent of private space in the public," the "putatively postmodern way" is still taken to be "slick" because it "believes in its shiny surfaces but less so in the meaning of its logic."[20] Is that the real case?

Enchanted by a Beauty with a Double Identity

Although the original novel is narrated in the first person of Wu Fang or Langlang, the central theme of this film adaption is Chen Mingliang's search for the true identity of the girl(s). This change not only makes it easier to knit the narrative of the film, but also renders it more convenient to introduce the personalities of the "two women." This adaptation is meant to produce a kind of filmic archetype of the search for the identity of a mysterious woman. In terms of this subgenre of "phantom sisters," critic Zhang Zhen incisively commented:

> On the fundamental level of epistemology and subjectivity, twins or multiples induce our fascination as well as uneasiness with the boundaries of perception, knowledge, and identity. They challenge our ability of discernment while giving us the comforting image of likeness or familiarity. They provide us with metaphors of self-reflection and intersubjectivity, while also haunting us with the very idea of an unreasonable facsimile and its spectral embodiment. On the one hand, the ubiquitous trope of the vanishing twin and dubious double is symptomatic of uprootedness and fragmentation, and occasionally split personality or multiple personality disorders that often beset the modern individual. On the other hand, the same trope invokes in us a longing for sorority, fraternity, and companionship. On these multiple, ambivalent registers, doubleness or double consciousness has become the hallmark of modernity, if not its very definition.[21]

She further notes that while "Kieslowski's 'metaphysical' parable mediates obliquely on the fate of a 'unified' Europe after the fall of the Berlin Wall," the two Chinese movies (*Suzhou River* and *Lunar Eclipse*) of the same subgenre produced in the late 1990s (also by Sixth Generation auteurs) are "primarily concerned with the fragmentation of the social fabric of post-1989 Chinese society."[22] The major difference lies in the fact that the Chinese films' "meditations on transpersonal selfhood and virtual sisterhood are more earthbound than metaphysical;" specifically, "they are directly aimed at the relentless social world and a moral universe not governed by celestial bodies or divine grace but by worldly desire and disenchantment."[23] Nevertheless, the question remains: does *Green Tea* offer the viewer a differing version of the narrative mode?

The first girl of the "phantom sisters" is Wu Fang, a postgraduate student studying comparative literature; she appears pale and insipid, wearing the kind of gray "uniform" adopted by older women, a style which is rarely seen today. This prudish image is a conceptual design hardly ever seen in reality; thus it could be taken as a "potential caricature."[24] The film begins with Mingliang dressed up in a black overcoat in the style of the Godfather asking for a date with her. His outfit indicates that he is not necessarily a vulgar *nouveau riche*; rather, he has a distinguished approach to what is considered right and wrong, which is obviously an intentional behavior. In the original work, he is "supported by the middleman in the back who seems to be pointing a gun against his waist... he is a P.E. teacher in a normal university, but wears the look of a post-doctoral mentor." He also judges others by appearance and ends up mistaking another girl in the cafe who is fashionably dressed as Wu Fang. Instead, Wu Fang wears old-fashioned garb from the 1970s.

Mingliang openly pursues Fang; and Fang keeps talking to him about the story of one of her friends. She says that they have been acquaintances for ten years or more, as they were middle-school classmates, and that she is also a postgraduate student. However, what Fang tells seems to be more about the girl's parents than herself. What surprises Mingliang the most is that a mysterious murder case is taking place in this girl's home. Since the girl's father often tortures her mother due to his dissatisfaction with her job as a beautician in a funeral parlor, the result is that the mother finally kills him. Later in the film, the girl claims that she is responsible; however, her mother eventually pleads guilty at the court hearing. Fang then explains that the father was actually killed accidentally when he attempted to rape his wife in a drunken state and injured his daughter. In an effort to protect her daughter, the mother finally knocked him unconscious and he accidentally fell on the blade of a knife (Fig. 4.1).

In the restless days during which he is unable to win over the love of Fang, Mingliang is urged by his friend Jun to enjoy himself with a pretty, sultry girl named Langlang who plays piano in a high-grade hotel lounge, where it is said she is readily available for paid sex. Mingliang is surprised to find that the charming, long-haired girl, dressed in a

Fig. 4.1   A screen shot showing Chen Mingliang pursuing Wu Fang

glamorous dress and having a flirtatious manner, looks exactly like Fang, although their appearances and personalities are vastly different. However, the girl blankly denies this is so to Mingliang's inquiry.

Following this, Mingliang becomes entangled in love affairs with these two girls. At a certain point, he needs to attend a party arranged by Jun. Since Fang is nowhere to be found, he takes Langlang instead and introduces her as Fang to his friends. Langlang then skillfully performs fortune-telling, which Fang has described as something her mysterious friend does. But Fang says something to offend a girl, and then her boyfriend. Thereafter, Mingliang pulls her hastily into a hotel room and the two consummate their feelings for each other, which is the last slow motion sequence in the movie.

On the surface, Mingliang, like the audience, wonders whether Fang and Langlang are exactly the same person. Is it true Wu Fang has fallen into a state of split personality as a result of her inner conflict and is, therefore, acting out her other half as Langlang in order to pursue material enjoyment and sexual indulgence? Or rather, does Langlang, who wants to improve her social status, begin taking college courses? Either way, the situation is inclined to be read via-a-vis Freud's theory, which explores the unconscious drives which motivate people to act in certain ways. For Freud, people are impelled by their desires, but also controlled by their conscience to behave; therefore, their personalities are a result of a power struggle going on deep within. In line with this reasoning, we can further interpret Fang or Langlang's double identity from Freud's differentiation of id, ego and superego.

It is in following this rationale that Derek Elley believes that "Whether the same dame or not, Wu and Langlang are archetypal flipsides of modern womanhood—and as such, the film becomes more about Chen's ability as a man to reconcile the two rather than choose between them."[25] Accordingly, in this tale about the contrast between the traditional and the modern, or a choice between the spiritual and the material, the final solution made by Mingliang seems to be a sort of reconciliation between the two opposites, as they are merely "flipsides of modern womanhood."[26] But is this really the subject the film is concerned with?

Another way of reading the movie could be pursued from a feminist perspective. The contrast between the "forest-style" and "Roman-style" girls as discussed by Jun shows the degradation of women's social status in a market-dominated society. As he boasts, "Langlang is a forest-style girl. On the surface, there are paths everywhere [to access to her]. But you find that you come back to the starting point after a long zigzagging journey. There is no path at all except traps and illusions." This metaphorical expression implies that women like Langlang just sell their bodies but do not lend their hearts. For him, the other type is the so-called Roman-style girl, who "has paths everywhere [to access] although outwardly you see none."[27] This metaphor is apparently an insult to women's dignity, treating the latter merely as an object of desire. Thus, on other occasions, we see the female characters' deliberate protection of their sense of dignity. Fang walks away when Mingliang asks her how many boyfriends she has had. When Mingliang chases after her suggesting that they get a room in the local hotel, she slaps him and takes a taxi to get away. During the party, Langlang predicts the fortune of Jun's girlfriend, revealing her to be shallow and manipulative. When the girlfriend retaliates, Jun slaps her. Langlang then walks up to Jun and slaps him in return, telling him that she hates men striking women. In light of this understanding, the movie becomes a fable about the diversified paths that Chinese women have taken in the market society.

Inspired by this reasoning, the close-up on the tea leaves twirling and swirling in boiled water during the date surely hints at opportunities and destiny, reminding people of the blurred channels of movement between different classes in Chinese society. Indeed, when we take a closer look we find three women with different identities: Fang, a master student in art; Langlang, a high-level bargirl; and the third girl (Fang's friend), who is also a postgraduate having experienced her childhood during the era of the Cultural Revolution. To understand the destinies and real identities of them, we have to delve into contemporary society as the subtext of the film.

Green Tea and Coffee: Class Polarization in a "Civil Society"

During the blind date, Mingliang orders coffee while Fang asks for a cup of green tea. One detail shows her special affection for tea—she smells the tea before gradually pouring the water. Fang says that she does not drink coffee, but her friend, Langlang, loves it and usually makes coffee at their dorm. She says Langlang's coffee pot is very tall, but she does not like it. Nevertheless, she says, "You won't believe it if I tell you how much it costs. It is even more expensive than two-months of my salary."

Not only insinuating the gap between rich and poor, these words also indicate that there exists a distinction between green tea and coffee, which signifies a kind of cultural difference not only between China and the West, but also among people of the same country with differing cultural distinctions and social status. It is well-known that tea-drinking has a long history in China, just as coffee has in the West. However, in contemporary China coffee becomes an emblem of fortune and high cultural tastes due to the Chinese desire to follow the Western way of life—which has become a common practice since the 1980s. Fang's comments here are reminiscent of a comparison that has been made by Zhou Libo, the famous stand-up comedian from Shanghai, in 2010. Zhou refused to perform onstage with Guo Degang, the renowned cross-talker from Beijing, on the pretext of regional cultural differences. The difference between his taste and Guo's is like a distinction between garlic and coffee, the symbolic foods of the northern Chinese and Shanghai people, respectively. By claiming that "Consumers of garlic only care about their enjoyment but never its stinky smell to others, yet coffee drinkers swallow down the bitterness and allow the good smell to spread all around," Zhou, in effect, sarcastically repudiates Guo's art. It is apparent that

Zhou's comments show a kind of class (and cultural) distinction. Here, Fang highlights the staggering price of a coffee pot, which also implies coffee to be a symbol of taste and of social status. It is interesting that, in this movie, Peter Hitchcock finds there exists "a properly bourgeois antimony, one where one no longer has to go abroad to cultivate class distinction but finds its privacy and privations built into the very infrastructure of cultural expression."[28]

Fang's sadness in her comparison of the price of the coffee pot and the level of her salary, as well as the final disclosure of her double identity, shows the helplessness and the surrender of a young woman within the Chinese market-oriented economy. This is further highlighted by a dialogue sequence: on a blind date with Wu Fang, her companion asks her, "Do all intellectuals like you care only [about] spirits rather than materials?" Fang looks embarrassed, "This depends on different people and different perspectives." Chinese tradition demands intellectuals to place greater emphasis on moral principles and not to yield to profits. However, this requirement becomes impractical in a market society where money talks the loudest of all. Furthermore, the surge toward the worship money has even blurred the bottom-line of morality. Therefore, upon Mingliang's inquiry regarding why she chose a menial job like performing (but also, implicitly, selling her body), Langlang replies, "It is my job, just like playing piano [is my job]." When Mingliang further asks her "What if you encounter a bad buy?", she confirms that "there is no bad person for everyone is a dealer." Her response clearly indicates the predominant role of the principle of profits in society, in which a girl who sells her body is called a "sex worker," in order to play down the nature of her profession and underscore her willingness to engage in this job. Accordingly, Langlang says to Mingliang, who comes to buy sex from her, "I have no oily tongue; this is my professional ethics. You paid and I have to make you happy."

The movie seems to remain silent over this attitude, though it also may offer an oblique criticism. In one particular scene, someone who has a blind date with Fang appears very grudging—he only orders rice, vegetable and salad for lunch, saying to Fang, "When a woman loves money, it makes me feel happy."[29] These verbal cues show that he takes dating as a kind of business deal that aims to satisfy both parties' needs. When he hints that he expects Fang to be his mistress and speaks in a roundabout way about the terms and conditions under which she would accept his proposal, Fang replies, "It is good to be a rich man. I have a friend who is very pretty. She always tells me that a man should not be too poor. If he is moneyless then he will become jealous easily. And the poorer he is, the more jealous he will become. It is hard to get along with this kind of person. So she only makes friends with the rich." She openly reveals the naked truth of contemporary China—that the gap between the rich and the poor contributes to the ongoing classification of the society. She continues, "Those guys are incredibly rich who drive either Benz or BMW, and talk only about big money. They are richer than you, but share the same standard with you. A successful man always has his standard." Apparently, here she is teasing him about his miserliness. She also attempts to distinguish herself from "her friend"; "Actually, I am not so interested in money. Money just like clothes, one more or one fewer piece (of clothes) doesn't matter much to me." But in the following sentence the way she articulates her thoughts changes the means of comparison: it is not that this mysterious friend loves money, but it is that she is prettier: "My friend is different. She never fails to attract the eye of men even if she wears a pair of cheap jeans,[30] because she is pretty. It is different for me though. I won't be as charming even if I am dressed up costly." Obviously, her poverty and the consequential self-contempt have deprived her of any self-assurance. She says to Mingliang, who expresses his love to her, that he only treats her as an object for poverty relief; that external appearance has become the gauge by which to judge status and to measure the social value of a person. Consequently, she makes money through proper and improper means. But, as an "intellectual"— in China, a postgraduate is regarded by the society as holding enough knowledge to be an "intellectual"—she also expects to maintain her self-esteem.

No traditional traits remain—either of the ancient tradition or the modern socialist tradition, which is demonstrated through the behaviors of these characters in the movie. In such an increasingly diversified and faithless society, pure knowledge of art plays an inferior role compared with scientific and engineering skills, and even superstitions, when it comes to making money. Fang at one point informs Mingliang that Langlang knows how to tell fortunes with tea leaves, from which she can tell the personality and the general fate of someone at first sight. Although Mingliang replies that he does not believe this at all, Fang insists that many people believe in it: "While I thought she was telling a lie, her customers came back to her with their relatives and friends; and they said she was accurate as a fortune teller." It shows that people living in this alien and depression-filled society have to rely on supernatural powers to keep psychological balance.

The truth-content of this new class society can be found through the Chinese middle-class concept of love. People often care more about physical beauty in their emotional quest. Therefore, Fang feels highly inferior even though she already holds a Master's degree. In the pursuit of love, people pay greater attention to physical satisfaction than spiritual exchanges. Thus, during the party Mingliang takes Langlang to, Langlang—who, in essence, combines both Fang and Langlang into one character—sarcastically says to a girl who competes with her for the sake of vanity, "You are a smart girl, and you really have your means, for you can know how to manipulate the psyche of a man, making them turn around you." However, the remark simultaneously demonstrates her anxiety.

The love that Fang is seeking and the affection she receives from Mingliang seem to be contrary to such a vulgar attitude. As a female holder of a Master's degree, Fang engages in blind dates in the hope of finding a reliable soulmate; in contrast, her friend Langlang "changes her boyfriends faster than the weather." But Mingliang reminds her, "Why do you want to marry? Because you feel lonely and solitary just like me." She is anxious to get married simply because she is worrying about her passing youth in light of the mainstream attitude to marriage. A man who has attained a reasonable level of wealth himself, Mingliang is used to being abandoned by capricious girls. However, he is part of the mechanism when he asks for sex upon the first meeting and courts Fang in such a way that she calls him a rascal; essentially, he follows the pragmatic principle of brazenly seeking to achieve his goals at all costs.

But Mingliang still seems to be a pure and humble person to Fang, for whom the other side of her is Langlang. Thus, Fang discloses the secret to Miangliang, "Actually, I know you at the first sight," as she has experienced various men. His inexperience is further highlighted as the story proceeds: he summons up his courage to give a fresh flower to Langlang, who is easily available in the minds of Mingliang's friends. Although his profession is unknown, his distrust of superstition and his disbelief in fate shows that he still devotes himself diligently in order to achieve success. This can be viewed as representing the dual persona of the Chinese middle class: they are degenerate, but also simple; cynical, but also eager for love; and hedonistic, but also entrepreneurial.

Schizophrenia Under a Historic Shadow

Most of the scenes in which Mingliang, Fang and their friends appear are shot in a gardened Chinese-style courtyard located in a hotel, which implies the existence of traditional awareness within the modern, middle-class way of life. On the surface, this story about the split personality of a woman reveals the tension between traditional values and the modern lifestyle found in Chinese market society; this dual identity is often interpreted through the concept of sexual repression. However, this perspective cannot fully account for the transformation of Wu Fang (or Langlang), and Chinese society is no longer one of sexual repression. In the meantime, neither Fang nor Langlang gives the audience reason to think she has a personality disorder. Therefore, we must find other reasons to explain the cause for her split personality.

Fang makes a comment about Langlang: "I don't think she is interesting at all. She is too cynical." However, she plays the same role that she repudiates. At first sight, her double identity is a product of split personality disorder, or a symptom of schizophrenia—the cause of which being an increasingly diversified society within the widening gap between the rich and the poor. Consequently, the destitute Wu Fang is envious of the luxurious life that a person like Langlang can afford to lead; thus, she (un)consciously seeks to live it by feigning the identity of that kind of woman even at the cost of selling her body. She is symbolic of certain Chinese intellectuals who possess a dual personality that leads to capriciousness and vulnerability. As a petty urbanite with a meager income, Fang has lost self-assurance in her identity, though in her mind she feels Langlang's lifestyle "not interesting" at all. She wears outdated clothing, which makes her look conservative. However, she is not insusceptible to the prevailing social atmosphere—intellectuals are not born to have a strong immunity to popular ideas. As a result, ordinary intellectuals are forced to take on such jobs as highly paid bargirls, which is possibly the message that the film intends to deliver (Fig. 4.2). As Fang says to Mingliang, "Some people look very strong on the surface, but they are weak underneath."

However, there is another undetectable historic motive for Wu Fang's spiritual state. She once tells Mingliang that her friend Langlang "has been brought up by her mother whose experiences have greatly influenced her." As mentioned, Fang/Langlang's mother is a funeral makeup artist who is rejected by her husband due to her "bringing back the

Fig. 4.2 Chen Mingliang is sympathetic with Langlang

odors and face of the dead" and "her hands smelling of the dead." The words indicate that she is engaged in a low-status profession avoided by all; but they also reveal that, nowadays, jobs are classified as high-status and low-status, unlike during the socialist era, when the most lowly laborers of old China, including a humble nightman, could receive the highest honor and were encouraged and acknowledged by the highest-ranking officials.[31] In Wu Fang's mind, the cause of Langlang's father's anger is her mother's concealment of her job. But, bearing in mind the historical ways of the socialist era, we should not take this excuse for granted. Therefore, Fang's explanation and Langlang's recollection is merely an unreliable memory (Fang/Langlang was only a child at that time) which is a projection of contemporary reality into a historical period.

In fact, it is still Langlang's words that reveal the true reason for the schizophrenia shared by her father as well as herself:

My father is a loser indeed. When he was young, he wrote a drama. It was the era of Cultural Revolution; he suddenly became famous and worshipped by everyone. He had frenzy fans, though they were not as crazy as the fans today. My mother was very pretty and won my father's love among hundreds of competitors. But for his whole life, my father only wrote that drama, which kept his fame for just a few months.

The writer was elevated to a high place during the Revolution and then pulled down into despair after the failure of the Gang of Four. This is the reason for his spiritual collapse, which brings out his insanity. This political experience becomes the turning point of his personal fortune, but also casts a shadow on the destiny of his daughter. As a teen, his daughter was neither interested in nor able to comprehend politics, although she had a vague understanding of her father's failure.

Actually, not only was it true that her father could not adapt to such an enormous change, but neither could her mother, who had been in jail for nearly twenty years, adapt to present society. Wu Fang remarks, "the mother of my friend" was "released the year before the last, but she returned to prison after a little while" because she "could not fit in with the outside world." The original novel explains her situation even more clearly, "She could not adapt to the outer world and feels better living in the prison. The prison has a factory, which was a glove-weaving factory. Her mother thus returns and resumes her position as a technician."[32] She prefers returning to prison to entering into an alien world, for the ideologies and social environments of the two societies are so vastly different that she could not adjust to it.

In this light, the split personality also becomes a mirror image of society, which is reflected in the music soundtrack, which "sharply alternates between hip electronica and orchestral sentimentalism."[33] In the market-oriented economy, some intellectuals lower their head in face of the seduction of materialism and become "high-level bargirls," while the true heroes of the era—rich men such as Mingliang (in his adventurer's image of Mafia apparel) and his friends—can satiate their desires with their wealth, while college students such as Wu Fang are willing to find a member of the new rich to become his mistress. In the meantime, the narrative can also be considered a record of the life experiences and the mentality of the Chinese middle class. They do not want to go back to history and prefer living a life of urban consumption, which is like a new utopia for them. As a result, facing the more complicated social-political and cultural experiences, this new generation lacks a social-political orientation and remains enveloped in a state of confusion. Consequently, as one of the particular ways of life of the Chinese, the consumption of "green tea" cannot compete with drinking coffee. Drinking coffee, being one of the major images associated with a Western middle-class lifestyle, has become the symbol of "universal" middle-class taste.[34] Under the shadow of the nightmare brought about by the authoritarian "total denial," the Chinese still live in a sense of inferiority and in the state of historical amnesia. The cultural-political identity of China's middle class is far from being established. But the historical trauma, just like a haunted memory, will return at any time like an evil spirit.

Finally, it is interesting to note that the director of this film also directed *Beijing Bastards* almost a decade prior. The fact that the two films share few common tastes and little intellectual orientation has brought about some thoughtful comparisons. Peter Hitchcock has trenchantly remarked that, "the trajectory from *Beijing Bastards* to *Green Tea* is not simply a passage from rebellion to conformity, as if what is tasteful about the latter sublates the riotous impudence of the former;" rather, "the stark contrast between his [the director's] early and more recent films if not a sign of compromise and conformism is certainly a measure of cultural schizophrenia."[35] But, for Hitchcock, this schizophrenia is nothing but "an acquired taste that refers not just to the taste buds but to the entire logic of acquisition in the People's Republic."[36] Apparently, the historical connotation of the movie—the cultural-political dilemma of this new stratum with a "new space of bourgeois taste"—has bypassed his intellectual comprehension.

THE CHINESE VERSION OF "PRETTY WOMAN"

The Contract shares a very similar opening with *Pretty Woman*. In the American film, the successful businessman Edward Lewis is a charming young man; yet, due to the negligence of his girlfriend, they have just broken up. Running an errand one night, he absentmindedly drives his car into the red light district. Losing his way, he has to ask a pretty young prostitute for directions. From this moment, he and the prostitute, Vivian, become involved in a series of events together. Vivian's beauty and vivacious personality attract Lewis. Enchanted by

Fig. 4.3   Guo Jiaju entertaining Lily in the bar

this woman, he continues to "employ" her and pays her 3000 dollars for the next seven days to be his female companion during social outings (Fig. 4.3).

Similarly, the story of *The Contract* also starts in a neon-lit nightscape in a prosperous city. Our protagonist, Guo Jiaju, is driving a minivan with his friend, nicknamed Monkey. Like Edward Lewis, he has also just broken up with his girlfriend; however, unlike Lewis, he is not very wealthy. Just an ordinary Chinese man trying to make a name for himself, the company he works for is nevertheless on the brink of collapse, so he is forced to pay his own debts. On a whim, his colleague takes him to the red light district, where they run into some police officers on their routine "battle against prostitution." They stop to watch the commotion and incidentally run into Lily, who is hurriedly fleeing the police. Jiaju's friend intends to take the advantage of the woman by offering her a ride home. Yet, by accident, he alerts Jiaju's creditor and is thus forced to flee the scene, leaving Lily in Guo's care. The plot up until this point is arranged to show Jiaju's naivety by comparing him with his treacherous partner. That evening, Jiaju is unable to engage in sexual relations with her but still offers her 3000 *yuan* to "rent" her services for a week, on the condition that she must pretend to be his girlfriend accompanying him to his home village to conciliate with his senile and ill parents.

Augment the Modern with the Traditional?

A series of montages show several trains and buses taking them from Beijing to a small village in the northern mountain region of Fujian Province in southern China. This journey is meant to imply that Jiaju's experience is symbolic of ordinary Chinese youth. His father, who has been paralyzed by a stroke, is now restricted to lying in bed or sitting in a chair. This can viewed as signifying the enfeebled patriarchy. In light of this, he looks withered and helpless. However, the ancestral authority that he represents in traditional culture still constrains Jiaju, whose name in Chinese literally means "a young horse in the family," which implies a sense of filial piety. Thus, right after Jiaju returns home, he stands in a temple worshipping the ancestors. An elder member of the clan mumbles before an altar. Speaking words that have been passed down through the generations, he exudes an air of "feudal awareness" that is so often witnessed in Mainland China today:

> To all the listed ancestors: Guo Jiaju, a respected descendent of the Guo clan and member of its 11th generation, has returned after completing his studies. He brings with him his wife Lily Wang to offer worship. Lily Wang comes from a learned family. She is virtuous and kindhearted, educated and sensible. The filial piety of Guo's and his wife's should be held as an example for others to follow. We beseech the ancestors in heaven to offer them their blessing.

Next, they perform the ceremonial kneeling and kowtowing; the same ritual is performed again during their formal marriage ceremony which takes place shortly after.

Since they have not yet become husband and wife, the feasibility of the ceremony is somewhat dubious. Can it be taken as a practice that is intentionally (or unintentionally) cheating his ancestors? In any case, the ceremony points to a new dominant culture that has been gaining popularity since the 1990s. That is to say, the country is exploiting the traditional ruling culture (mainly Confucianism and ceremonial rites) to replace socialist ideals and institutions, which stress equality and justice, in order to cover up the worsening phenomenon of class division and contradiction. Unable to effectively curb the rising protests from the lower class, it resorts to the tenets of Confucianism, which underscores social-political order premised on class hierarchy as an instrument for attaining "harmony". Yet, when a half-hearted "filial son" brings a mischievous call girl to fulfill the expectation of the ancestral culture, the whole situation becomes a farce, which signifies the invalidity of this ruling strategy.

But we cannot underestimate its formal utility. As a restrictive, stratified discipline of human interaction, this ideology has its strict rules and brings into play formidable effects on people's psychology. The fact that Jiaju's sick father asks Jiaju to come home with his girlfriend and get married to "honor their ancestors," shows the alliance of traditional values (and their remaining power) with the newly emerging capitalist culture becoming the dominant cultural ideology. Jiaju's mother tells him the reason that his father had the stroke is that he woke up at midnight to count the money they had put aside for their son as the dowry to get him a wife, which is apparently meant to arouse sentimental or maudlin feelings. Even the overly frivolous Lily gradually becomes inspired by their loving acts and becomes domesticated in the process. This is particularly portrayed when she forsakes her usual greedy motives and refuses Jiaju's betrothal gift, as well as the jewelry that Jiaju's mother gives to her. The Chinese "pretty woman" finally returns to the "right path" by the interpellation of conservative, traditional values.

Similar to its American counterpart, the conversion of this rebellious woman requires the learning of moral behavior and the shedding of her old ways. A sequence of events aims to impress the audience that her change of habits is the result of an emotional struggle due to her witnessing the pressure Jiaju's parents are putting on him to marry and start a career, as well as their earnest wish that she could become a "good wife and loving mother," which are the traditional expectations for a normal family.

But Lily's emotional struggle during this time almost betrays her during the marriage ceremony. When she is unable to control her feelings, she runs off in distress, which throws the family members into uproar and causes Jiaju's paralyzed father to stir in his chair and shed tears. Although this scene meant to deliver a touching atmosphere, it also uncannily brings back an image of the ludicrous response of the moribund patriarchy when confronting rebellious acts by the impious offspring, an ironic picture often portrayed by the Chinese May Fourth writers when they were undertaking their iconoclastic anti-traditionalism. As Lily's behavior arouses suspicion, she is asked to stand in for a sick teacher in the village school, apparently to test her ability to teach. She is illiterate, however. The fake identity that Jiaju created for her is one of an experienced elementary school teacher whose parents are both professors, which is a respected social role expected for a contemporary Chinese "middle-class" family. On the surface, she gets by with this false pretense with the assistance of Jiaju, but several things betray her from the very start, such as her thoughtless rejection of the proposal that she teach by suggesting that, "I've only graduated from elementary school," and her impolite beharior during the marriage ceremony, as well as Jiaju's careless attitude toward the marriage ceremony.[37]

At first sight, it is the characters' mistakes that contributed to the disclosure of the real situation; also, for the sake of maintaining face for their family, the parents play their part in helping Jiaju see it through. It is not until the father dies that the mother demands that Jiaju to find a real wife, which implies that they have long been aware of the secret. But it is better for us to say that the audience has to accommodate the barely credible plotline in order to receive this fable.

Lily's domestication needs more patience. Even though Lily's cooperation puts her in good standing with Jiaju, he is ultimately unable to overcome his disdain of the profession, which is common among ordinary Chinese. Thus, he becomes irate when he finds that she puts makeup on Xiangcao, a naïve local girl who is attracted by life of the outside world and dreams of leaving the village. Lily bitterly feels the disgust Jiaju holds toward her job and tries to drive off, but he eventually persuades her to stay. However, during this incident they are spotted by two men who are sent by Jiaju's creditors and Jiaju is forced to return the money he owes. In this moment of desperation, the plotline of Shakespeare's *The Taming of the Shrew* finally comes to fruition. When the creditors threaten to take Lily as their hostage, Jiaju declares loudly that she is just a hired prostitute in order to save her from being harmed. Disappointed, the two guys intimidate him by threatening to chop off his hand. Seeing what is going on, Lily turns her back on her greed and instantly repents. To spare Jiaju from this dire fate, she takes out her bank card, which represents all the money she has saved while working as a prostitute. Sitting in the wilderness, she bursts into tears.

The movie could have ended at this point. Clearly, the Chinese version of "pretty woman" does not end up with her shining prince. The protagonists do not even fall in love with each other. But the movie gives us an epilogue. The subtitle "three years later" appears on screen, and we see Jiaju driving on his way to pick up Lily from a detention center. The plot-line is that, after eventually returning the money he owed to Lily,

Jiaju lost contact with her for two years. However, one day he overhears that a woman named Lily has been captured during the government's seasonal "battle against prostitution," and he decides to look for her. In response to his partner's warning that his company has just got back on the right track and that they should not play with fire, he grudgingly retorts, "Did I say that I wanted to marry her?" The division between social classes is not something that can be easily bridged. In reality, it was probably Jiaju himself that severed relations between them once he had repaid the debt he owed her.

But, in the detention center, Jiaju finds that the woman named Lily looks much more innocent and pitiable than his Lily. There are so many prostitutes like Lily that he could not save them all, so he turns around and leaves. In the last scene, Jiaju is on the road back, as the light turns red. Jiaju is talking on the phone and we witness Lily, several months pregnant, walking across the road. When the noise dies down and the world becomes quiet, the director decides not to choose the scenario of a sensational reunion; instead, he respects the principle of realism by letting them regrettably pass without paying attention to each other. Throughout, there is no chance for them to be together.

In reference to the theme that he means to convey, the director says that the movie "has a really rich ideological denotation. It explores the antagonism and the conciliation between modernity and tradition; and in the meantime, it tells the story about human dignity. Moreover, it sets aside people's different opinions toward morality. This is what attracts me the most."[38] As a critic, we must ask: did the director actually complete these goals that he set for himself?

The movie narrates a story about the chance interaction between a man who wishes to become a typical middle-class businessman and a low-level prostitute; it also shares a comparable ending with *Pretty Woman*. As in the latter, the heroine's arguably uncivilized, greedy character is absolved of her sins and eventually reforms. But the Chinese director takes an unconventional approach here: whether Lily gets out of prostitution is unclear, for she has just lost a huge sum of money that she has been saving, which would have resulted in her having to work twice as hard in order to earn it back. In this light, rather than saving her from a descent into crisis, the hero, Jiaju, makes her situation even worse. Unlike the romantic ending of *Pretty Woman*, the movie declines to allow Jiaju to develop real feelings for her; the two are still set on completely different life trajectories. This is not entirely out of the restraints of traditional values but is attributable to the weakness of the Chinese "middle class" in terms of its economic vulnerability.

In this social melodrama, Jiaju and Lily are the main characters, and the parents and debt collectors play the minor roles. Together, they show the diachronic tension between the traditional and the modern, as well as the synchronic interaction among various classes in Chinese society. But the interactions and societal network are not broad in scope, and there are several problems within the narrative itself.

Solidification of Stereotypes and Illusory Satisfaction

In line with his personal style, the director reveals and criticizes certain aspects of Chinese society. In the debauched and corrupt environment of the nightclub, the air is filled with eroticism and desire. The bargirls are shuffling back and forth while waiting in line for customers, and the brothel keeper calls them only by their assigned number. The businessmen are singing the revolutionary song "Sending Off Our Comrade-in-Arms," which implies that, if they were not once revolutionary soldiers, then they were part of the generation that was baptized under Mao's revolutionary culture. However, they have become corrupted amid the market fever.

This criticism is also subtly shown in its revelation of the omnipresent impingement of consumer economy and capitalist ideology on every aspect of contemporary Chinese society. The director tries hard to show the benevolence of human nature almost to the point that the audience begins empathizing with the two brutish debt collectors. As the film progresses, they even earn the audience's admiration. In the very beginning, the debt collectors inform Guo that they are "forced" to drive off with his car.[39] After chasing Jiayu to his hometown, they constantly stress the need for Jiaju to pay back what he owes: "If you don't give the money back, our business is going to collapse!" They spend a great deal of time hanging around outside the village, and they even stay two extra days at the long-distance train stop after Jiaju's father dies, so that Jiaju can arrange the funeral. In all, they choose not to interrupt and take advantage of Jiaju's personal troubles; they even let him off the hook for a few more days. In this light, Jiaju is less honorable than them. However, eventually, when they could have chopped off Jiaju's finger to settle his debt, they take the 80,000 savings of a prostitute Instead, which is cruel and opposite to the sympathetic portrayal thus far. In the spirit of realism, the director shows the power of capital, which defeats any humanistic virtue.

Still, the director is unable to maintain this incisive criticism throughout the film. Although it carries a strong sense of humanism, which inquires into the issue of the dignity of the lower class, there are many problems with this assessment. Jiaju's friend, Monkey, appears to be a less honorable person (which intended as a contrast to our hero). On one occasion Jiaju asks him, "these girls are quite pretty, why would they do this?" Monkey responds flippantly, saying "They earn millions every year;" and "They are all experts; not a single honest word ever comes out of their mouths." Jiaju is amused, replying "In this case, are they not just like you?"

This exchange, along with Lily's insistence on charging a higher payment, solidifies the impression that ordinary people hold of bargirls: they are cold-hearted and make large sums of money, or they even do the "job" voluntarily; it is never shown or implied in the movie that Lily is being forced into this profession. This confirms the director's lack of understanding of this group of social underclasses because, based on China's daily news reports about the "battles against prostitution" and the special talks given by the officials in charge of the initiative, we all know that most Chinese women involved in prostitution are being forced into this profession. Also, most of the income they earn is taken away by the brothel owners or the Mafia. Furthermore, the movie seems entirely disinterested in looking into the social causes behind prostitution. When Jiaju and Monkey are discussing the Chinese government's "battle against prostitution," they focus on the issues of employment: "How many prostitutes will lose their jobs [as a consequence of this act]?" and "They won't have any jobs!" The message delivered from this conversation is that it unwittingly supports the idea of prostitution being a necessary "job."

Nevertheless, this avoidance of delving into the roots of this social problem not only leads to the superficiality of the movie's humanist message, but also brings out a vicious side effect. Lily seems unashamed of her profession, even making several attempts to challenge Jiaju for looking down on it by challenging him, "What's wrong with my profession?" Jiaju's distain is not directed toward Lily, who is a victim, but represents most people's loathing of this social phenomenon.

Furthermore, it displays the repugnance of the Chinese to the resurrection of capitalism, as well as their unconscious persistence in the concepts of socialism, which defy the exploitation and victimization of jobless women. But the movie is incapable of showing this. Instead, it just shows Lily defending herself premised upon a shallow sense of self-respect.

More than once, the film gives us a beautiful picture of the village scenery, as well as showing the boisterous villagers washing their clothes at the edge of the river. These village scenes, which deliver the simple and honest reality of country living, are meant as a contrast to corrupted metropolitan life. However, although Lily's fondness of the country might imply that she has finally returned to a kind of primordial paradise, her own family background is never disclosed. She tells Jiaju's niece, Xiangcao, that when she first left home she too wanted to learn and to improve herself, but that "it wasn't long before I realized that this wasn't how the world worked." When replying to Jiaju's inquiry as to whether her parents know what she is doing, she says "They would kill me if they knew." However, she immediately adds a contradiction, "It wouldn't matter even if they knew. I haven't made a lot of money yet. Once I earn enough, I'll go back home and open a beauty shop." It is unclear whether this means that her parents would not care, or she herself would not care if they discovered her profession. But her own ambiguous family background suggests that her role is just "symbolic" of prostitution, or that she is just a plot device manipulated for the purposes of the storyline.

Therefore, the film solidifies the stereotypes the audience is likely to have toward prostitutes—they are cold, heartless, and immoral. Lily is so pragmatic that she has no illusions throughout the film about her prospects of marriage with Jiaju; and she quibbles over every penny with him. It seems that she always maintains her strong willpower and is never swayed by emotion (not until the last moment). Even on the eve of their marriage, she makes a phone call to one of her regular customers to "strengthen emotional connection," whispering giddily that she is going to "get married." She is shown to be lazy, even spoiled at times. For instance, she insists on taking a soft-bed in the train and is very unhappy about sitting in a hard seat. In this light, she is not a real woman living in reality, but merely fulfills the popular imagination of the life of luxury enjoyed by prostitutes. This way of characterizing her personality, together with the problematic rendition of Jiaju not entirely being a positive hero,[40] constitutes a sharp contrast to the archetype portrayed in the American film *Pretty Woman*.

Apart from this, the ending of the movie withholds certain essential information. A plain-faced, pregnant Lily calmly walks along the road, which gives the audience the impression that she has already reformed and returned to her regular life. However, how has she become pregnant? Has she married a rich man and started a normal family already? Or does she finally earn her own living and has met a man like herself? Whether or not this finale is an embellishment in face of the censorship, the sluggish nature with which she straightens her belly gives people an illusory sense of conciliation.

On the surface, the movie shows a realistic picture in which reality surpasses the traditional, as well as the negotiations between the two cultures. However, what is really presented is the articulation of tradition (the Confucian culture of familial piety and class hierarchy) with modernity (the pursuit of individual wealth in the spirit of capitalism), as well as the domestication of modernity (namely, freedom) by traditional values, which altogether form a new cultural dominance. In addition to this, there is one more dimension worthy of exploration.

The Reincarnation of a "ROC Girl"

At a certain level, Lily's role shows the commodification of the female body under capitalism. The terms of the contract that stipulate the price of renting one's bodily services unrelated to any human affection reminds us of Marx's critique of the bourgeois marriage in capitalist society, which he says turns marriage into long-term prostitution. However, to comprehend this dubious image fully, we have to note two other characters: a crazy woman who constantly appears in the village, and Xiangcao, a local girl who is yearning to go to the city (Fig. 4.4).

The first time the crazy woman appears is when Lily strolls along the village road in the early morning. She spots an oddly dressed girl stooping on a pile of dirt waving at her and following her all the time. But when Lily fails to run her off, as though warding off some evil spirit, and turns around to ask her why she is following her, the woman gives a confused response, saying that Lily has gained some weight. When Lily gets annoyed and plans to leaves, she demands Lily's attendance at her wedding, which is to be held shortly after. The woman appears once again at Lily's wedding ceremony, silently standing there in the corner watching what is going on and then quietly leaving. It is not until right before the movie ends that her life experiences are disclosed by Xiangcao.

Fig. 4.4 The lady dresses like the reincarnation of a "ROC Girl"

It turns out that she had some time before worked as a prostitute in the city, sending the money she earned back home for her family to build a house and buy the necessities of life. But the people in the village despise her, and her family feels that she made them lose face. Ultimately, her family had kept her money and forced her to marry an elderly bachelor. Refusing to resign herself to her destiny, she eloped with her lover. However, one year later she came back home and went crazy.

This sad ending should have set off warning bells in Lily's mind. Upon hearing the lamentable story when she is applying makeup to Xiangcao's face, her hands unconsciously stop moving. Yet, when she tries to leave the village due to her indignation at Jiaju's repudiation, she gives the crazy woman a lipstick as a farewell present, which confirms that she has yet to give up her vanity. But when the crazy girl continues to follow her like a shadow, Lily loses her composure and yells at her, "Go home! Stop following me!" and then starts crying, "I don't even know where I'm going; how can I take you with me? And why did you go crazy? Didn't you know that people like us cannot earn our dignity?"

The tragic experience of the crazy girl not only discloses Lily's past, but also foreshadows her future. Her clothes tell us even more. She wears a top hat and a scarlet robe; her face is pale, making her look like a living ghost. This abnormal choice of clothing was only witnessed in the ROC period; nowadays is only seen in TV programs and movies from Hong Kong and Macau. This indicates that she, like Lily, is also a symbolic figure. Her fate is Lily's future,[41] and her experience also Lily's "former life": the profession of prostitution was a phenomenon that existed in the Republican period but was wiped out during Mao's era. It now resurfaces in mainland China, thanks to the resurgence of state capitalism: the ghostly shadow has not disappeared.

While the crazy woman from the "ROC" is Lily's former life, Xiangcao, the other girl, is her future generation. From her appearance, the audience can figure out the past images of Lily and the crazy woman. She is Jiaju's niece, and she really likes Lily's cosmetics. But this appreciation comes from the "cultural capital" Lily supposedly owns. She is unaware that Lily falls short of this capital back in the city; rather, Lily is an object of contempt. She hopes that Lily can take her into the city to find a job, as, due to poverty, she is forced by her family to quit school and marry someone she does not like. Therefore, all she wants is "to just get out of here, whatever I have to do is fine." To her, a metropolitan life is one that not only provides material goods, but also affords complete liberty, which only demonstrates the limited extent of freedom in village life.

When Lily is applying makeup to Xiangcao, she unconsciously pushes Xiangcao toward her own profession: "If you ever go to the city, you would definitely be able to earn a lot of money. Here, these two earrings are for you!" Her distorted sense of beauty comes from contemporary Chinese social mentality, which despises nothing more than being poor, seeing even prostitution as preferable to poverty. Upon seeing his niece dressed up like a hooker, Jiaju becomes infuriated, ordering her to take off the earrings and clean off the makeup.

It is this refusal and reprimand that show the difference between the Chinese and American versions of *Pretty Woman*. It does not mean that the American middle class is more liberal and open-minded (up until the ending of *Pretty Woman*, the story just informs us that the prostitute is willing to change her ways in order to live up to the expectations of the middle-class man, since she does not want to be just a mistress). But it means that, in Mainland China, the reincarnation of this "ROC girl"— or, rather, the resurgence of prostitution—has been despised and rejected by the various social groups in society. Unfortunately, however, we do not see more epochal elements within this refusal in the movie.

Because there is no way for the film to show more societal factors, the director can only resort to his "humanistic feeling" to highlight the positive aspects of Lily's personality, which possibly lifts her out of prostitution and having her change her ways. However, the merits and the weaknesses of this humanistic move (as an action stimulated by "the politics of dignity") can both be found in the sudden illumination of her conscience. If she is given a second chance, will she still do the same thing again? Does this action mean that she decides to quit her present way of life? Does the mutual understanding and support among the disempowered social groups really work like this? And how should we view the estrangement between Jiaju and Lily that occurs later after this touching moment? The reason that we cannot find a satisfactory answer to these questions is because the director only examines prostitution and the other lower-level Chinese populations from the perspective of an elite or an outsider, although it seems that he genuinely believes that, only in this way, can we delve into their intrinsic world.

Notes

1. Alice Ekman, "The Distinctive Features of China's Middle Classes," 2.
2. Yuezhi Zhao, "The Challenge of China," 567.
3. Ban Wang, "In Search of Real Images in China: Realism in the Age of Spectacle," 502.
4. Ibid., 501.
5. Alice Ekman, "The Distinctive Features of China's Middle Classes," 2.
6. Alice Ekman, "China's Emerging Middle Class: What Political Impact?" 2.
7. Alice Ekman points out that "Chinese middle class households often share a strong feeling of instability. In a context of economic transition and absence of rule of law, they anticipate further expenses of the household and extended family. They save a particularly high share of their disposable income in anticipation of hardship, given the underdeveloped welfare system and the rising cost of healthcare, education and housing." Alice Ekman, "The Distinctive Features of China's Middle Classes," 2.
8. Ibid.
9. Peter Hitchcock, "Cong Pizi Wulai dao Shangceng Zichanjieji."
10. Ibid.
11. It is illusion because their life is not guaranteed and not as leisurely and free as the film depicts.
12. See Jameson's comments on the symptom of historic amnesia in postmodernism. Fredric Jameson, *Postmodernism, or the Cultural Logic of Late Capitalism.*

13. Peter Hitchcock, "Cong Pizi Wulai dao Shangceng Zichanjieji."
14. Derek Elley, "*Green Tea* Review."
15. Zhang Lei, "Zhang Yuan Sanda Guanzhong."
16. Xuelin Zhou, *Young Rebels in Contemporary Chinese Cinema*, 126.
17. Peter Hitchcock, "Cong Pizi Wulai dao Shangceng Zichanjieji."
18. Ibid.
19. Ibid.
20. Ibid.
21. Zhang Zhen, "Urban Dreamscape, Phantom Sisters, and the Identity of an Emergent Art Cinema," 353.
22. Ibid., 354.
23. Ibid., 355.
24. Derek Elley, "*Green Tea* Review."
25. Ibid.
26. Ibid.
27. This differs directly from the expression of the original novella, which says: "He (Chen Mingliang) has no knowledge of green tea. But he is confident on his study of women, For him, there are only two kinds of women: forest-style and Roman-style. In the forest, you see countless roads and countless possibilities; consequently, before the forest-style women, men would be easy losing their ways. However, before Roman-style woman, men would be easy losing themselves, for they do not know how many other men are embarking on the differing roads towards the same object." See Jin Renshun, "Shuibian de Adiliya."
28. Peter Hitchcock, "Cong Pizi Wulai dao Shangceng Zichanjieji."
29. In the novel, this is originally what Mingliang says.
30. The camera then moves to the man dating her, showing that the seat has been vacant.
31. Shi Chuanxiang (1915–1975), a nightman, had been received by the PRC's chairman Liu Shqoqi's (1898–1969) in 1959.
32. Jin Renshun, "Shuibian de Adiliya."
33. Peter Hitchcock, "Cong Pizi Wulai dao Shangceng Zichanjieji." He also aptly notes that, in the movie, "If the visuals are often intimate and almost claustrophobic, the music has the air of random download." Ibid.
34. The following comments by Peter Hitchcock on the meaning of comparison between green tea and coffee in the film are also notable: coffee-drinking is "a fetish much cultivated by the nouveau riche and one that is fed in Beijing by the proliferation of Starbucks. Wu Fang's love of green tea has something both pure and Chinese about it and its distinction here is connected to Wu's intellectuality...Yet the cafes and restaurants featured in the film underline that there is green tea and the real green tea, and that its consumption at high prices in upscale surroundings

is about the new space of leisure and its hierarchies, not simply its history in China. No doubt Zhang was aware of green tea's increasing popularity in the West as a health drink, fragrant but bitter, so its role here may also have a measured transnationalism about it." See Peter Hitchcock, "Cong Pizi Wulai dao Shangceng Zichanjieji."

35. Ibid.
36. Ibid.
37. He does not ask the parents of the bride to attend the wedding, and he disregards the local tradition in which the husband should avoid the wife on their first night of marriage—breaking significant rules.
38. See Anonymous, "Ziliao: Yingpian Zuqi Daoyan Lu Xuechang Chanshu."
39. In the car, one of them makes a call to his family, tenderly asking if his child has finished his homework, saying that he would be home soon. Apparently, they too need to earn money to support their family.
40. Jiaju takes the advantage of Lily's situation requiring that she demand a lower price for her services; also, he never falls in love with the woman. Meanwhile, when dealing with the debt collectors, he always tries to cheat and take evasion action, though he does not get away with it. This forces him to present a dual character.
41. If Lily continues to engage in this "profession"; but Lily's decision to save money so that she can return home to start a beauty shop is exactly the same as that of the crazy girl in the past.

References

Anagnost, Ann. "From 'Class' to 'Social Strata': Grasping the Social Totality in Reform-era China." *Third World Quarterly* 29 (3) (2008): 497–451.

Anonymous. "Ziliao: Yingpian Zuqi Daoyan Lu Xuechang Chanshu" (资料:影片《租期》导演路学长阐述) [Reference: The Explication of the Director Lu Xuechang on the Movie *The Contract*]. http://ent.sina.com.cn/m/2006-03-13/11201014067.html. Accessed December 12, 2015.

Ekman, Alice. "The Distinctive Features of China's Middle Classes." *Asie Visions* 69 (June 2014): 1–40.

Elley, Derek. "*Green Tea* Review." *Variety*. (2003, October 28). http://variety.com/2003/film/reviews/green-tea-1200538309/. Accessed November 12, 2015.

Hitchcock, Peter (彼德·希区柯克). "Cong Pizi Wulai dao Shangceng Zichanjieji: Dangdai Zhongguo Dianying zhong de Xin Zichanjieji Xianying" (从痞子无赖到上层资产阶级:当代中国电影中的新"中产阶级"显影) [From Hooligan to Haut-Bourgeois: Refractions of the New Middle Class in Contemporary Chinese Films]. Translated by Liu Yuqing (刘宇清). *Shanghai daxue xuebao*

(上海大学学报) [*Journal of Shanghai University* (*Social Science Edition*)] 13 (4) (2006).

Jameson, Fredric. *Postmodernism, or the Cultural Logic of Late Capitalism.* Durham: Duke University Press, 1991.

Jin, Renshun (金仁顺). "Shuibian de Adiliya" (水边的阿狄丽雅) [Adiliya on the Waterside]. *Zuojia* (作家) [*Writers*] 2 (2002).

Wang, Ban. "In Search of Real Images in China: Realism in the Age of Spectacle." *Journal of Contemporary China* 17 (56) (2008): 497–512.

Zhang, Lei (张磊). "Zhang Yuan San Da Guanzhong: Lùcha shi chedi de aiqingpian" (张元三答观众:《绿茶》是彻底的爱情片) [Zhang Yuan Replies to Spectators Three Questions: *Green Tea* is Completely a Love Film]. *Beijing qingnianbao* (北京青年报) [*Beijing Youth Daily*]. August 25, 2003.

Zhang, Zhen. "Urban Dreamscape, Phantom Sisters, and the Identity of an Emergent Art Cinema." In Zhang Zhen (ed.), *The Urban Generation: Chinese Cinema and Society at the Turn of the Twenty-First Century*, 344–387. Durham: Duke University Press, 2007.

Zhao, Yuezhi. "The Challenge of China: Contribution to a Transcultural Political Economy of Communication for the Twenty-First Century." In Janet Wasko, Graham Murdock and Helena Sousa (eds.), *The Handbook of Political Economy of Communications*, 562–563. Hoboken, NJ: Wiley-Blackwell, 2011.

Zhou, Xuelin. *Young Rebels in Contemporary Chinese Cinema*. Hong Kong: Hong Kong University Press, 2007.

CHAPTER 5

Memoire of Socialism and the Chinese Enlightenment

If there is one thing that can bring about emotional antagonism and intellectual controversy in Chinese society, it is none other than the appraisement of the Cultural Revolution (and, implicitly, its helmsman Chairman Mao). When the class struggle in contemporary China is reaching a new stage, in which the so-called "proletarian consciousness" of the laboring class is still hard to attain, the issue of whether the idea and practice of the Cultural Revolution was, and still is valid, triggers diametrical opposition between the left and the right. Berenice Reynaud thus perceptively notes that "different memories from the Cultural Revolution are creating a sharp divide within the Chinese population—depending on whether these years were spent in the countryside or in the city—triggering generational conflicts between father and sons, as well as between the Fifth Generation and the Sixth."[1]

In this regard, the two movies, In the Heat of the Sun (*Yangguang canlan de rizi* 1994) and Eleven Flowers (*Wo shiyi* 2012), reveal the lives of the Chinese people during Maoist socialism, which is particularly important when discussing the historical significance and repercussions of the Cultural Revolution during this time. The films themselves share many comparable narrative forms, as well as thematic concerns. Both ostensibly narrate the coming-of-age tale of the teenager-protagonist from his the vantage point; both focus on his pubescent libido and intellectual growth; both offer episodes of revenge and rape, pondering on what is the import of being a hero; and both ruminate over the meaning

© The Author(s) 2018   139
X. Wang, *Ideology and Utopia in China's New Wave
Cinema*, Chinese Literature and Culture in the World,
https://doi.org/10.1007/978-3-319-91140-3_5

of loss of innocence. In line with the fashion of postmodernism and following the vogue of new historicism, they are also both concerned with the dichotomy between collective historical consciousness and personal recollection, undertaking a personal and subjective retelling of history and musing on the (un)reliability of memory. In this way, they are both filled with a humanist spirit and avoid the pitfall of blank realism.

Yet, not unexpectedly, their intellectual inclinations are vastly differentiated and their cultural-political orientations divergent. If we acknowledge the tenet "the personal is the political," then both of them do touch on this cardinal issue. But if enlightenment traditionally means learning to judge what is right and wrong by one's own rationality based on the standard a person sets up for themself, then the protagonists of both movies regretfully do not reach the key point in the diegetic space. Thus, a comparison of these two films not only teaches us how a similar subject with apparently similar technical means can yield different renderings with diverse cultural-political ramifications, but also informs us what is radical/idealist and what is conservative in China's New Wave cinema, in particular, and in Chinese society, in general.

Jiang Wen's film *In the Heat of the Sun* (1994) came as an exciting shock to Chinese audiences. It appeared at the same time as many other Sixth Generation directors were producing films within China. However, unlike those other movies, it did not concern itself with contemporary Chinese society; also it did not rebel against the official narrative in China and thus was granted public release. This film was the earliest made during the 1990s that launched an alternative reflection of the Cultural Revolution. Unlike previous films, which were frequently premised on an openly accusatory position, it shows the era in a more complicated way by recounting "the daydreams of the youths under the sunlight of [the] Maoist ideology."[2] Therefore, its fresh brutality and unconventionality set it apart from the works of the other directors in the same group at the time. Unsurprisingly, it won several important awards, including the Golden Horse Award in Taiwan; the best film, best director, and best photography in Hong Kong; and the best actor award at the International Film Festival in Venice.

The most salient feature of *In the Heat of the Sun* is that it is "vastly different from the existing negative judgments of the ten-year 'madness'."[3] In this nostalgic narration, the director "puts into practice a new understanding or even an audacious rewriting" of "the whole discursive genealogy of the Cultural Revolution."[4] To those discontent with it, the film "unusually closes its eyes to the state violence and terrors, brutality, injustice, and coercion prevailing in this historical period;" instead, it "focuses on the splendid memory of youth, or the metaphorically 'gorgeous sunshine' of the romantic life of several wild kids in the 1970s."[5] How can these "kids' stories with the poetics of violence, a sense of humor, and an antiheroic tendency" become both "realistic and fantastic, both conformist and reformist"?[6] And how does this "ambiguous mixture of 'Maoist ideology' and the rebellious discourse of the youth subculture"[7] challenge, and simultaneously concur with, the existing conservative (if not reactionary) understandings, interpretations and explanations of the radical period?

Couched in a family drama, Wang Xiaoshuai's film *11 Flowers* (2012) is a "nostalgic" remembrance of the experience of Chinese adolescents during the height of Mao's socialist revolution. In the film, the protagonist receives his father's passionate love and obediently follows his instruction to study painting, while his father, who is filled with resentment towards Mao's program of "reeducation of bourgeois intellectuals" by sending them to work laboring, surreptitiously inculcates his son with the knowledge of classical Western art. The ideological connotations of this demonstrate that the film complies with the Chinese government's indictment of "Mao's persecution of intellectuals and eradication of culture" and, essentially, joins the strident chorus of anti-Maoism. This gesture is not only departing from the exposure of the patriarchal autocracy as expressed in the director's earlier film *Shanghai Dream* (2005), but also violates the general assumption held by the Sixth Generation of directors, which claims itself to be intellectually, if not institutionally, "independent."[8] One can therefore conclude that this film symbolizes the director's alliance with the state ideological apparatus.

Moreover, the two films display two ways of regarding the concept and practice of enlightenment. Being an academic term with its idiosyncratic connotations, the jargon in China has particular references:

> the frequent reference to "enlightenment" (*qimeng*) in Chinese academic writings may seem odd at first glance because Chinese intellectuals are often obsessed with "catching up" with all that is new and trendy in the West. Yet the term harkens back to the eighteenth-century French Enlightenment. However, upon closer examination it becomes clear that the term "qimeng" in the Chinese context really goes beyond its original meaning and is a subtle reference to individual autonomy, liberalism, and democracy.[9]

However, this understanding is merely one of its many usages. As early as the late 1930s, the Chinese Communist Party had applied the term "new enlightenment" to refer to its program of inculcating Marxist theory to the masses in order to arouse their class consciousness of claiming collective, political-economic rights. In the Chinese intellectual world, the Mao era has also been designated by some leftist scholars as one period of enlightenment. In this regard, the two films unconsciously lend themselves to the debate concerning the diversified versions and orientations of Chinese ways of "enlightenment."

REMEMBRANCE OF THE MAO ERA OF ENLIGHTENMENT

In the Heat of the Sun was adapted from a novella published by Wang Shuo in 1992, which can be taken as a personal reflection of the writer's childhood experience. In the 1970s, a group of kids living in army barracks in Beijing are filled with idealistic passions and youthful energy, and longing for emotional fulfillment. Amid the danger of immaturity, they gradually come of age. The fundamental message of this movie, which fondly recalls the warm, sunny and (mostly) happy experience of the era, makes it look like a "youth film" filled with the tune of nostalgia cherishing the unregretful old, golden days—which, however, rendered many staunch anti-Maoist critics quite unhappy, as they blamed it for trying to reverse the official verdict of the Revolution as a complete disaster.[10] Even the mildest comment still accuses it of "Neither telling a lie... nor making a confession...Jiang Wen's cinematic distortion is an intentional embellishment of the rebel youth in the Cultural Revolution."[11] However, more people tend to enjoy the movie from an artistic perspective. What is more intriguing is that the same cinematic texture yields quite different, and even antagonistic interpretations from the left and right, which shows its rich and complex nature.

To understand why the movie incurred so much controversy and what it really brings about, we need to delve into both the cinematic text and the cultural politics of the eras of both the past and the present. Through these we can understand that the "seemingly irreconcilable dichotomy of resistance and conformity, transgression and submission...fused in the ambiguity and duality of the fantasy" is not simply due to the "Beijing youth subculture" at that time[12]; rather, the ostensible tension and anachronism is coming from a contrast between the revolutionary, idealistic past and the post-socialist, conservative present, which speaks to the cultural politics of recollection or the phenomenology of remembrance in the post-socialist era. Moreover, this ambiguity, as well as "its very refusal to attend to what is usually called politics and its insistence on focusing on ordinary teenage life,"[13] explains why the film is condemned by one group of conservative critics while simultaneously is acclaimed by another group from the same community.

An Incomplete Coming of Age Story

Focusing on "the splendid memory of youth, or the metaphorically 'gorgeous sunshine' of the romantic life of several wild kids in the 1970s,"[14] the audience witnesses that, within 10 years, the younger generation grows from children into young adults. But this coming-of-age story "avoids the twee sentimentalism that often mars the genre without losing a magical sense of charm."[15] At the very start of the movie, we are informed by the hero-narrator, Ma Xiaojun, that his father works for the military and is often gone for months. This situation is shared by the rest of his peers. Thus, the kids live in an environment where they are rarely subject to the direct supervision and education of the father's generation. Two scenes involving the cap-and-feather days are particularly relevant. The first scene shows the characters throwing their schoolbags into the air, which signifies their yearning for emancipation from discipline; the second reveals Xiaojun standing on the tips of his toes peeping through a window observing three girls dancing in a classroom bathed in warm sunlight, which is meant to express his curiosity for girls.

It is well-known that most coming-of-age stories center on two cardinal subjects—the characters' rebellion against authority figures at school, and a budding fondness for girls spurred on by libido; these often intertwine with each other. This film is no exception, though the motif of passionate libido is here more evident and is continuous throughout. From the very start, the narrator informs us of the specific environment: "My stories are always set in summer. The extreme heat forces people to wear less and less, and leaves them internal desire hardly concealable. That time seemed like an endless summer, and the sunlight always followed me. It was strong and extremely bright, always making me feel vertiginous." Near the end of the movie, he concludes his experience: "I still remember that there was a smell of burning wild grass which was really pleasant...in my memory, the events of that summer was always tied in with that smell." In such an intense atmosphere of hormonal release, a libido-driven story would be inevitable.

Ma Xiaojun teaches himself how to make keys and uses that knowledge to break into other people's houses and discover the owners' secrets. Unexpectedly, he finds a picture of a girl, Mi Lan, and, from that point onwards, he becomes infatuated with her. But when he sees Mi Lan, he has no way of attracting this older, more experienced woman's attention. His embarrassed smile, compared to Mi Lan's calm composure, shows that Mi Lan sees him only as an inexperienced child looking for an older sister figure. When he really demands her to play that role, he is doomed never to win her affections. Thus, when he invites Mi Lan to come and play in their barracks, Mi Lan ends up meeting the tall and handsome Liu Yiku, and the two of them quickly hit it off. Yet, Xiaojun is so excited to show off his masculinity that he acts out a scene from the movie *Stalin in 1918* for her by climbing on top of a high chimney. However, ultimately, he finds that, no matter what he does, he has no hope of earning Mi Lan's praise. Next, in a personal feud, Yiku, who is a veteran, heroically stands up to the provocations of Mi Lan's former boyfriend, whereas Xiaojun again shows his cowardice. After he comes back inside one day, he finds that Mi Lan and Yiku have already become intimate with each other, and he can only look on in helpless jealousy.

It has been noted that "Liu is both the hero's ego-ideal, the desired self-image...and the rival, whose very existence serves to frustrate the same desire."[16] Thus, the conflict between Xiaojun and Yiku imply the disintegration of Xiaojun's idealistic self because of the contradiction between personal desire (individualistic jealousy) and heroic passion (collective altruism). The urge to possess a desired object runs counter to the revolutionary ideal, which calls for a self-disciplinary morality that Xiaojun is in no way capable of attaining at the moment.[17] Thus, the frustration that Xiaojun has been holding inside for so long finally bursts out during a dinner gathering at the Moscow Restaurant, a name showing the idiosyncratic social-political climate of the time. Xiaojun picks a fight with Mi Lan and exchanges blows with Yiku. When he brandishes a broken beer bottle and rushes at Yiku, the scene suddenly changes and the hero-narrator reveals to the audience that this scene is just an illusion; what really happens is that he draws back and puts on a fake smile. Through and through, he never develops the virility of a man. His cowardice and grievance comes to the surface in the form of sobbing in the rain. Even though Mi Lan is moved when she sees this and hugs him, he still clings to his immature shyness and is unable to tell her his true feelings.

Yet, what suddenly occurs—and critics always feel that it is improbable—is that, under the (rebellious) social atmosphere of the times, Xiaojun comes to an high-handed decision to rape Mi Lan. Whether or not this actually happens, we need to understand it as intended to expose a serious symptom of the times. In the original version, Xiaojun goes through with the rape; however, in the final release he was not physically strong enough to overpower Mi Lan. These children were coming of age in an environment devoid of either parental guidance or societal control. Young people had to rely entirely on themselves to figure out their path of intellectual growth and to reach maturity. The call for fearless spirit from the party left the "the children of the revolution" with a strong sense of pride, but also brought out the possibility of going astray. Because of this, even though they were supposedly enlightened by revolutionary ideals in regard to upholding equality and justice, they had not yet acquired a fully formed reason. The absence of this continues to the end of the movie. Since his envy is obvious to everyone, Xiaojun is all but abandoned by his friends. Defeated and dispirited, he resigns himself to floating in the indoor swimming pool. His socialization is forever left unfinished; thus, is his future left to wither? In this regard, there is another scene worthy of dissection:

> Near the end of the film, Mi Lan comes out of a swimming pool. Walking toward Ma Xiaojun, she smiles at him exactly as in the picture, wearing exactly the same red swimsuit. When she asks him how she looks in this swimsuit, Ma responds with disgust that she looks as if she just had given birth to a baby. By identifying herself with her fantasy image in her real life, Mi Lan has returned to the position of an ordinary object of everyday life, and has thus lost the sublime beauty of the object small other in the fantasy world.[18]

The relegation of the heroine from a sublime position to a profane, vulgar location signifies the disillusion of the ideal (and the ideology),[19] as well as the loss of innocence of the hero, due to his regard for a cherished object being contaminated or polluted. The failure to attain the object of his love and the ensuing jealousy, hatred and revenge also signifies the impossibility of forging a pure totality for the community even during the tide of revolutionary zeal, which is partly because of the homogeneous quality of "human nature."

Since Xiaojun is unable to achieve maturity through his romantic experience, will he be able to attain a sense of manhood through any other channels (such as participating in political events) and gain the "rationality" necessary for a robust subjectivity? Actually, one of the significant elements of nostalgia here is that youthful hormones are closely tied in with political idealism and heroism. In the beginning, Xiaojun proudly announces his fancy dream of becoming a hero. "I am sure that in a New World War, the PLA's iron fist would smash the Soviets and Americans. A new war hero would be born and become a legend." Since the film shows Xiaojun's "apparent freedom is…a trip to the very core of the symbolic order;" to Lu Tonglin, this "nostalgic portrayal of the protagonist's enjoyment during the political movement shows the dependency of fantasy space on the dominant ideology."[20] But to another critic Song Weijie, although Xiaojun builds "his own imagination of or longing for the Icons of Revolution, Hero, Great Mission, Situation of World Politics, and other key words with capitals," these words now appear to be merely "funny imitation of clichés," which is "a revolutionary parody of Maoist discourse."[21] The reason that these expressions may seem ridiculous to a contemporary audience is due to the de-politicized atmosphere of the present age; yet, for many Chinese who have experienced the Maoist era, the scene still bequeaths a sense of déjà vu, which shows their passionate idealism. Without doubt, for these adolescents this heroism is an imagined and individualistic one, rather than the collectivistic heroism as required by Maoism. When the urge to attain it cannot be achieved in real politics, it must be released in other channels, the most salient being the spirit of rebellion.

When Hormones Meet Politics

The rebellion against authority is vividly shown in a comical way. Before the story actually begins, the narrator tells us that because "there were not yet so many skyscrapers in Beijing at that time, nor were there many people and cars on the street; the elder youths and adults all went off to the army or to the countryside for reeducation." Therefore, in the minds of this youthful generation that was inadequately supervised, "this city belonged to us." Their lack of respect for teachers—which is a cliché nowadays as a denunciation of the Mao's political line—is recalled here in a humorous manner, which turns out to be just another way of mocking any form of supervising authority. In a classroom, a lump of coal finds its way into the cap of the teacher, Mr. Hu, when he is giving a lecture. The teacher, played by the well-known director Feng Xiaogang (1958–), slaps his desk and throws the books on it in great anger. To the youngsters in the front row, who are watching him in amusement, he roars out, "Who did this?!" Just at this moment, a young man outside the classroom asks for Mr. Hu's assistance in retrieving a basketball that has been thrown into the classroom. Initially enraged by this sudden disruption of his high-pitched reprimand, he nevertheless immediately surrenders by softening his stance when the man poses a mild threat ("You wait and see!"). What he does is find a laughable excuse to return the basketball and extricate himself from the embarrassing situation. This somewhat ludicrous scene reflects the changing power relationship at the time between teachers and students, demonstrating the weakening social status of seniority/authority deprived of arrogance, as well as their cowardice and hypocrisy in the new political atmosphere. This salient critique (but also subtle exposure) is also shown when Xiaojun uses a telescope from a room he has broken into using his key-making skills to look around the school. While doing so, he happens to spot Mr. Hu rushing to the restroom. On his way there, Hu begins flirting with a female colleague; however, when he gets into the restroom he starts shaking uncontrollably (Fig. 5.1).

Fig. 5.1 The teacher reprimands the unruly students in the class

These particular scenes are meant to reveal the effects of Mao's political line on society, and apparently sides with it by showing the real
goings on in the school, which is varies markedly from the popular anti-
Mao literature. In the latter, the period of Cultural Revolution is taken
to be one in which teachers were badly treated by being beaten, insulted
and even killed. Recent scholarship on these incidents indicate that they
did occur; but they were mostly perpetrated by the second generation
of the high-ranking officials who wished to feign being ultra-leftists in
order to protect their parents from being kicked away by Mao's anti-bu-
reaucratic policy. These criminals were arrested and punished during
Mao's time, but were absolved after the Cultural Revolution. In contrast
to the demonization, the movie shows that, even though some students
mock and take liberties with the instructors, the latter are still respected.
Therefore, the students are mostly just a little suspicious of authority,
which is reflected in the way Ma Xiaojun behaves toward his father.

Here, the rebelliousness of youth is not shown through the "patricide
complex," which appeared after the Revolution when the moral-polit-
ical authority of the Revolutionary Father was completely lost. Rather,
Xiaojun keeps a reserved respect for his father. In the very beginning
of the film, the father leaves to assume the role of military representative for the local government, which was a policy aimed for strengthening socialist morality and discipline. Ma Xiaojun, still a child at this
time, stands dignified at the front of the line to bid farewell to his father
and runs after the plane before it takes off. The dogmatic manner his
father assumes is shown in his strong disapproval of Xiaojun's association with Mi Lan. When this proves too much for Xiaojun to disguise,
he strikes Xiaojun in anger. However, out of the official's encourage-
ment of challenging authority at the time, the narrator also recalls his
gradual development of suspicion regarding the moral character of the
father. On one occasion, the narrator tells us that he has inadvertently
broken the condom his father stashed in his book, which directly leads
to the unintended birth of his little brother. This retelling of an unfortunate incident in a farcical way harbors the intention of making fun of
the solemn composure of the ruling figure. The most serious observation is made through the narrator's straightforward words: during the
"Campaign to resist U.S. aggression and aid Korea" (namely the Korean
War), "many people bravely sacrificed themselves, but he came out completely unscathed. Even my mother suspected that he had spent those
years hidden away in some caves of the Korean mountains (Fig. 5.2)."

Fig. 5.2 The father dressed in his military form caresses Ma Xiaojun

Since the father has no opportunity to educate his son on how to be a hero in reality, Xiaojun has to teach himself. Even though he has the audacity to teach himself how to make keys and break into other people's homes, he is still powerless to realize his manhood. In the scene in which he is mistakenly taken into custody by the police, he is unable to restrain his sobs and cries for mercy during the tough and rough interrogation. He could only allow himself to fantasize about a spiritual victory after he returns home by looking into the mirror imagining how he would exact his revenge on the police. The movie finally shows us how he gets himself involved in a conflict between two gangs in order to regain his lost dignity and lessen his embarrassment.

Contrasted by the valorous tune of "The International," the lens of the camera shifts back and forth, highlighting the tension of the atmosphere. To keep people from looking down on him, Xiaojun wishes to act through the bravery of cruelty and violence. He takes a brick from a wall and proceeds to strike a man over the head with it repeatedly, continuing to do so long after the man stops resisting. His actions here bear the shadow of the notorious military fights during the Cultural Revolution, which confirms the argument that "an undercurrent of threat, menace and violence gives what could otherwise be nostalgia [with] an added edge."[22] In the following scenes of the larger conflict taking place between the two gangs, we do not see this kind of brutality again.

Because of his recklessness, Xiaojun gets dragged into the subsequent retaliatory scuffle, which now involves weapons. As if by magic once again, the next few scenes show kitchen cutlery, screwdrivers, metal pipes, and bike locks being stuffed quickly into a bag in preparation for the fight; these people get on their bikes and speed off toward the location of fight. But all these things fail to materialize into real brutality. Instead, the highly combustive situation is diffused by a wise, older person. The two sides raise glasses in a toast at the old Moscow Restaurant in mutual praise of this experienced ruffian. They all chat with each other amicably, and everything returns to normal. Perhaps to the director Jiang Wen (as well as the author of the original novel, Wang Shuo), this harmonious ending would be more indicative of the times than violence. Furthermore, rather than suggesting that their conflict had been triggered by any "ultra-left-ist" politics, here the movie seems to imply that a more accurate explana-tion is that these characters only utilize this struggle as an opportunity for a sort of "coming-of-age" experience in a society devoid of any real "ene-mies of the people" from whom to claim justice.

However, the unruly nature of youth could not exhaust the rampant libido of Ma Xiaojun (and the predominant demographic within the Chinese society of the time that he represented). This exuberant passion is a result of the social and political climate, which is shown through a series of scenes that seemingly digress from the plotline. In one scene, we witness an official parade welcoming a foreign leader, among which is a fully dressed up Mr. Hu dancing with cosmetics on his face. Through the idiosyncratic mannerisms of the leader waving his hands, we can guess that he is the King of Cambodia Sihanouk (1922–2012), who is well-known throughout China. The diegetic music is of a song entitled "The Legendary Fragrance of the Flower of Friendship," which very accurately presents the fanfare of the ceremony commonly witnessed in Mao's era. The gestures of the crowd are exaggerated, yet genuinely show the happy and positive life attitudes of the masses at the time. In another case, when a musical performance by the North Korean Orchestra is to be held in a magnificent theater, a middle-aged man tries to pass himself off as the North Korean ambassador so that he can get in and watch it, but he is harried by the police and sent away. The episode epitomizes the high level of exchange among countries of the socialist camp during the time, and the populace's enthusiasm for experiencing socialist art-forms. Art in the collective era is a form of group appreciation; thus, a scene is shown where the masses gather together to watch an outdoor showing of the Soviet classic *Lenin in 1918*. Although it is not the first time that they have watched the movie (because Xiaojun has watched it so many times that he can recite some lines from it), the laughter the audience bursts into still confirms their genuine fondness for the artwork.

The atmosphere of a new form of "enlightenment" is introduced everywhere. Through Mi Lan's conversation with Xiaojun, we learn that they are well-versed in the popular revolutionary literature of the time, domestic and abroad alike. Revolutionary ideology was seeping deep into the minds of the masses, who genuinely believed in the socialist ideals at the time. Thus, Xiaojun says that he disapproves of the bourgeois girl Dounias while praising the revolutionary hero Paul, both of whom are leading characters in the Soviet classic *How the Steel Was Tempered*. At the time, foreign art was also popular, such as the wide circulation of the pamphlet *200 Famous Foreign Songs*. Highly influenced by these revolutionary cultures, idealism and revolutionary heroism were ubiquitous. Even though Xiaojun is not very happy with the fact that his father did not receive any injuries and had no proof of heroism, he is still proud of his righteous militaristic image: "I get my (key forging) skills from my dad. During the Korean War, he taught himself how to dismantle the firing pins out of countless Americans' grenades."

Cultural Politics of Retrospection

The movie proceeds from a first-person perspective. A further analysis of the phenomenology of this recollection is warranted. This film shares many common features with the film *Once Upon a Time in America*. However, what we must take into account is the cultural-political connotations of memory. It is precisely with reference to this issue that the director is singled out by some anti-revolutionary critics as an "evil holdout of the Cultural Revolution era," and the movie is denounced as disseminating the pernicious elements of the era.[23]

As previously mentioned, the youth's disillusionment with and rebellion against the authoritative power is not shown through any bloody whippings, or even the torturing of individuals as recounted by some anti-Mao literature. What is presented is a comedy or farce, not a tragedy. Instead of echoing the political denunciation of the Cultural Revolution as the cause of social chaos and disaster in which school education was all but disrupted and discontinued, we are greeted by the narrator's voice informing us that, to the contrary, the "engagement of learning industrial skills and farming" (a request to become a fully developed revolutionary New Man, as Marx and Mao teaches us) lasted for only one month, whereas "the rest of the time you still had to go to class." During finals, students could still be found diligently preparing for tests, which is evident by the fact that Xiaojun regretfully tells Mi Lan that he does not have time to see her due to the forthcoming test. We are also told by the same narrative voice that the students are studying practical skills in school, which consist of the reformed educational curriculum during the era.

It is hard to deny that when the film tries to honestly portray the era, it diverges from propaganda, providing an "objective" presentation of both the positive and negative aspects of the period. The sound of a flute in the opening scene signals a dirge of a bygone era. Yet, immediately, the subtle tune of sorrow is replaced by an excited atmosphere. In recollection, we are informed, "people at the era were positive and hard-working." A series of montages in the very beginning is meant to convey this passionate, idealistic social atmosphere. With an establishing shot showing the blue sky and the impassioned tune of a revolutionary song (the lyrics of which read "The revolutionary storm is raging in all its fury; the soldiers harbor the rising sun in their hearts"), the camera zooms in to give a close-up of the statue of Chairman Mao waving his hands; and the curtain of the story officially rises. In the next shot, orderly lines of revolutionaries stand in file ready to depart and show their respect to the people. Afterwards, a plane is trailing smoke and flying resolutely into the distant sky. All of these rapidly changing shots are being used symbolically to portray the lively atmosphere. In a calm and unperturbed way, the narrator very naturally gives his opinions of that time: "None of us had any money then. The electronic appliances that everyone relies so much on nowadays were unheard of back then. All the furniture we had in our houses was provided by our work units... Apart from a few cadres with dubious political caliber, instances of political corruption and greed were exceedingly rare." These words provide an objective assessment of the social situation of the times. Furthermore, "At that time, no one ever slacked off on the job; and because they never lost anything, they never had to be wary;" which surely afford a sharp contrast to the post-socialist Chinese society when and after the movie was released. Therefore, these seemingly careless statements directly deliver the director's particular feelings toward this period. In general, the zeitgeist is "conveyed with lively group activities, bustling cars, running children, and billowing dust, which are displayed with the accompaniment of the impassioned and heroic music."[24] A bittersweet memory of the selfless innocence, the phrasing "back then" presents a mocking comment on contemporary society with its lack of idealism and conscience.

However, far from avoiding touching upon the social ills and contradictions of that era, which some critics accuse the director of, the film relentlessly exemplifies Xiaojun's merciless beating of the unresponsive man, which directly portrays the cruelty of that period. When the "closed-door, internal film" (a rule at the time restricting the so-called Western, bourgeois movies containing venomous intellectual elements to the investigation of officials with that privilege) is shown at the theater, a senior official sits in the front row along with his beautiful secretary. The official, upon the disruption of the showing by naive children who wish to sneak into the theatre and watch the movie out of curiosity, arrogantly reproaches the misbehaving children by making a farcical statement that the film is a "very pernicious" work unsuitable for them to watch. This scene thus indirectly showcases the bureaucratic prerogative and hints at the existence of corruption. In addition, the narrator also informs us that Ma Xiaojun's maternal grandfather kills himself in fear of punishment, for "he has four hats: a big land proprietor, a big capitalist, a Nationalist Party member, and a historical anti-revolutionary. Since the Revolution, his house has been ransacked countless times, and he has been forced to give in his money and the alleged 'proof of appointment.' He dies after enduring extreme pains, both physically and spiritually." One can conclude that this unfortunate tragedy is a microscopic examination of the widespread phenomenon of ultra-leftist crimes at the times. Even the policy of deciding personal marriage and promotion on the basis of one's family background is exposed with the fortune of the hero's own parents: "I later found out that my parents' marriage had not been approved by their superiors since they belonged to different social classes. But because of their stubborn obstinacy, they got married anyway, resulting in my father losing any prospect for promotion in his professional career, and my mother her job as a teacher." Through the narrator, the audience is given the multi-faceted reality.

Certainly, no narrative can be immune from the political and ideological impositions of this time. In the opening, the narrator expresses his feelings as such:

> Beijing has changed so fast! Over twenty years, it's already become a modernized city. There's almost nothing left of the Beijing that I remember. In reality, this change has already begun to affect my memories. I no longer know for sure what was real and what is my imagination.

To some critics, this voice shows the narrator's "gradual loss of confidence in his memory and fantasy;" the "ambiguous, doubtable, and problematic" nature of which displays "a significant skepticism about the narrator's memory of the 'grand (dominant) narrative' and the individual, unquiet, and imaginary past."[25] In other words, "the dubious relationships between the individual, history, memory, and ideology"[26] reveal a postmodern trick.

There are several different implications in this regard. First, the story is told from the perspective of someone twenty-odd years removed from the actual events of the Cultural Revolution, a person who now lives in "modernized" Beijing. Looking at it this way, the past already belongs to the lost age of pre-history. Moreover, the statement is neither a condemnation of the alleged official stance of declining a genuine reflection of the "ultra-leftism" of the Cultural Revolution, nor is it charging the masses' lack of memory of the past violence, both of which are popular discourses in Chinese intellectual circles. It is, instead, a reference to the incredible change that has taken place in the city—namely, how people have become spiritually lost within the materialist trends nowadays. Moreover, the inability to clearly distinguish between reality and imagination does not refer to the phenomenon of historical amnesia, which is popular in Western postmodernist culture, which Fredric Jameson has explained. Instead, it is indicating that the historical memory has been so inexorably affected by this transformation that it has lost its reliability. It transforms the memory of ordinary people regarding the Cultural Revolution by its high-pitched "complete denunciation" of the "10 years of chaos and disasters." It also implies that the memories of those people that experienced the Revolution are now influenced by their political unconscious brought about by their new identities. During the coda towards the end of the film, the color of the movie changes to black and white, symbolizing the bland, homogenous nature of the consumer society. Ma Xiaojun and his friend sit atop a luxurious limousine as it drives off. Judging by their appearances in this scene, it is clear that they have become quite successful. The scene suggests that these youths, who led the life of the lumpen proletariat during the Cultural Revolution, have become used to the new market economy with their indomitable spirit and, having gained through theie past experiences, taken the business world by storm, becoming new heroes in this brave, new world.

Even so, there are exceptions. We are informed by the narrator here that Xiaojun's rival in love, Liu Yikou, is mentally disabled because of an injury sustained during the Sino-Vietnamese War (1979–1989), in which he participated after he reenlisted in the army. It should be noted that most of the survivors of the War have now become a disenfranchised social group reliant on government relief. Their inability to "succeed" could probably be traced to the incompatibility of their idealism and the vulgar, materialist society, which explains the mental anguish that Yiku suffers. Another reason can be attributed to the controversial nature of the War, which is different from all the earlier wars that took place during Mao's era. What we must remember is that this is the second time Yiku had joined the army. Also, except for Yiku, everyone else seems to have reaped a huge capitalist success, having given in to worldly desires.

But there is yet another survivor of that era. At this moment, we have the reappearance of a mentally retarded man, in real life named Gu Lunmu, who shows up now and again. Similar to his actions in the past, he rides on a chunk of wood, which looks like a massive gun barrel (a gigantic phallic symbol, certainly). By contrast, the successful businessmen, including Xiaojun, are riding atop the fancy limousine, calling to this old acquaintance. However, Gu Lunmu does not speak in the stuttering manner he previously had. Instead, he carefully enunciates his words, scolding the characters, "Punk-ass!" The anachronistic profanity he uses (the word has only become popular since the 1990s) appears surprising and even ludicrous to the viewer. But what exactly does this signify? And who is the object of debasement? Is it the physically disabled man, the "big shots," or even the audience, who have lost the ability to reflect critically on the past and present? The vagueness may be an intentional addition, which serves as a subtle form of ridicule.[27]

However, even though the movie does not conform to the dominant ideology nowadays, which regards the Revolution as entirely negative, it is not able fully to escape the official rhetoric, the most significant case being its ubiquitous representation of the so-called "sexual repression." In addition to Xiaojun's repressed libidinal urge, which sometimes transforms itself into a kind of political enthusiasm, as well as the sexually charged symbolic gesture performed by the mentally challenged Gu Lunmu, the ballet performance "The Red Detachment of Women" shown in the film also focalizes the high kicks of the Chinese female revolutionaries, which insinuates the popular opinion that the revolutionary era was an age in which the masses' sexual desire was heavily suppressed. Rather than a fact, however, the thesis of "repression" or "suppression" is merely a projection of the present age of mass consumption when sex becomes a marketable good and desire is stimulated by all sorts of advertisements that serve to prompt consumption. Indeed, little attention was given to sexuality during the Revolutionary period, which is not only related to the socialist values and the urgency of establishing a strong socialist nation, but is also based upon the ethical principles and customs found in Chinese traditional culture. In addition, most of the characters are adolescents; people of the same age are not encouraged to access adult materials, now or then.

One of the reasons that the movie is indicted as "an intentional embellishment of the rebel youth in the Cultural Revolution" is that, throughout the cinematic space, the characters' "everyday life and even their erotic dreams reflect some basic elements of Maoist discourse and share some common cultural logic or political expectations of the mainstream ideology in the Cultural Revolution."[28] In other words, by showing the fact that the youth's "spiritual heritage is inevitably derived from the logic and terminology of the Cultural Revolution itself"[29] in a non-negative way, or by revealing that "the kids are unconsciously driven by the impulses of youth released by the unprecedented Cultural Revolution"[30] to become idealistic and passionate in the name of human nature, which is departs considerably from the conventional, popular rhetoric and ideology of the present, the film titillates the uneasy nerve of the anti-radicals of this conformist age.[31] But, intentionally or not, this portrayal of youth's coming of age in the bygone "era of enlightenment" reveals both positive and negative aspects of that period.

Because this generation did not receive a complete education—either from their revolutionary, elder parents, or from life with real revolutionary struggles—they had no way of developing their intellectual caliber fully. Since they could not intervene in political life (the Red guards of the early stage of Cultural Revolution was only a short-lived phenomenon), they could only make symbolic gestures to emulate the political fights (such as hitting their opponents with bricks), thus incapable of fully acquiring the political experience. They are far from attaining their "reason" and they do not grow up, at least not until the end of film. This means that, although the days of the Cultural Revolution were shown as warm, bright days, they were not an accomplished "era of enlightenment." Thus, this film is ultimately not a story of *Bildungsroman*.

Conservative Projection in the "Enlightenment" of a Father

The movie *Eleven Flowers*, produced by Wang Xiaoshuai in 2011, is quite similar to his earlier film *Shanghai Dream* (2005). Both films demonstrate the lives of Chinese people who lived in the so-called "third-line cities" during the Mao era, and involve such scenes as the living conditions of close neighbors, collective dorms, school gymnastics, collective bathing pools, revolutionary banners and slogans, and many other images of collectivism. Moreover, they both focus on a fetishized object and a rape scene to illustrate the tragic destinies of intellectual families, which experiences initiate the growth experiences of the protagonists. They are even embedded with a similar plot structure beginning with the sound of a loud speaker broadcasting disciplinary messages, and ending with the noise of a piercing gunfire. On the surface, the most salient difference lies in the perspectives from which the stories are narrated. In *Shanghai Dream*, the event is observed from an omniscient point of view; in *Eleven Flowers*, the story proceeds from the perspective of Wang Han, the protagonist of the film. The heroine in *Shanghai Dream* is the victim of a rape; the hero of *Eleven Flowers* is a character who learns about the adult world by observing and hearing others. But, towards the end of the analysis, we will find that the two movies share vastly divergent ideological inclinations.

Like *Shanghai Dream*, the presentation of an unusual incident and its repercussions in a short period in the life of a youth comprises the overarching narrative content of *Eleven Flowers*. Wang Han, an eleven-year-old boy, is given the chance to lead the school gymnastics every day because he performs the poses well. His teacher suggests that he wear a white shirt, which accentuates his actions. His mother, who has grown up in the widespread poverty of that era, is barely able to satisfy his aspirations. Learning the importance that this clothing has on her child's well-being, she nevertheless spends the whole year's cloth coupon to make a shirt for him. However, the shirt is taken by a fleeing murderer as a bandage for his wound when Wang Han is playing with his friends by a river. As a result, Wang Han gradually comes to know the murderer's identity. The character Jueqiang, a descendant of an intellectual's family from Shanghai and working at a local factory, kills a factory leader in revenge for the rape of his 16-year-old younger sister. Threatened by Jueqiang, Wang Han agrees to keep their acquaintance confidential. However, he unintentionally releases this secret to a friend, which leads to an extensive search by the. Some days later, Jueqiang is arrested while he is setting fire to the factory and is sentenced to death shortly afterwards, from which, Wang Han learns his first major life-lesson.

There are numerous "first time experiences" in the movie, which confirm its interest in the coming of age of Chinese youth. Thus, one can raise the following question: does the film complete a narration of the genre of *Bildungsroman*? If so (or not so), then in what sense? It has been noted that the film is "in part a portrayal of the deprivations, both material and spiritual, of the Cultural Revolution."[32] But how can this be the case?

A White Shirt and a Rape Case as Symbolic Objects

We can start our analysis from the two symbolic objects: the high-heeled shoes in *Shanghai Dream* and the white shirt in *Eleven Flowers*. Being the physical carrier of the personae's psyches, they both become emblems of "the suppression and contamination of...the children of intellectuals of the Cultural Revolution."[33] Yet, in effect, they are vastly different in their connotation: the red high-heeled shoes are symbolic of beauty, but taken to be something evil by Qinghong's father because of their sexual or adult overtones. It does not mean her father is an abstinent. Instead, he hates the object because it threatens to "contaminate" his daughter, whom he deems as his dependent. For its seductiveness, this object is also a symbol of the commodity fetishism that began to emerge during the late 1970s. On the other hand, the white shirt is a token of purity. As a common summer clothing that was popular in China throughout the Maoist era and extended into the 1980s, it signifies the healthy, spiritual pursuits of the Chinese people during that era and becomes its aesthetic embodiment.

However, Wang Han loves the shirt not only because he prefers fashion—he already has some old, white shirts—but because he desires to wear it to become a model student leading the practice of gymnastics, which shows his sense of honor and responsibilities. A compulsory, collective activity aimed at strengthening the physical constitution of students, school gymnastics is still practiced today. Moreover, it is an effort in light of Mao's call to boost the general physical health and spiritual strength of the Chinese in order to eliminate China's centennial national image of "Sick Man of East Asia." In the last couple of decades, it has effectively attained that goal; this the exact reason why it is still preserved today. During gymnastics, each student must wear the same uniform and make the same exercise in order to foster the spirit of collectivism required for national development. The team leader is a representative of "model education" like the Chinese socialist hero, Lei Feng, who has often acted as a paradigm to set off a national fever of emulation in China. This model education, which establishes a positive paradigm for all, is taken to be a necessity to enhance people's ideological awareness and reform the existing ethnic and moral principles restricted by prior production relations; hence establishing a new-type socialist "new man" with high morals. In this light, collective gymnastics symbolizes the new socialist values; leading the gymnastics signifies being a model character for the others, which means the model for the socialist ideology. By honoring an outstanding personality, it is a kind of award for the hero of the era.

Therefore, Wang Han feels a strong sense of a holy mission when he is chosen. This is why he pulls a long face at his mother and even refuses to eat the scanty available pork that his mother has acquired. This is also why his teacher strongly expects him to wear a white shirt, even though she knows the general poverty of the family. For the same reason, the impact of his white shirt being stolen is enormous. It unfortunately happens when he is playing with his friends on the riverbank. When he sees his precious shirt snatched by the fleeing murderer, he plunges into the forest to get it back at all costs. The murderer is the elder brother of Wang Han's schoolmate Juehong, and therefore knows him from his younger sister. Apparently understanding the meaning of the shirt to Wang, he says to him, "Just take it that I borrow the shirt from you. I will give you a new one the other day." He specifically explains how to give back the new one, "I will give you money later on for you to buy a new piece." But Wang Han refuses, "I will not take your money!" He immediately understands it and says bitterly, "Because I am a bad guy?"

Such extraordinary switching of images via shot-reverse-shot to demonstrate their intense emotions foreshadows the subsequent story revolving the white shirt. During their conversation, Jueqiang voluntarily reveals his identity although it is almost impossible to work out in reality. Apparently, the movie earnestly expects the audience to know their relations with a third party: "You…are 5 years younger than my younger sister. Do you know Juehong, my younger sister?"

We soon know it well enough from the gossip of people around and from what Wang Han hears from the adults in the public bathhouse. Tranquil and orderly life is thus disturbed. The contamination of the white shirt with blood symbolizes the beginning of value changes in Han's mind. Is Jueqiang the bad guy as the officials (and the populace) understand it? How does Han apply his own moral principles to distinguish what is right and what is wrong? On the surface, Wang Han's personal philosophy is not fundamentally changed throughout the film; and he does receive a parcel of a white shirt from Jueqiang, although it is given to him by Jueqiang's family.

Juehong's rape is not directly viewed in the movie, but it is contained in the subtext of the movie. The significance of this event must be recognized in order to appreciate its direct consequence and the social repercussions it brings about. A person who has been raped may be penalized in China, today, if her resistance causes the rapist to die or to be severely harmed. But, at that time, chastity is taken not only as one's "integrity," but is also identified symbolically as his or her political worthiness. Therefore, the concept of chastity or purity is comparable to that of the white shirt: both harbor new political connotations. It is in light of this fact we can understand why Jueqiang is so cruel as to drown the corrupt carder and castrate him, as well as in light of the remark the people make: "If Chen has really committed this crime, he is a bastard!"

However, the film never makes a clear judgment on whether Jueqiang is a criminal, but only provides hints that he is, by nature, not a villain. Despite the extensive gossip by the public, the movie does not allow them to demonstrate their attitude towards him more clearly. However, does the film do so because of the censorship? Or could Wang Han not make his appraisement due to his lack of moral judgment? However, it is without doubt that, in the eyes of youngsters such as Wang Han, Jueqiang has always been a "murderer."

This question forces us to take the specific factors of particular eras into account. Before the film's title is shown, a caption appears: "an arsenal at a third-line city in the southwest of China, 1975." A long shot, with the camera apparently located inside a narrow room, shows a green sprawl of mountains outside the window. The sounds of the broadcast stressing production and construction repeat now and then, "Under the guidance of Mao Zedong thoughts, (XX Factory) has completed the task of general assembly of No. 5 product. All our staffs have fully demonstrated the spirits of…having regarded class struggle as the base and persistently and diligently stood at the forefront of our production line." Sometimes, the broadcast says, "our output has decreased slightly, mainly because…." These non-diegetic vices show the fact that the government still sticks to the policy of "placing the revolution in the center position to promote the economic development" before the end of the Cultural Revolution.[34] However, there is a scene in which Wang Han's father sees a teacher being severely beaten and decides to mediate, because of which, he himself gets punished. Such an extreme situation only happened for a particularly short period during the Cultural Revolution, around 1967–1968, and we have witnessed the social order (including the production order and class order) being well-maintained throughout most of the diegetic space[35]; thus, the deliberate arrangement of the extreme, chaotic scene is uncannily self-contradictory. In other words, it is actually a kind of anachronism: the physical fighting as portrayed is not typical of the mid-1970s (Fig. 5.3).

Nevertheless, at that particular moment, the bureaucracy that used to be effectively curtailed by the masses was revived, with increasing emphasis on social-political order. Therefore, when hearing of the crime perpetrated by the cadre Chen of the Revolutionary Committee, the

Fig. 5.3 The scene of a physical fight delivered in a long shot

populace dare not carry out Mao's teaching of public supervision in line with the principle of allowing "free speech, free criticism, free debate and free poster," nor even dare to have further discussions in private. When Wang Han's father knows about the truth from Jueqiang's father, he only says, "Is Chen really the rapist? Shit!" He is angry but dare not say more. The film also shows that corruption begins to brew: people gossip, "It seems that Xie requests Chen to change his position." When Wang Han is playing hide-and-seek one evening, he hears the adults speaking about Chen's engagement in sabotage during the Cultural Revolution: "Chen of the Revolutionary Committee...instigated the physical fighting between the royalists and 411"; "It is said that he has also problems in his personal affairs;" "He has backers and can go wherever he likes to go." Because the masses have now lost their right of supervision in the re-institutionalized bureaucracy, the corruption of the bureaucratic bourgeois has returned. Having seen no likelihood of resisting such a bureaucratic system, Jueqiang has to take personal risks to exact revenge. However, the film was unable to present this causality.

On the surface, the director does not show his position and present his individual perspective. Instead, through the use of the point-of-view shots or a subjective camera, we see through Wang Han's eyes as he circles a table of gossipy grown-ups, peeking past arms and elbows; in addition, the film "also simulates the kid's perspective through windows and steam when hanging his head upside down and during the wooziness of a fever."[36] In other words, the story is narrated from Wang Han's perspective when he was a child who, like the other children, was too young to understand the world around him. However, upon scrutiny, we would find the truth is not the case.

Paternal Education and Its Effects

The movie sets up a particular situation in which Wang Han is forced to respond to the fleeing "murderer." This particular instance can be viewed as a kind of personal struggle that he must face in order to reach a higher level of maturity. Thus, the white shirt being stained by blood symbolically represents an idea that the character's purity has been contaminated. In China, ordinary people are taught from their childhood that the red scarf is turned red by the blood of revolutionary martyrs. One can therefore ask: what symbolic connotations does the blood-stained shirt carry? Is Jueqiang a martyr or a criminal? This is the key question that the movie poses for the audience and for characters in the film.

But we need to note that this question could not have posed a problem to Han at the time because, for Wang Han, who had not yet developed sophisticated thought processes like the adults, Jueqiang is nothing more than an escaped criminal. The movie tries to convince us that Jueqiang's nice behavior (if any) bewilders Han, so he is sympathetic to Jueqiang. However, since Jueqiang merely threatens him with a dubious promise, how could Wang Han trust him? Besides, he knows nothing of the corruption of the cadres. To brush away the doubt, the movie also refuses to consider Wang Han as a socialized person—i.e. a boy susceptible to the political education of the revolutionary era. Thus, when he is facing the "criminal," he never decides to fight him, although a more politically educated youth would surely have in similar circumstances. On the contrary, Wang Han follows the orders of Jueqiang (who appears, at least at the time, to be extremely vicious) to find herbal medicines for him, agreeing not to reveal his whereabouts to anybody else so as to receive money from him (to buy a new white shirt). The former scenario implies a sort of humanism, whereas the latter shows his egoist motive. Both are oblivious to the revolutionary atmosphere which, however, is nothing but an illegal projection of an imaginative situation from the post-revolutionary perspective, in an era of de-politicization, by establishing an egoist without any political awareness.

What is more, after Wang Han returns he voluntarily lets out the secret in order to win the understanding of his friends who have wrongly accused him, further emphasizing that "he will come back and kill me if you release the secret!" They hesitate whether "it is necessary to tell the teacher about this case?" For egoist motives, they decide not to tell the seniority. Such a post-revolutionary imaginative scenario continues further: these kids, who showing no political consciousness, never bother to distinguish right from wrong, and even decide to play with the "criminal" for fun in the evening. With this unimaginative plot, the movie also has these kids give the audience an egoist idea: "So long as we offer him food, he will not kill us." It is not merely the incredible idea (of playing with a murderer just for fun in the evening), the subsequent occurrence is also improbable in light of the particular social-political circumstance. Within the darkness of the forest, one child begins to shout "A ghost is coming," which scares away Wang Han's friends even though he yells, "Don't run away!" Why they do not behave like the little hero Yulai (who was not only a popular revolutionary hero, but also a teenager, a model for the Chinese kids at the time) who has the courage to fight the criminal? This question could only become an issue in the Chinese post-revolutionary and de-politicized era.

Although these kids decide not to reveal the whereabouts of Jueqiang to the adults, one of them discloses the secret soon afterwards. On the surface, this is a moral dilemma: they are breaking a promise. Although the movie creates ingenious circumstances so that the spectators do not feel the arrest of Jueqiang is a result of their disclosure, we still need to consider whether this is a real dilemma: this fake predicament appears simply out of the movie's portrayal of these individuals to be atomized individuals lacking political awareness. Therefore, the turning point that occurs in the growth of these teenagers is only a hypothetical event.

This hypothesis is not totally unreasonable, because that revolutionary society was already disintegrating: the bureaucracy that emphasizes order discourages people from criticizing the dignitaries; the re-institution-alized society stresses procedural legal justice, rather than the substantive justice which the revolution had promised. Therefore, we see that the warder sympathizes with Jueqiang when Wang Han's parents go to prison with the mailed parcel: "The rapist should have been sentenced to death. But another person becomes his victim…It is a crime of murder anyway; no excuse for it." The words show that the rule of law was followed even during the Cultural Revolution (at least for a significant period of it).

If the children really behave that way, we will feel surprise at their lack of political education; what astonishes us more is that the parents of these kids are devoid of political awareness. The film specifically presents a scene which confirms this point. At dusk, neighbors are chatting and singing a traditional Shanghai Opera "Yanyan as a Matchmaker." One elder worker recommends singing some revolutionary songs; but the singer says, "those revolutionary songs are too old and familiar for us! You even want to hear them? What a shame on you!" For this singer, as well as Wang Han's father who echoes him, these soft and melodious traditional songs (which were rejected by the revolutionary discourse as "feudalist" at the time) with lyrics such as "Let me make a match to your satisfaction" appear to be pure art, whereas the revolutionary songs are nothing but a nuisance. Surely, people with a different class of habitus have diversified aesthetic distinctions and thus different preferences. People such as the elder worker surely prefer the revolutionary songs with their energetic vitality. But they finally make a compromise: they allow Wang Han's father, who is a performer in a Peking Opera troupe, to sing the revolutionary lyric song "In Beijing's Golden Hill." However, he waves and stops singing halfway through and says, "No more singing, no more singing." The elder worker smiles, "Chairman Mao and the Communist Party have brought us up. How can you forget it?" Apparently, he is protesting with a pun, for the words he has just articulated form the next sentence of the song.

Surely, it is not that the father forgets the lyrics, but he simply has decided to refuse to sing the song of paean. He vigorously sings the first half of the song, which lauds the beauty of his hometown because it most likely satisfies his petty bourgeois appetite. But he stops singing the second half of the song, which glorifies the party. The exact reason for doing so is demonstrated through additional details to be analyzed, which are clearly portrayed by the movie because they are closely related to the growth of Wang Han, who is shown hiding behind them during the hide-and-seek game when they are singing.

The father does not appear many times in the movie, but he plays a significant role in the growth of our hero. He is a political outcast; but also the figure who gives Wang Han key guidance. In effect, the father–son relationship is the implicit narrative thread running throughout. The English title of the movie is *Eleven Flowers*, whereas eleven signifies Wang Han's age, the flowers symbolize that the boy is in the prime of his youth. The metaphor that "the youthful child is the flower of the motherland" is well-known among Chinese. What is more, the flower is the object in the painting scene in which the father instructs Han not only in the skill of art, but also in the wisdom of life. He is not authoritative but almost like a spiritual/cultural mentor, which symbolically replaces the grand historical narrative/politically authority as the intellectual guide.

What the father teaches is Western oil painting, instead of traditional Chinese art. Apparently, he admires these Western skills and takes them as the authentic, pure art form. A particular scene shows how he tells his son, "This is a world-famous painting collected by Uncle Xia when he was young. Do you remember the Impressionism that I used to tell you? Impressionists advocate observing and painting the nature and the changes of sunshine on the ground instead of staying in a studio. Look! This is a work of Claude Monet the great master of Impressionism. Everything is vaguely painted, including the tower crane, the fishing boat and the sun reflection in water. Just a few strokes and you seem to see the flowing of water." With his instructions, the admiration of the authority of bourgeois arts is instilled into the mind of the child (Fig. 5.4).

Fig. 5.4 The father "enlightens" Wang Han with the knowledge of Western art, shown in a closeup

The "impressionist" painting signifies the influence of the West, although from which source the father gets this "impression" is never explained in the film. The father's instruction also subtly conveys the message of leaving the studio and looking at reality, which could be taken as a metaphor for departing from the common point of view of society. By comparing the individuality of humans with the individual shape of each flower, the intention is clear. He essentially calls for the Enlightenment of the value of individualism.

The father also tells Wang Han about the nature of society, "The adults could not decide where they go to work;" in a half-sentence the audience barely hears, he says "You can live in freedom"—the movie intentionally leaves out the approaches and ways to achieve freedom, possibly because it is a sensitive topic. He even drops hints to his son through metaphors: "Underneath the brightest place is the darkest..." He also instructs his son in a particular way, including teaching the son how to drink: "Be a man and have a sip of it!" When Wang Han complains "It's too pungent" and refuses to have more, he still stimulates Han's vanity to complete his objective.

This amateur artist, who is indulged in his own world of bourgeois and traditional art, seemingly avoids politics. Therefore, after he is assaulted while mediating in a fighting, he becomes hysterical once he is back at home and, in a sudden outburst, cries "Have I offended anyone? I don't care which sect it is!" These individuals who try to evade politics simply cannot get away from it in their daily life, either it is foist on them from the revolutionary politics or by the bureaucratic bourgeoisie. Thus, his refusal to sing the lauding lyrics shows his internal resentments to them.

Such resentment has nothing to do with the so-called "capitalist spirits." Instead, it arises from the degraded social status of the elite class and its worsening living standards. A particular episode evinces this fact. When Wang Han's father takes him out to sketch, they encounter Juehong and her father on the way to pay their respects to Juehong's mother at her tomb. It begins to rain and all of them have to take shelter at Juehong's home. Wang Han is taken by Juehong to another room, and we can hear the loud complaints of Juehong's father, an expert from Shanghai, to Wang Han's father, "What happened to us? We came to this mountainous region for no reasons; I would have done much better with my profession if I was in Shanghai...but I could do nothing here. I am useless here;" "Ten years, how many ten years does one have in a life time?" "I am not used to the life here. I very much expect to go back to Shanghai. Maybe I did something evil in my previous incarnation. It is my choice anyway!" Different from the voluntary response to the call of the Party to support the construction of third-line regions by Qinghong's father in *Shanghai Dream*, he completely resists the situation.[37] The film does not provide relevant messages and therefore we do not know his discipline and why he feels himself so displaced at the current job. However, we can clearly feel his strong yearning to return to Shanghai. In contrast to Qinghong's high-handed father, he seems to really care for his children. When Wang Han's father advises him, "Take it easy and open your mind, just for your kids!" he is pained. "I feel sorry for my daughter; she has experienced such great wrongs. How can she live on in the future?" His repentance may have something to do with his personal choice because we have heard the discussions of the masses: "How can he solicit sympathy from such a person [Old Chen]?" "Who knows? He is an elite intellectual anyway." This might imply that he tries to bribe the cadre Chen but unexpectedly lets his daughter become the victim.

This dialogue must have a deep impact on Wang Han, who is in the next room. The film switches between the scene in which he is being attracted by and peeping at Juehong (whom he secretly loves) while she is undressing and the other scene in which he is turning back to listen to the fathers' exchange. This specific moment gives him two means of enlightenment—initial sexual attraction, and vague but deep political awakening.[38] The whining of the uncle could not but have left an inexorable shadow upon the boy. As one critic points out, "the director illustrates the physiological and psychological changes of Wang Han in a 'dynamic vs. static' manner. Wang Han has been completely changed unintentionally by the family of the murderer: the father (enlightenment of counterrevolutionary thoughts), the murderer (enlightenment of value philosophy) and the murder's younger sister (sexual enlightenment)...The age of eleven marks not only the beginning of his physiological adolescence, but also the formation of his psychological complex of 'educated youth'. His personal growth and interrogation of the era thus meet each other at this particular moment."[39]

What Is the Root Cause for the Loss of Innocence?

Similarly to the film *Shanghai Dream*, the characters' parents in *Eleven Flowers* maintain a safe distance from politics—the primary difference being that, in *Shanghai Dreams*, the children feel the harshness of, and hence distance themselves from, their fathers. However, in *Eleven Flowers*, Wang Han receives emotional warmth from his father, which contributes to his admiration of him. What is important to note is that the viewer needs to address the problem of truthfulness of memories here, which refers not only to the practicality or probability of historical facts, but also to one's definition of growth.

The film shows that even when the father becomes involved in the battle between the royalists (the persons in the Cultural Revolution supporting those in power) and a particular sect named the 411 (apparently the rebel faction aiming to topple the ruling officers), he spares no effort to teach his son life lessons. However, the battle between the two parties was no longer sufficiently vehement towards the end of the Cultural Revolution. Yet, to highlight the atmosphere of the Cultural Revolution, the movie still presents a scene with the characters involved in a physical confrontation. That said, we need to diagnose more carefully how the father approaches educating Wang Han. His way of teaching his son is to understand life through painting. At one point in the film he says, "Each flower has its own life. They look like they are breathing. Each one of them is different, like us human beings. In this world, there are so many of us. But each one of us is different." Such emphasis on individuality highlights the value of individualism, which composes a sharp contrast to the often perceived oppressive and collectivist Chinese life at that time. It also implies a yearning for personal freedom, which is not meant in the philosophical sense but, rather, a freedom derived from a de-politicized and secular life. As a cowardly person (such cowardliness was typical for some people in that era, particularly the suppressed elites; it was also the choice of those who wished to keep away from politics and the turmoil), the father burdens his next generation with his dissatisfaction for the era and his wishes for the future.

Wang Han catches a cold and stays in bed for three days after he comes home, and learns what has happened from visiting friends. When he almost develops meningitis, Jueqiang is caught for attempting to set fire to the factory (the fire is extinguished by a sudden shower). We need to understand the ingenuity of this situation: it exonerates Wang Han of responsibility for the leaking of Jueqiang's whereabouts; since the shower extinguishes the fire and no casualty is involved, one would feel the inhumanity of the death sentence. According to the final broadcast about his crimes Jueqiang is labeled a "counterrevolutionary murderer and arsonist." Apparently, even if his murder (of the rapist) could have been pardoned, sabotaging the factory was enough to hold him responsible for the crime of being a "counterrevolutionary arsonist." In other words, while his killing of the corrupt official represents the spontaneous antagonism of the people, which also demonstrates the public distrust of a procedural justice that resumes the order of the bureaucratic rule, nevertheless, him setting the factory on fire is simply done to exact revenge from society, which can be viewed as rooted in class hatred. In essence, the factory has become a token of the "dark society"; burning the factory shows his desire to break away from this darkness, rather than representing his indignation for the present bureaucracy.

This member of the second generation of the former elite class thus expresses his hatred towards his degraded social (and class) status (being demoted from a superior descendant of the bourgeois to an ordinary worker). The director probably intends to express his mockery of the socialist concept of "the working class being the leading class," which can be viewed in the scene when there is a close-up of a Maoist slogan on a column reading, "The people's democratic dictatorship requires leadership of the working class because of their lofty vision, absolute self-lessness and thorough revolutionary spirit." However, what the movie overlooks is that blind revenge does not reflect a kind of ignorance of the working class. Rather, it merely shows the failure to establishing political awareness in this second generation of the elite class. This personal revenge, out of class hatred and a private feud, is against the corrupt bureaucrats in a nation-state which is allegedly led by the working class but that, in reality, has degenerated and transformed into one of the "bureaucratic authoritarianism" that Mao has indicted during that time.

However, the director provides us with an unnecessary explanation for the fighting during this time. In this scene, a worker, named Afu, has been fighting; he is severely injured and is rescued by his colleague. The next scene shows the following conversation among the four kids:

> "Who has beaten him so severely?"
> "Afu's girlfriend kisses with another man. Afu knows it and so they have a fighting."
> "Oh, it is all because of a woman!"
> "Don't you know that men fight only for women? How can Juehong's elderly brother become a murderer and arsonist if it is not for Juehong?"
> "That is different. I will surely revenge for my younger sister if she is humiliated."

For these kids, men fight only for women. Yet, this is still a post-revolutionary projection—and as we said, the masses, including the kids, do not think the same way that we do in this post-revolutionary age. Ironically, though, what could be inferred from the scene is that all the physical fighting is merely "for women." Sexual implication plays such an important role that we witness another scene in which a character nick-named Little Mouse points at Juehong and says to Fatty, "Do you think she has grown mature?" Fatty points at his breasts and says, "You know it when you see here."

These pictures, which do not fit in with the features of that era, indicate that the era could not be authentically presented by simply displaying those images with epochal traits and in a Shanghai accent.[40] Critics also notice that "the director attempts to include more scenes of collective memory in the story, e.g. the physical fighting that has a spectacular beginning but a less anticipated ending; but they are done in a less reasonable and logical way, because all the characters other than the heroes are vaguely portrayed."[41]

Towards the end of the movie, we witness a lengthy epilogue (as a long take) of Wang Han and his four friends chasing the police vehicle taking criminals under a sentence of death to the execution field. It surely reminds us of the last scene of the French film *400 Blows*. But Wang Han gives up his plan to go to the execution ground; instead, he stops, turns around, and only listens to the gunfire from a distance. This turnaround could be interpreted as a turning away from collectivism to individualism, from engaging with revolutionary devotion to focusing on personal development. He is finding his own morality out of an emerging skepticism.

Likewise, the rape event symbolizes the loss of morality within the revolutionary society, as it is perpetrated by a figure of political authority who is not get punished for his crime. However, the execution of the killer raises a moral question as to what is a hero and what is a murderer, as well as what is the extent of equality or fairness in society, which is bewildering to the child. In this light, the rape event and execution of Jueqiang symbolize two instances that cause a moral disorientation of that generation. In medical science, a serious sickness is equal to a crisis, which displays a turning point within physical development. Thus, Wang Han's recuperation from his fever and his subsequent departure from the execution site also implies his farewell to political passion, which is a turning away from political idealism towards individualistic awareness.

Wang Han's loss of innocence originates from the education of his father, who is resentful of the Party's policies towards the elites and instructs Wang Han to distance himself from the Party's teachings. It also comes from the oppressive atmosphere arising from the recurrence of the bureaucracy that emphasizes ruling order and prohibits public debates. His loss of political faith also arises from alienated feelings towards the ruling authority, which now takes procedural justice instead of substantive justice, as a result of which those who—in the eye of the kids (and the ordinary people) should not be sentenced to death—are subject to the death penalty. All these matters deprived the people, including Wang Han, of their strong identification with the regime: the country under the new governance is no different from the old administration that it has overthrown, because they are both inhumanly bureaucratic.

However, the movie does not take this position. On the contrary, Jueqiang's revenge and his being sentenced to death are not attributed to the corruption and revival of corrupt bureaucracy (which was revived towards the end of the Cultural Revolution when political idealism had subsided and political fatigue spread everywhere). Instead, these events are attributed to the chaos of the "extreme leftism" of the Cultural Revolution. As such, we see the less appropriate inclusion of physical violence in the film. Because of this mentality, even the lyrics of the song "Ode to the Motherland," which has been popular since the 1950s until now, is referred to as a kind of extreme leftism. When the physical fighting is going on, the camera shifts to show a scene of natural landscape and the song is heard in the soundtrack: "Ode to our beloved motherland, with best wishes for its prosperity and strength." This is obviously a satire; but this device ignores the fact that the ruling party is no longer the one that promised to eradicate all of the exploiting classes and all injustices in the world. Instead, it is a revived, rigidified, bureaucratic machine, which succeeds with the concept of a people's revolution only in name. In reality, the so-called "extreme leftist" people's politics—the people's democratic participation and supervision of the bureaucracy as encouraged by Mao's policies—was been suppressed at that moment.

From this perspective, the fact that Wang Han stops and retreats after running during the last scene of the movie is not because of his juvenile cowardliness and mercy. Rather, it symbolizes the birth of a conservative awareness among this younger generation. Under the influence of Claude Monet's landscape paintings and his father's mentality, he begins to doubt the revolutionary teachings he has received thus far. This conservative consciousness has been preserved until today; so, the same director who dares to expose the hypocrisy and selflessness of the parents in *Shanghai Dream* has to feel repentance for the father's generation and sincerely identify with their affection and "education" in *Eleven Flowers*.

The story is a retrospective memory examining and narrating past events; but, essentially, it is only a projection from the perspective of the present. The movie does not deny that the story is a product of recollection. At the beginning, the narrator (the adult Wang Han) says in his voice-over: "We are always looking at others in our life, assuming us to be born elsewhere, with an aim to conceive a totally different life. But one day, you will find that it is too late, because you are who you are now. You are born in a certain family and in a particular era. Your life trails won't change simply because of your imaginations. What you can do is accepting and respecting it." At the end of the film, the voice-over returns, "I don't remember if I heard the gunfire far away in the execution ground. But one year later, many things that happened in China have always remained fresh in my memory. I was eleven years old then." The first voice-over emphasizes the special historical events of one's existence: "born in a certain family and in a particular era;" and nobody can change the reality through their imagination. But such a superficial brand of "historical materialism" is interpreted according to the principles of conservatism: "What you can do is accepting and respecting it."

The next voice-over stresses a clear memory of the major events taking place during 1976. The death of the three leading figures of the Chinese revolution and the consequential end of the Cultural Revolution are well-known to those Chinese who had experienced that era. But the statement "many things…remained fresh in my memory" should not be taken for granted because the narrator is incapable of remembering whether he ever heard the gunfire, which shows that his memories are not absolutely reliable. The conservative ideas that his parents have instilled in his mind, which is due to their dissatisfaction with and indignation at Maoist socialism, prevent him from making an authentic retrospection. This conservatism, which yearns for the "stable and free" life, fails to understand the real meaning of the crucial events and circumstances of that era; the film therefore fails to grasp the meaning of the lives of the Chinese people during that time. This is why we see such an abrupt and anachronistic episode as the fighting scene in the film, which prevents the film from becoming a structurally integrated masterpiece.

NOTES

1. Berenice Reynaud, "Zhang Yuan's Imaginary Cities and the Theatricalization of the Chinese 'Bastards'," 278.
2. Weijie Song, "Transgression, Submission, and the Fantasy of Youth Subculture: The Nostalgic Symptoms of *In the Heat of the Sun*," 179.
3. Ibid., 172.
4. Ibid.
5. Ibid.
6. Ibid., 173.
7. Ibid., 176.
8. The image presented in this movie can be compared to Zhang Yang's film *Sunflower* (Xiangrikui 向日葵), made in the same year as *Shanghai*

Dream. Critic Cui Shuqin has succinctly summarized one part of its essential plotline, "*Sunflower* demonstrates the clash between father and son through its representation of hands, a phallic symbol representing at once power and castration. The father, who is an artist, has his hands crippled in the tumult of the Cultural Revolution, a kind of symbolic castration by political violence. To compensate for his own loss, the father forces his son to practice painting, To his surprise, the child will do anything to ruin his own fingers—injuring them in a sewing machine or with firecrackers—to protest his father's authority. This self-denial or self-castration reveals the vulnerability of the rebellious son in the Oedipal struggle." See Shuqin Cui, "Negotiating In-Between," 104–105.

9. Chen Mo and Zhiwei Xiao, "Chinese Underground Films: Critical Views from China," 144.
10. See Dongcheng Wang, "Yong Zhenshi de Jiyi Weizao Lishi." Weijie Song also complains that, here, the Cultural Revolution is "less a collective or individual trauma than a colorful backdrop to a summer pastrol," which "intriguingly turned out to be 'the best time' of their lives and represents a golden era in their memory." Weijie Song, "Transgression, Submission, and the Fantasy of Youth Subculture," 171, 176.
11. Ibid., 174.
12. Weijie Song, "Transgression, Submission, and the Fantasy of Youth Subculture," 180.
13. Chris Berry, "Review: *Yangguang canlan de rizi*," 24.
14. Weijie Song, "Transgression, Submission, and the Fantasy of Youth Subculture," 172.
15. Chris Berry, "Review: *Yangguang canlan de rizi*," 23.
16. Tonglin Lu, "Fantasy and Ideology in a Chinese Film: A Zizekian Reading of the Cultural Revolution," 547.
17. The symbolic meaning of Liu Yikou has been noted, "As the group leader, Liu Yiku represents the intersubjective Other. As the Other, Liu does not possess a human body. His indifference to Ma's beating reveals his status as a presymbolic object beyond physical harm." Ibid., 548.
18. Ibid., 549.
19. Since Mi Lan's picture has been idolized by Xiaojun, Lu Tonglin points out that she "occupies the position of a sublime object of ideology." Ibid., 552.
20. Ibid., 554.
21. Weijie Song, "Transgression, Submission, and the Fantasy of Youth Subculture," 174–175.
22. Chris Berry, "Review: *Yangguang canlan de rizi*," 23.
23. See Dongcheng Wang, "Yong Zhenshi de Jiyi Weizao Lishi."
24. See Mengge Mali, "Ren he Ta Suochu de shidai."

25. Weijie Song, "Transgression, Submission, and the Fantasy of Youth Subculture," 178.
26. Ibid., 179.
27. Chris Berry notes that "When they appear in the final shots as the nouveau riche thugs and yobs that populate China's littoral cities today, the entire film acquires a more troubling set of connotations about the ongoing effects of the Cultural Revolution today." Apparently, the connotation of this scene again could yield to two interpretations which are antagonistic to each other: whether the past is to be condemned, or the present is dull and boring. Chris Berry, "Review: *Yangguang canlan de rizi*," 23.
28. Weijie Song, "Transgression, Submission, and the Fantasy of Youth Subculture," 174, 180.
29. Ibid., 180.
30. Ibid., 179.
31. In particular, Xiaojun "follows the propaganda of 'Rebellion is reasonable' and subverts the social order and authority;" "he himself identifies with the Maoist ideology." Ibid., 181.
32. Mark Jenkins, "'11 Flowers': A Revolutionary Childhood."
33. See Xunyicaoshang de Baotu, "Bai Chenshang yangai de shidai mimi."
34. We could not accurately know if the Cultural Revolution has come to the end in the diegetic space. Yet, according to the caption at the end of the film, which is about the major events occurred in the year of 1975, we can infer that the diegetic story happened before that.
35. The school is presented in very good condition and in full authority; there is no disorder there.
36. Mark Jenkins, "'11 Flowers': A Revolutionary Childhood."
37. But, just like the previous movie, the second-generation Wang Han feels at home within the village with his friends, whereas the father insists on leaving there as soon as possible and returns home to Shanghai.
38. In an interview, Wang Xiaoshuai says, "Those detailed scenarios that are seemingly based on personal experiences in the film, e.g. the father and son drinking together and watching the impressionist paintings that have nothing to do with them, actually show the roots of my spiritual growth," see Sohu Yule, "'Diliudai daoyan' xilie zhi dianyingli xungen de Wang Xiaoshuai."
39. Ibid.
40. Critics notice that, in order to display the "authenticity," "the representative symbols that have appeared in *Shanghai Dream* are further underscored in *11 Flowers*: even the sequence is the same. They are used at the beginning, turning point and ending of both films." See Xunyicaoshang de Baotu, "Bai Chenshang yangai de shidai mimi."
41. See Zuyi, "Ruhe yu Wangshi Ganbei."

References

Berry, Chris. "Review: *Yangguang canlan de rizi* (*In the Heat of the Sun*)." *Cinemaya* 31 (1996): 23–24.

Chen, Mo, and Xiao, Zhiwei. "Chinese Underground Films: Critical Views from China." In Paul Pickowicz and Yingjin Zhang (eds.), *From Underground to Independent: Alternative Film Culture in Contemporary China*, pp. 143–160. Lanham, MD: Rowman & Littlefield, 2006.

Cui, Shuqin. "Negotiating In-Between: On New-Generation Filmmaking and Jia Zhangke's Films." *Modern Chinese Literature and Culture* 18 (2) (2006): 98–130.

Jenkins, Mark. "'11 Flowers': A Revolutionary Childhood." *NPR: National Public Radio* (2013, February). http://www.npr.org/2013/02/21/172395278/11-flowers-a-revolutionary-childhood. Accessed April 13, 2016.

Lu, Tonglin. "Fantasy and Ideology in a Chinese Film: A Zizekian Reading of the Cultural Revolution." *Positions* 12 (2) (2004): 539–564.

Mengge Mali (萌哥马狸). "Ren he Ta Suochu de shidai" (人和他所处的时代) [Man and the Era He Lives In]. http://movie.douban.com/people/peterwolf. Accessed December 1, 2015.

Reynaud, Bérénice. "Zhang Yuan's Imaginary Cities and the Theatricalization of the Chinese 'Bastards'." In Zhang Zhen (ed.), *The Urban Generation: Chinese Cinema and Society at the Turn of the Twenty-First Century*, pp. 264–294. Durham: Duke University Press, 2007.

Sohu Yule. "'Diliudai daoyan' xilie zhi dianyingli xungen de Wang Xiaoshuai" ("第六代导演"系列之电影里寻根的王小帅) [Series of Sixth-generation Directors: Wang Xiaoshuai and His Tracing of Origin in Films]. http://yule.sohu.com/20120613/n345511271.shtml. Accessed December 31, 2015.

Song, Weijie. "Transgression, Submission, and the Fantasy of Youth Subculture: The Nostalgic Symptoms of in the Heat of the Sun." In Haili Kong and John A. Lent (eds.), *100 Years of Chinese Cinema: A Generational Dialogue*, Signature Book, pp. 171–182. Norwalk, CT: EastBridge, 2006.

Wang, Dongcheng (王东成). "Yong Zhenshi de Jiyi Weizao Lishi: Ping Dianying Yangguang Canlan de Rizi" (用真实的记忆伪造历史:评电影《阳光灿烂的日子》) [Fabrication of History with an Authentic Memory: On the Movie *In the Heat of the Sun*]. *Zhongguo Qingnian Yanjiu* (中国青年研究) [*Studies of Chinese Youth*] 1 (1996): 19–20.

Xunyicaoshang de Baotu (薰衣草山上的暴徒). "Bai Chenshang yangai de shidai mimi" (白衬衫掩盖的时代秘密) [The Secret Covered Up by a White Shirt]. http://ent.qq.com/a/20120510/000437.htm. Accessed December 12, 2015.

Zuyi (祖伊). "Ruhe yu Wangshi Ganbei" (如何与往事干杯) [How to Toast with the Past]. http://movie.douban.com/review/5435043/. Accessed December 31, 2015.

CHAPTER 6

Elitism or Populism? The Problematic of Imagining the Other

Jia Zhangke has always been taken as the benchmark of China's New Wave cinema; even though he joined the filmic world quite late, he is regarded as the representative figure of the second wave of this cinematic trend. It is commonly accepted that his films "have attempted to fathom the gaping and contradictory schism between the compressed capitalism of Dengist modernization and the worker/peasant state envisaged in 1949."[1] Accordingly, one might ask, does Jia Zhangke's style of artistic representation intend to critique the incompatibility between the pro-capitalist reality and the socialist scenario/propaganda? Regardless of whatever objective truth may exist, the commonly accepted opinion is that his sense of upholding public responsibility and expressing concerns over the destiny of the lower classes has continued unabated. Even after he was allowed to release his works through officially permitted public channels, his "social consciousness hasn't faltered."[2] Since Jia is the key figure typifying the practice and ideology of China's New Wave cinema, in this chapter, I will examine the three films Jia produced after he went mainstream. This will provide the reader with a clearer picture of what is cherished by fellow Chinese directors that have left the independent film industry, as well as investigate the merits and flaws of their perspectives.

Although the Sixth Generation of filmmakers always proclaims the spirit of independence, Jia, just like the others in this group, was often under financial pressure of, if not always the strains of the market. Therefore, while the "early films of director Jia Zhangke...represent

© The Author(s) 2018
X. Wang, *Ideology and Utopia in China's New Wave Cinema*, Chinese Literature and Culture in the World, https://doi.org/10.1007/978-3-319-91140-3_6

an attempt to make art that is independent of both political power and market forces,"[3] it has been observed that he "soon became dependent upon the transnational market for art films, insofar as his producers expected his films to gain success through screenings at film festivals and subsequently in art-house theaters around the world."[4] While his dependence on the market may have compromised some of his artistic and cultural-political visions, however, the more significant problem lies in the political unconscious of the director, which over-determines the cultural-political connotations of his final works.

Is Jia Zhangke's cinematic vision guilty of a kind of elitist or populist tendency? It is well-known that Jia himself opposes the elitist stance of producing so-called "personal films" taken by some self-styled "independent" cinematic producers, and promotes a sort of "amateurism,"[5] which "refers to a mind-set in approaching his subject-matter, not to the technical quality" of the film produced. However, undertaking an alternative film style as Jia does, in order to delve into the lives of marginal subjects and sensitive subject matters, does not by itself mean that he essentially chooses the point of view of the ordinary Chinese people. Rather, it is closely related to the political unconscious of the artist himself when he makes his judgment on social affairs and assumes his own personal motivations. To answer the question of elitism/populism, one useful method is to examine the way of dealing with the problems of the "other" in cinematic works. In Jia's case, the "other" appearing in his works comprises the "new poor" and the lower classes. Through our inquiry, we will find that, to a degree, he takes the stance of the elite in many respects.

The World (2004) is the first film for which Jia won the approval of, and even funding from, the Chinese government; however, it "retains a lot of the socially conscious edge of Jia's earlier works."[6] Primarily a social-realist film, it concerns the fortunes of migrant workers in urban China by exploring their everyday lives in the foreign, exotic and metropolitan city. They are trying to realize their dreams in the harsh environment; however, their existence is empty and depressing. Dedicated to showing the unvarnished reality of life, the film nevertheless has to address the tastes of the audience and censors. Although limits on the freedom of artistic expression seemingly do not weaken the critical spirit of realism, the director fails to develop the bigger picture as to why the characters cannot escape their socially determined destinies.

Four years later, in 2008, Jia produced a "fake documentary," *24 City*, which blends documentary footage with fictional elements based on his interview of one hundred ex-workers in a factory undergoing unprecedented changes. The mutative destiny of the factory merely serves as the background, while the foreground expresses the vicissitudes of the lives of its staff—both of which serve as an ethnographical account of the working class and the nation-state in general. The film is meant to account for China's macro-transformation, which departs from the Party's official version of the historical narrative.[7] Yet, what a de-politicized recollection ultimately reveals is that the downfall and tragedy of the working class is shown merely to be a phenomenon of certain strata and professions, and the transformation of the fortunes of this community a result of industrial restructuration. Consequently, the historical experience that shaped the Chinese national identity in the socialist era is once again masked by commerciality, instead of being revealed.

Four years after *24 City*, Jia produced *A Touch of Sin* (2012), which is usually taken as a film of social conscience portraying the omnipresent conflicts and violence in Chinese society, displaying the hapless lives of the lower classes. Yet, although to a certain extent the movie exposes the direct causes of violence, corruption and increasing social stratification, it uncannily places the blame for these tragedies on the flaws and petty-mindedness of the lower classes, which weakens the depth and strength of the film's criticism. The reason for this lapse is that the film observes societal conflicts and the under-classes from the director's elitist point of view; consequently, the film is incapable of delving into their inner motivations and social-political over-determinations to account for the inevitability of the characters' inexorable choices. Partly because of this, it merely presents an unrealistic, fantastic picture of the lower classes by portraying and insinuating their eccentric dispositions and cultural-psychological idiosyncrasies.

Postmodern Paradise or Post-socialist Fantasy?

When miniatures of famous buildings and monuments from around the world exist in one place (such as portrayed by the "The Window of the World," Shenzhen, in the film *The World*), does this necessarily imply that the Chinese laborers working and living there can freely live a cosmopolitan life while China enters into the "global village"?

In Jia Zhangke's 2002 movie *The World*, most of the stories occur in a theme park named "The World Park." Although there are many kinds of amusement parks (such as Disneyland), the one shown in the film is most likely only observed in China, which shows the fanatical urge the country has experienced, ever since the reform and opening-up that started in late 1970s, to explore Western countries and catch up with the "international community." Today, there are two amusement parks in China, one located in Shenzhen called "The Window of the World," the other situated in the unglamorous Beijing suburbs of Tongzhou. Although most of the movie was filmed at Shenzhen's Park, the movie fictionally "transplanted" this park to Beijing, which could be due to the belief that Beijing would be a better location in which to signify the Chinese fantasy of foreign countries. Ironically, the film is reluctant to show the native Beijing residents in its diegetic space.

On the surface, the setting of the film is a paradise of a cosmopolitan postmodern world. The park's slogan indicates the possibility of touring the world without leaving one's home country, which was exactly the dream in the "high culture fever" of the 1980s in China. However, just as Fredric Jameson informs us, "At the cultural level, globalization threatens the final extinction of local cultures, resuscitatable only in Disneyfied form, through the construction of artificial simulacra and the mere images of fantasized traditions and beliefs."[8] Thus, the form belies itself by virtue of its own illusory fantasy.

What is more, the happiness and sorrows of the characters in the film show us that China's postmodernism is not the fragmented phantasmagoria of the post-industrial West; but, rather, it is the post-socialist centrifugal network. There are many worlds and many dreams in contemporary China, which constitute a sharp contrast to the fantasy of "one world, one dream," a slogan propagated by the Chinese official propaganda for its 2008 Beijing Olympic Games.

New Proletariat and the Commodity World of Alienation

First and foremost, the space of the park itself is allegorical. Cui Shuqin has noted that this world is "divided into underground and aboveground spaces and between onstage and backstage spaces. On the theme park's performance stage, singers and dancers play various roles as world citizens. 'Backstage' – in [the] basement dressing room, on construction sites, and in nearby garment factories – tangled life stories unfold."[9] In the underground dressing room filled with pipes, the actors and actresses hurriedly prepare themselves and rush to the stage. On the stage, as they display their bodies electric music and fantastical lighting that flickers back and forth accompanies their performance. However, after they retreat from the stage, they remove their makeup and change clothes in the narrow room, returning to their real identity as migrant peasant-workers. Every day, they alternate between the real and the unreal, which makes these youthful girls feel the anxieties of life more and more heavily.

Thus, the film's overarching storyline revolves around emotional entanglements, which is in line with the director's past creations concerning the affections of the people from the bottom of society. This focus reveals their insistence on an invaluable principle irrespective of the maelstrom of historical changes, which is quite different from mainstream society, which follows a more pragmatic way of handling daily life. By showing the gradual fragmentation and differentiation of the under-classes, *The World* also exemplifies the deep impingement of globalization.

In this world, females abound; but they are "marginalized and victimized by a sexually commercialized society."[10] Xiaotao is one such woman, having come to the city from the countryside. She takes a job as a performer in a song and dance troupe. Sometimes, she displays her body on stage; at other times, she is an air hostess. In comparison with the girl Qiaoqiao in Jia's previous film, *Unknown Pleasures*, she is not searching for a man to provide financial assistance in return for sexual gratification; therefore, she on one occasion she rejects the advances of a businessman in the bar. Instead, she is attracted to the character Taisheng, from her hometown, who works as a security guard at the park (Fig. 6.1).

Xiaotao becomes bored with her mundane and routine life at the park, telling her girlfriends, "I feel like I'm dying here. I really want to leave this place and experience life outside." In one shot—an animation of her flying in the sky, could be considered as the representation of one of her dreams. According to Cui Shuqin, the scene implies that "if real life means confinement, computer technology brings one the illusion of freedom."[11] She also often emits huge sighs, wondering why it still has not snowed. Here, the snow has become a symbolic image of breaking free from her alienated state. The illusory, virtual world does not bring about a postmodern feeling of liberation and detachment; rather, China's real

Fig. 6.1 A wide-angle, medium shot showing Xiaotao seduced by a nouveau riche

world is far more exciting than the illusory one, even though this real world is also filled with technological gimmicks; entering the so-called *real* means facing the real world and its potential negative consequences. In the latter half of the movie, when Xiaotao is taken by her sisters in the troupe to a nightclub, she is immediately tempted by a rich business-man and, conversely, becomes the object of sexual consumption. She also unexpectedly runs into a past member of the dance troupe, Anna, who appeared at the very beginning of the film. When she finds out how Anna has been forced to work as a prostitute, they hug and cry. Xiaotao appears to becomes aware that it is impossible to live within "the real" in a dignified manner.

However, there is not much characterization of Xiaotao's personality in the film. Rather, her image is established only through her relation-ship with her boyfriend Taisheng, who becomes the major character later on. He is the person most worthy of attention, for his transmogrification shows the trans-signification of the under-classes, appearing for the first time in the works of the Sixth Generation of auteurs.

Coming from the bottom of society, Taisheng was initially an honest and upright character. Pursuing Xiaotao, he follows her from Shanxi to Beijing and, over the next three years, he for her remain constant. The film continually shows him talking to Xiaotao on his walkie-talkie when-ever they are apart. In one scene, when he is eating lunch and hears that Xiaotao has left the park with another man, he chases her down to a res-taurant right away. He straightens Xiaotao's hair in front of the man—ho is Xiaotao's ex-boyfriend Liangzi—and intentionally puts on a show for him. Later, Taisheng also drives the car taking Liangzi to the train station, which is meant to demonstrate his strong ability to be sociable. However, he is also susceptible to the temptations of the society and demands that Xiaotao permits their physical intimacy to confirm her feelings for him. When Xiaotao refuses to do so, the words he chastises Xiaotao display his moral degradation, "What time are we living in now? You are still pretending to be a virgin?!" Xiaotao, infuriated by this outrageous insult, slaps his face. But, although Xiaotao begins to doubt that Taisheng is in love with her, eventually she gives in to his request. During this scene, she says, "Taisheng, do not trick me! This is all I have left." She knows that her body is the only capital that she can invest in so as to gain lifelong happiness and security in a relationship. Apart from that, Chinese society gives her no security whatsoever, for she is just an ordinary girl from the countryside.

However, Taisheng does not make her any promises. "In this world, there is no one you can trust. You can only trust yourself." Like many literary works dealing with similar subjects, here, the movie hints that Taisheng's metamorphosis is a result of his experiences in the city. He helps to make counterfeit ID cards for his boss to earn extra income and is entrusted by him to be a bodyguard when he is sending his relatives back home. Taisheng's morals have degenerated and his values distorted. We can see this particularly clearly when he admits to Xiaotao that, during the first night in Beijing, he had made himself a promise to earn a living by whatever means necessary. However, his decision to "make his livelihood count" turns into a kind of wild ambitiousness. Becoming the security chief at the park, he orders all the security guards to salute him. During a scene that shows him riding a horse while patrolling the recreation of Stonehenge, in England, he can be thought of as exhibiting the semblance of a self-entitled authority figure. His professional ambition has thus far surpassed the ambitions of his peers, which eventually produces contradictory personality traits.

On one hand, he has not forgotten his humble upbringing and does what he can to help the villagers that he grew up with. With a strong sense of pride, Taisheng takes these people around the various sights in the park like an expert—these people who have left their village for the first time and are touring "the world." An episode shows that after his fellow villager Little Sister—who now becomes his subordinate—has an accident, he immediately goes to take care of event and sort the issue out appropriately. Apparently, he is a product of the era. When a person coming from the bottom of society tries to exert their will to succeed, their perspective on things will experience a clash between the old and the new—the new now being the outside world dominated by the logic of capital. While Xiaotao persists with her moral principles, Taisheng just follows his impulses. After three years of living in the city, he becomes acclimatized to the usual way of doing things. Accepting the advances of the wealthy Liao Aqin, he prostrates himself underneath her pomegranate-colored skirt.

Taisheng's degeneration is not a matter in isolation. Xiaotao's friend Liu Youyou, another performer in the troupe, also sells her body in order to attain an opportunity for professional promotion. The logic of commodity exchange in the commercial era alienates the relationships between people, changing them to a sort of transaction in the purest sense. In this environment, migrant workers have become an object for exploitation and domination, living in the most debased position imaginable. Thus, the will that "Little Sister" leaves instructs that there are various debts to be repaid ranging from 3 *yuan* to 50 *yuan*. His parents, coming from their hometown, appear silent and senile while picking up the monies, demonstrating the inevitable seediness of the Chinese countryside.

Different Worlds, Differing Dreams

When Taisheng escorts his boss's relatives to their hometown, he gets to know a businesswoman from Wenzhou named Liao Aqun. After she returns, she invites him for a date and begins flirting with him. She tells Taisheng that her husband was willing to die in order to go to France, while most of his compatriots perished in the ocean while trying to immigrate illegally; he luckily became one of the few who survived; but he has not returned to China for ten years. Her description reveals a popular phenomenon during the 1990s when many Chinese, especially those from the coastal areas, stowed away illegally in an attempt to achieve a better life in another country.

Liao herself is running a clothing factory, which makes money by producing fake brand-name items. In the film, when she says, "Craftsmen rely on their hands to make a living," it reminds the viewer of a similar statement the pickpocket Xiaowu made in Jia Zhangke's film *Xiaowu* (1997), which suggests their similar nature. When Taisheng invites her to the park, he boasts: "We there have all those French things you're looking for." Mrs. Liao smiles and brushes the remark aside by saying, "But it doesn't have the place where my husband lives." Taisheng does not understand what she means and responds, "So where does your husband live?" "Belleville," Mrs. Liao answers back. "Belleville" in all actuality is a Chinatown in Paris, France. While Taisheng's proud comment merely indicates his narrow horizons, Aqun's protest also proves that the Chinese like her, although they have never been abroad, always imagine foreign things to be better than they are. The exchange inadvertently shows that there are different dreams for these people living in differing worlds. Taisheng's ambiguous relationship with her continues until she ultimately succeeds in immigrating to France.

Although globalization has seemingly promoted the globalized circulation of commodities, what is not circulated is the free flow of labor. Those who can "join" the global circulation in China are the entrepreneurs who blindly envy the west. In the end, Aqun makes her wishes become a reality and leaves for Paris. However, her future prospects are still undetermined. While this scene delivers "the blurring of rural and urban dichotomies and of commitments torn asunder by a global economy marked by travel and migration,"[12] we also witness those workers in her factory busy engaged in their employment. After Liao departs, how will they make a living? What we are sure of is the fragmentation of the people living within and outside the park. Critic Chen Xihe thus aptly notes:

> The film exposes two worlds. One is represented by the park, which is an artificially structured world. It looks like a magnificent theater. Yet, when Jia Zhangke shows this world, he also deconstructs it. For example, on the screen we can see someone passing by, and the audience knows this is only a performance but not the real world. When the tourists are taking pictures in front of the Italian leaning tower, we also see workers passing by lifting bundles of items, which immediately brings us back to reality. There are two worlds: one a beautiful, splendid world, and the other the real society and the people on the edge. Thus, Jia Zhangke casts his camera to this group of people and he represents their excitements and sorrows as well as their living conditions. They come to the city from the countryside and they are struggling at the edge of this society, which are among the many phenomena inevitably arising in this era of economic transformation. Actually, we should ask who is paying the bill for the modernization? It is the lower class of farmers and migrant workers...We can see this very clearly from the destiny of Little Sister in the movie.[13]

The character in the film that is nicknamed Little Sister is an introverted boy who has just arrived at the park. He is very envious of the security position at the park, which pays 200 *yuan* per month. He even goes so far as to ask the security guard whether the salary is 210 *yuan* or 290 *yuan*, and whether the uniform is free. Not until he accidentally dies of fatigue while working a night shift does the audience learn from his note that his entire debt does not even exceed 200 *yuan*. It is precisely because he is trying to repay the money as quickly as possible that he works overtime. When the boss sends Little Sister's parents away by paying them a small sum of money, a sum of money that Taisheng has negotiated for and won, he puffs out smoke into the air, feeling as though he has resolved a minor inconvenience. However, the audience witnesses Little Sister's father stuff the money in his breast pocket and pat it several times, as though he is patting his own son to his chest.

Little Sister's destiny is an extreme case, but representative of the unfortunate experiences of many Chinese migrant peasant-workers. But the plights of the performers in the troupe are more usually seen in daily lives, which show that within "the world" (the park) there are different types of people and they do not share the same dreams. Among them, there are characters dependent on rich men in exchange for sexual favors, as well as others directly working as prostitutes. The destinies of Laoniu and Qiuping, a couple that appears in the opening of the film, make a stark contrast to those of Xiaotao and Taisheng. However, the portrayal of their love seems overly idealistic. Laoniu is crazy about Qiuping and, throughout, he only says two things to her: "Where are you going?" and "And then?" It can be viewed as showing his determination, but also can be understood as displaying his egocentrism. After Qiuping decides to break up with him, he sets his clothes on fire. The director gives us to believe that this behavior brings Qiuping back to him. Eventually, there is a satisfying conclusion in which the film shows the couple holding a party celebrating their marriage. Laoniu's insistence on love poses a contrast to another group member named Youyou, who devotes all her attention to becoming the mistress of the manager in order to get promotion. The third couple's story involves a male performer Erxiao and an elevator operator named A Fei. They have an emotional connection. However, before the two can express their feelings for one another, Erxiao is implicated in embezzlement and is fired. His degeneration reveals the moral failure of the migrant workers who, just like Taisheng, lose sight of themselves within market-oriented society. However, what is ironic is that although Taisheng reprimands him, Taisheng himself has collaborated with the powerful boss in undertaking much bigger illegal acts.

Many characters in the film are thinking about a particular place, Ulaanbaatar; this is reminiscent of dialogue in Jia Zhangke's early film *Platform* (2002) undertaken between two protagonists who discuss the same location there. The dialogue takes place in an era when scarcity of resourses greatly constrained people's knowledge of the outside world. Ulaanbaatar was the most exotic place they could think of—a place that can be linked with the so-called "social imperialism" of the former Soviet Union.[14] At the time, they know nothing of the world the other side of the ocean—namely, the States and the European countries of the capitalist bloc. Twenty years after economic reform and after globalization has seeped into every major city of China, youngsters now can superficially discuss Western cities such as Paris, London, New York and Rome. However, in reality, many ordinary citizens are limited to touring virtualized reconstructions. Although they have been bombarded by advertising and mistakenly believe that they can "travel around the world without leaving Beijing," the reconstructions are merely a "kitschy mimicry of architecture"[15] of the Eiffel Tower, The White House, Big Ben and the Egyptian Pyramids. In more exact terms, while "the simulacra of the World Park tantalizes the Chinese with daily visions of foreign countries,"[16] their imaginations of the world are still a Chinese version of the American Dream, or a Chinese fantasy of the capitalistic world, which is uniquely demonstrated in elaborate fashion shows.

Before economic reform, many Chinese dreamed about the "big family of socialism (or internationalism)" under Maoist idealism; now, baptized by the gospel of globalization, they have fallen into a kind of illusion of enjoying worldwide materialistic welfare while being fully integrated into the capitalist, global market. This phenomenon points to the ideological features of the concept of being modern: after discarding the Marxist methodology of class analysis, as well as the ideal of undertaking an international socialist movement, the idea of being modern gradually moves from the notion of establishing a strong socialist country in which people can enjoy socialist welfare to outrageous consumerism and hedonism. However, for these migrant workers, they are unable to travel to the West; they can, however, go to Ulaanbaatar and resort to hard labor or engage in small business ventures. One scene in the film shows that Little Sister and Xiaotao are chatting together when they hear the booming sound of a plane. They lift their heads and see a plane whizz by at low altitude. Little Sister asks Xiaotao: "Who is aboard on the aircraft?" To which Xiaotao responds, "Who knows? In any case, none of those I'm familiar with has ever taken the flight."

Emergence of the Bud of Internationalism

The revelation of the impossibility of globalism or cosmopolitanism indicates that China lies at the bottom of the world's production chain. However, this impossibility has also brought about the birth of a new internationalism, which is mainly articulated through the foreign perform-ers appeared in the film, especially Xiaotao's Russian friend Anna. Their friendship goes well beyond the bounds of language differences, for they could communicate through body gestures. Not only does Anna speak out the renowned tenet of cosmopolitanism, "We speak different languages but are still friends;" but also we witness that a male member of the troupe takes hold of Anna's telescope the first time they meet and looks out over the surroundings, which brings him the nickname Columbus.

Anna and Xiaotao's relationship runs throughout the plotline. When Anna and the other three Russian actresses are taken to meet the dance group, her passport is confiscated by human smugglers by means of a security scam. She is then forced to sell her body in order to earn money for her captors. She gets to know through selling her a smuggled watch. Later, Xiaotao discovers layer upon layer of scars on Anna's back and begins to realize the dark social reality for these woman. In the hotel, Anna tells Xiaotao that she has to do "another kind of job," and that she hates doing it. She also informs Xiaotao that her little sister is living in Ulaanbaatar and that she must earn enough money to visit her. The last time Xiaotao sees Anna is in a nightclub where Xiaotao's friend has taken her to have a fun. The two meet each other in the bathroom; upon seeing Anna's dress, Xiaotao immediately knows Anna's situation and the two hug each other to vent their grief.

Anna's appearance provides the audience with the migrant workers' perspective of the neoliberal circulation of global labor. She plays the role of "the other," through which we can view the social environment faced by the characters. She also leaves her home, Russia, in search of wealth or happiness; however, ultimately she realizes that it was nothing but an illusion, and she finds herself trapped in the dim reality of the under-ground sex-world (Fig. 6.2).

Fig. 6.2 Again, a wide-angle, medium shot reveals Anna and Xiaotao are sympathetic with each other in the troupe

In this way, the picture of the collective destiny of the lower classes is thus imprinted with an ideological tone of internationalism. This, without doubt, is still a helpless, largely unconscious and half-hearted internationalism, just like the fact that China's neoproletariat classes have not yet formed their own political consciousness. In the film, the peasant-workers have almost completely shed their traditional consciousness; none of the political class-consciousness found in the Mao's era is found. In their minds, the new mainstream values are consumerism and hedonism. When they initially arrive in Beijing, they are, for the most part, blindly optimistic. They do not know that the job market into which they must throw themselves is one manipulated by capital. They appear numb and confused: although they experience hardships, being atomized individuals, they lack the organization and theoretical guidance to revolt. Their destiny is doomed.

This social class's inability to establish its self-awareness is ultimately shown in the sudden climax of the film. Taisheng and Xiaotao, who are temporarily staying in their new wedding home which is owned by Laoniu and Qiuping, succumb to death by gas poisoning. We do not know whether this is an unexpected accident, or an incident deliberately arranged by Xiaotao who discovers that she has been betrayed in love. The viewer only witnesses the two characters fading into darkness while their heads are layed down in the snow—a uniquely eerie scene. In the darkness, two people's voices are heard: Taisheng asks, "Did we die?" and Xiaotao responds, "No, we have just begun."

As one renowned Chinese saying goes, "Confront a person with the danger of death and he will fight to live." At this point, Xiaotao has just begun to take up a new consciousness against the mainstream logic of commodities. She is unable to endure her alienated state any longer. When she realizes that the last "capital" of her body as an exchangeable commodity has been used up, she is left without hope and, ultimately, has to fight back with her life. Apparently, this is a tragedy; and it is the symbolic failure of both a particular social class and a particular gender. Is she cowardly or heroic? For Walter Benjamin, the choice of suicide is the product of passion existing in the era of modernism, showing one's solemn attitude towards life in general. For Xiaotao, too, her decision is a tragic way of fighting back and breaking away.

In this light, Jia Zhangke does not "fail" "to realize that the local finds little space to establish its own identity and experience,"[17] as Cui Shuqin suggests. Neither does he become "mesmerized" by the park "like a besotted tourist," as Manohla Dargis contends.[18] Rather, the film reflects upon the class-ecology and gender state of China's migrant workers in the neoliberal age of globalization. For these people at the bottom of society, the world in the World Park is unreal but is within reach. By contrast, the world in reality is real but is full of false hopes. This confirms that the park's slogan (which is also the false promise provided by the government) that "Never leaving Beijing you can still experience the entire world" is just a lie or the illusion of globalization.

In the meantime, while the use of animation throughout the cinematic space shows the director's efforts "to get closer to the mainstream commercial culture," Jia probably also hints that "When the local is plugged electronically into the global, local identity and experience give way to an image-making system controlled by computer technology,"[19] which does not fall short of providing us with a critical message.

However, the film shows less class oppression and exploitation. Apart from a possible self-censorship (due to the director's compromise for the sake of public release) and the director's own estrangement from class analysis, it also exemplifies a social reality in which the consolidation of class structure is one side, and the conscious and unconscious suppression of any discourse of class analyses the other. Moreover, none of the feminist connotations here point to the issues of commodification, commercialization and consumerism; neither do they tie in with class discourse. Sexual exploitation of migrant workers receives weak representation in the film; sometimes it only shows females actively throwing themselves forcefully into the arms of "power." Therefore, the last resistance is merely a revolt at the anatomical level, which inevitably encounters death and failure.

Presenting the characters with no real details of their past, and weaving a "narrative of unfulfilling love, spiritual desolation and apprehension,"[20] the film documents their fragmented existences, in which the newly internationalized world in China is explored through the eyes of the under-classes. Everyone is trapped in their destinies, lost within the epochal currents of the era and forced to fight to survive. Critics thus find that "by juxtaposing the gay festivity of the park with the gloomy real life of migrant workers, Jia acutely expresses a dismal view of present-day China."[21]

This situation calls to mind the maxim articulated in Walter Benjamin's imagery of "Angelus Novus" (lit. Angel of History): "a storm is blowing in from Paradise; it has got caught in his wings with such a violence that the angel can no longer close them. The storm irresistibly propels him into the future to which his back is turned, while the pile of debris before him grows skyward. This storm is what we call progress."[22] This famous entry was originally a response to the encroachment of modernity. In China, which is flooded with all sorts of postmodernist fantasy, there exist different worlds—worlds whose intersections have inexorably blurred China's form of modernity/postmodernity. In the opening sequence, Xiaotao is looking everywhere for a band-aid for her wounded thumb. In this postmodern amusement park, the under-classes experience all kinds of injuries. Where can they find their "band-aid" to save themselves from being harmed? We are left with no answer. Therefore, while exposing the illusion of "China's dream," the movie does not show the struggles of the lower classes; neither does it offer any kind of solution (Fig. 6.3).

The opening scene is intended to entice the audience to "marvel at the sheer audacity and kitsch beauty" of the performers at the Park.[23] In a static long shot, glamorous images with the Eiffel Tower in the background are callously placed together with a peasant-like figure holding a garbage can in his shoulder and with a passive expression in his face. He passes by without noticing the spectacle while turning his face to the audience for a few seconds. Towards the end of the film, images of this garbage collector are once more presented, since they are reminiscent

Fig. 6.3 The opening scene of *The World*

of the famous essay by Charles Baudelaire entitled *"Scavenger."* Is the man indifferent, or is he mesmerized by the postmodern simulacrum? He takes a glance at the skyscrapers and leaves; everything around him is beyond his concern. Yet, Baudelaire put great emphasis on the function of the role of this rag picker (trash collector):

> [The ragpicker] is responsible for gathering up the daily debris of the capital. All that the city has rejected, all it has lost, shunned, disdained, broken, this man catalogs and stores. He sifts through the archives of debauch, the junkyards of scrap. He creates order, makes an intelligent choice; like a miser hoarding treasure, he gathers the refuse that has been spit out by the god of Industry, to make of it objects of delight or utility.[24]

For Baudelaire, the trash collector is an allegorical figure that delivers the essence of consumer capitalism, which provides much inspiration for Walter Benjamin, who takes it as a recurring motif in his writings.

Indeed, the essence of trash collecting is re-imagining and reinvesting new value in what is treated as rubbish. By reorganizing the material, the trash collector dreams for a better world. A social critic similarly sifts and searches through the pile of debris that the "storm of progress" trails. Thus, Benjamin takes it as the objective of an authentic cultural critique, which redeems objects and people repudiated as worthless by dominant values. Also, in this sense, the image of the trash collector has a revolutionary edge. It is known that Benjamin called Siegfried Kracauer "a rag-picker, early, in the dawn of the day of the revolution":

Kracauer was a rag-picker because he paid attention to the scraps, both the abandoned treasures and the acknowledged detritus, of civilization. These rags, these fragments that he collected, would, he sensed, reveal more about his age than the haute couture and grand self-estimations of the snobs...Along with Benjamin and Ernst Bloch, Kracauer perceived early on that his was an age of momentous social, political, and cultural transformation and...the "revolution" that this change implied.[25]

When he set up the particular screen shot, Jia Zhangke probably has thought of Baudelaire's poetic sentences; but Baudelaire's meditation of a revolution probably never comes to his mind.

ORCHESTRATING WORKERS' MEMORIES AND CHINESE NATIONAL HISTORY

Jia Zhangke admitted once that he had a strong desire to rewrite the national history of China when he produced the film *24 City* (*Ershisi Cheng ji*二十四城记) in 2008. He explained that the reason for his "leaving for Chengdu without hesitation...to produce a new film" was that:

At the end of 2006, news outlets reported that a local factory in Chengdu named the "Chengfa Group" (or "Factory 420") with a total workforce of 30,000 workers and 100,000 dependents transferred its lands to "China Resources Land Ltd." One year later, this factory...would finally disappear like ashes. Simultaneously, however, a modern real-estate project would emerge on its ground...From the transformation of land, from the planned economy to the market-oriented economy, from collectivism to individualism, all of these would tell a story of the system and the collective memory of the Chinese people.[26]

Jia Zhangke acknowledged his positive response to this change. "I was excited to come across this real-life case: it represents the gigantic – and miraculously rapid – transformation of modern China."[27] Thus, his new movie also signifies the director's shift of attention from individual, marginalized characters (such as bargirls and thieves) to a broader group of people; those who used to be members of the leading class in the country but that are now considered part of the "underprivileged" stratum of society, i.e. the working class. He attempted to make a record for them that is also about a recollection of the history of the People's Republic. Therefore, it has been noted, "Grander themes like historical turmoil, seismic shifts in economic and human infrastructures are in the periphery but always informing these characters' destinies."[28] In other words, this narration is "about two interrelated stories. One story recalls and narrates the fifty-year evolution of a factory on the basis of personal experiences, as well as the contemporary history of China demonstrated by the experiences of the factory and its staff. The other story relates to how the fifty-year history is narrated through certain subjects, and how it is elevated to be the common memory of the Chinese through personal or 'local experiences.'"[29] Does this mixed genre of a practice of "oral history," combining documentary (about real people) and fiction (played by professional actors and actress), authentically reveal the Chinese history of the workers as well as the evolution of the People's Republic?

According to many of the reviews at the time, critics acknowledged the positive merits of the film in this regard. *Hollywood Reporter* praised the film as a "moving elegy to modern-day China" with its documentary strain that "prevails to simple, yet emotionally reverberating effect"[30]; The *New York Times* sang its praises that, "Without nostalgia but with sensitivity and depth of feeling, Mr. Jia is documenting a country and several generations that are disappearing before the world's eyes."[31] Even *Time* joined the chorus: "the film interweaves the political overview...with personal anecdotes that are poignant and charming."[32] On the other hand, Jim Hoberman regards it as "an ambivalent exercise in Communist nostalgia" with a "subversively old-fashioned hymn to production."[33] Scott Tobias takes the arrangement as "jarring without necessarily being illuminating," since there is not "much continuity" within the film.[34] These with divergent comments speak to the ambivalent nature of the movie, which confirms its complex significance.

On the surface, the film chronicles the stories of workers using the narrative structure of a pseudo-documentary consisting of two parts intercut with each other. In the desolate industrial complex of the factory, five elderly factory workers poignantly describe their life and work in the factory. In addition, three other "witnesses" who have observed changes taking place in the factory, portrayed by actors, appear as composite characters. As the director claims, this peculiar arrangement is to "emphasize the value of imagination in the film":

> I found several film stars whom everybody [in China] knows, to make the public aware that this is a film comprising of both factual and fictional parts. No film can be absolutely accurate and objective in its factual account; there is inevitably some treatment processing involved.[35]

However, this "controversial use of actors playing fictional roles, inserted silently amidst real people" incurred many reservations among critics, who suggest that it "arguably evaded the responsibilities of both fact and fiction." They also consider that "by failing to signpost the difference between reality and fiction...it was underhand, even phoney." However, other critics contended that this "formal daring is what is impressive"[36] and this "synthetic vision of docufiction...gives Jia the philosophical freedom to contrast, juxtapose, and integrate the real and the fictional in ways that defy and overwhelm conventional cinematic storytelling."[37] To judge whether this creative decision achieved its intended aesthetic and cultural(-political) objective, we need to examine the formal effect on the content, and vice versa.

Before going into the textual analysis, a brief introduction of the historic background is necessary. Factory 420, founded in 1958, was formerly the top secret aircraft manufacturing Shenyang Factory 111. Following Chairman Mao's strategic plan to develop remote regions of China in the early 1960s, it was relocated from Northeast China to Southwest China, together with its workforce of several thousand staff members. This particular policy is known as "Third-line Construction," a major decision concerning the Chinese industrial system and national defense, and the first large-scale and concentrated movement to develop the western area. Although China's key strategic factory in the 1960s and 1970s, the fortunes of Factory 420 have nevertheless undergone several rounds of upheaval. Accordingly, the vicissitudes it has experienced show the fifty years of social-political disruption within the People's Republic. After the 1980s, the factory experienced its first short boom period on the eve of China's economic reform due to the Sino-Vietnamese War (1979–1989). It subsequently suffered economic depression that began in the late 1980s when the War ended. Finally, it collapsed totally after the 1990s during national industrial restructuration. In 2008, the factory was relocated to a new industrial zone and the original lands located in the downtown area were sold to a developer, which then developed a real estate project called 24 City. In this regard, it has become "an obvious symbol for China's transformation from communist behemoth to capitalist powerhouse."[38] How does the movie take its stance towards this sea-change? Is it that the director "offers neither criticism nor celebration" but "simply chronicles and pays a gentle tribute to the unnoticed and unappreciated people who devoted their lives to the old factory, and to China's pre-capitalist state, just as they disappear into oblivion,"[39] as many critics generally believe?

Three Generations of "Flower of Factory"

The most salient feature of the movie is that it presents three generations of the so-called "flowers of factory"—Hao Dali, Gu Minhua and
Su Na, who recount their experiences. These roles are all performed by
well-known professional actresses whose acting careers correspond to the
three phases of the factory.

Dali, the flower of the first generation, appears with a transfusion bottle held high in her hands. In a long shot, we witness her walk past a
long block and a passageway before she reaches her office. Such bold
behavior arouses a sense of discomfort among the audience.[40] Dressed
in a plain manner, she does not appear particularly mature; however,
she responds to the greeting of the clerk, who calls her by the title of
"auntie," "Why are you calling me aunt? You should call me Grandma!"
The impatient answer shows her deliberately flaunting her seniority. She
does not appear have a positive opinion of the polite young girl in this
scene and sarcastically remarks, "Are we allowed to wear makeup at work
nowadays?" In response to this meddlesome and aggressive "Marxist-
Leninist woman" (a nickname for women who spout revolutionary
phrases but who do not themselves set a good example), who is not old
by any estimation, the girl patiently and politely explains, "In foreign
enterprises, the staff members are even required to wear makeup!" Dali
replies contemptuously, "Isn't this a state-owned enterprise?" The girl
is then speechless. Taking her entrance in an irritating manner, the lady
then begins her narration.

Her narrative comprises four parts: the first is the privilege of the
factory—a monthly confidentiality fee of 5 *yuan* and a monthly benefit
of 1.5 kg of pork per staff member during the days of great starvation in
the 1960s when everyone else could barely feed themselves. The second
part of Dali's nasrrative is about the staggering income earned by the
staff at the time. "I remember the bank was opening a temporary outlet
next to the gate of our factory when we were reimbursed. I earned 58
yuan per month in 1975 and could deposit in the bank 30 *yuan*." As the
"leading class," they received full welfare packages from the state, including work uniforms and gloves, and Dali had sent the additional sets to
her younger sister, who then unraveled them and knitted woollen clothes
and pants. The third section of her account consists of comparisons of
the past and the present: the son of her sister, who ran a small drugstore
in the countryside, sent her 500 *yuan* because he knew that her "factory

is in trouble." But the best part of her narration is the last part, which is about her personal sacrifice when her child went missing during the chaotic factory relocation. In floods of tears, Dali recounts the experience as though to an interviewer. It is uncertain, however, whether this would have the desired dramatic effect, as the character is being played by an actress who is well-known across the country. The last scene shows her eating and watching television. A barely audible voice-over is heard from the TV: "an enemy airplane is approaching from the southwest..." Apparently, this is a war movie shot during that era. She is enjoying a moment of nostalgia (Fig. 6.4).

Upon the initial appearance of the second flower, Gu Minhua, (acted by the internationally renowned actress Chen Chong), she is performing a scene from an opera with other elderly female staff members. After her performance is over and the other actors have dispersed, she returns home wearing her makeup, which intimates that, in real life, in her mind she is still a fairy from heaven. In the next scene, she appears in front of a mirror in her inner room applying rouges and eyeliner, which again shows that she is fond of dressing herself up. She is then begins talking to a man sitting in front of her (whose face is never shown) using the Shanghai dialect. Strangely, the conversation begins with her visit from her younger sister in Shanghai and goes on to the anti-Japanese

Fig. 6.4 A long shot deliberately presents Gu Minghua returning home after the performance with her makeup on

war: as the "Japanese invasion started," many Shanghai residents fled to Sichuan. After the victory, they saw themselves as anti-Japanese warriors and ate spicy food to demonstrate their experiences in Sichuan. This narration, apparently of the Nationalist Party's experience during the anti-Japanese war, appears strangely unique. We can only surmise that the director has a special message for the audience here, because the actress had played the role of the wife of a high-level Nationalist Party traitor in the hit movie *Lust, Caution* not long before.[41] To audience members born before the mid-1970s, her nickname—Little Flower—also brings to mind the memory of her acting in her debut movie *Little Flower*, which laid the foundation for her reputation in 1978 (the same year as Gu Minhua, the character she plays, was allocated to "Factory 420" as a graduate of the Shanghai Aeronautics University). The two intertextual messages seemingly imply that the director aims to keep the audience's distance from this character. Even more interestingly, after Minhua performs *Dream of Red Chamber* in a Zhejiang Opera play by a group of people dressed up in ancient costumes (her role here is the leading heroine, the sentimental Lin Daiyu), she wears her opera costume when she goes home and carries a basket. She flaunts her way past a block to get home, just as Dali held her transfusion bottle high in her hands when she first appeared. The comparable scenes indicate that they are similarly vain and conceited.

To begin with, her narration breaks the myth of her spirit of sacrifice. She, indeed, was the only one who chose to leave Shanghai for the frontier when all the others were trying to stay there after graduation. However, as she confesses, this is because there were seven people living in her highly congested attic. Next, her life in the factory was not difficult. She was well received, for there were few female workers in the factory. A piece of intertextual information is offered to show her popularity. We are informed that many factory workers said that she was very much like Little Flower, the principal female character in the homonymous film widely shown across China at the time, which was also the first movie to arouse national sensation after the fall the "Gang of Four." Minhua narrates two stories; these cover the working conditions of the factory and her experiences in dating, which were microscopic of the society of the early 1980s.

The first tale shows the highly responsible level of discipline in the factory of the period. A picture of handsome youth hangs in the window; this attracts the workers' curiosity and numerous possibilities were posed regarding his identity. Days later, the director of the factory told them that he was a pilot who sacrificed his life for public safety when his airplane was in trouble. His was death due to a malfunction because of a defective component that had been produced by the factory. The director then requests everybody to "take self-examination."

While this scene reflects the revolutionary consciousness at the time, the second tale narrates her loss of youth. Minhua used to date a teacher from an open university (something like a workers' evening school) at the factory, whose parents were both high-ranking officials. Someone else was infatuated with her and wrote a love letter to him in her name. This caused misunderstandings between them and they parted ways. By the end of the Sino-Vietnam War in the mid-1980s, the need for military products were greatly decreased, so the factory's business profits were deteriorating; this meant the factory had to turn to making civilian industrial goods such as refrigerators. Minhua was then dispatched to Shanghai to the sales department. Next, following the subsequent rise in the number of private enterprises in China, she left the company and started a company by herself. She was over thirty then and could only be introduced to divorced men with children; however, she was reluctant to be a stepmother. Recently, she had come to know a successful businessman with "satisfactory conditions," who used to be a mason. But when she learned from him that he used to know her when he was younger but had not thought he deserved to be her boyfriend, she was greatly offended, "Even if I am not 'standard' now, I am not useless!" Only at the end of her narration do we learn from the caption that she was a quality inspector of the precision workshop. Yet, the nature of her profession was inconsequential here, which means her contributions, just like her sufferings (if any), were insignificant.

Most critics believe the narrations of the two "factory flowers" are about their sacrifices, and such stories about the system and the costs are narrated in as a dichotomous of family versus nation.[42] When we note that one of them has lost her child and another has remained single throughout, it indeed appears so. However, careful examination reveals that this opinion falls short of firm evidence. Dali lost her child simply because of her negligence, rather than a tragedy caused by the mission. Also, Minhua's single status is not due to the intervention of the political authority (which was frequently a stereotypical practice in the past), Rather, is the result of her own conscious decision (she always had high expectations of potential lovers) and her self-conceit, which is particularly shown by her wish to marry a successful businessman.

Although it is far-fetched for the director to orchestrate the stories to demonstrate the antagonism between a "naturalized family" and an "alien state," their reminiscences of the bitter past really reflect the "backfire against class theory and collectivism" by the generation of people after the 1990s, as well as the "loss of order, despair and bewilderment arising from sharp social diversification and restructuring" in this era.[43] When the director attempts to arouse sympathy from the audience towards their "tragedies" with the theme song of "Little Flower" (the lyrics of which read, "the girl is in all tears looking for her brother"), what he does not observe is that, when these characters are showing off their contributions to and sacrifices for the state in the "old days" with the pretension of seniority, the seemingly nostalgic sentiments only backfire, exposing their repentance for and the betrayal of their past behaviors in this era of transformation. It is more a projection of their contemporary feelings than a genuine recollection.

When the "factory flower" of the third generation shows up, we are surprised to learn that she does not take a formal job. Su Na—pet name is Nana—was born in 1982. Interestingly enough, her first appearance is the same way as for Minhua, doing her makeup in front of a mirror. And then, like her two predecessors, she fastidiously walks past the same block dragging her suitcase; she is greeted by a passing acquaintance, which also demonstrates her narcissism. But her egocentrism has a higher form. After driving a car past a motorway, she comes to a field of cauliflowers and stops there to look into the distance. Following her line of sight, we witness the high-rise buildings under construction protruding into the sky. Then she comes to the old, dilapidated and empty "Chengfa Children's Middle School" where she used to study. As she saunters along in a conceited manner, reminiscing on her times there, a voice-over filled with her sense of self-satisfaction is heard. "I was 1.66m tall when I was in Senior Grade 1. With such excellent physical conditions, I was even expected to become a model. But unfortunately I stopped growing taller from then on." At this moment, she is passing a building with a lamp post on the wall; and she carefully examines the lamp post which shows a hand holding up the "torch" of Marxist gospels, a typical design of Mao's era. Apparently, she is unfamiliar (and thus curious) about the past.

Like her predecessors, she then starts to talk eloquently as though to an interviewer. She was not admitted to university due to her poor academic performance; but neither did she want to work in Factory 420.

Immediately shifting to another topic, her conceitedness is seen again on her face and in her hand gestures. "I feel I am doing a good job now. I am a buyer and I need to go to Hong Kong to shop for my patrons once every two weeks. There are many rich people in Chengdu…those rich ladies have too much free time. They want to be fashionable but feel too tired to shop by themselves. So I am their agent." These ladies fed by the nouveaux riches prefer the most trendy luxury products but are reluctant to go there. That is the reason why she can become an agent for them. She says, in a proud and shameless manner, "I will take one thousand per item. I think the profit is ok for me. Not too much anyway." The interviewer flatters her by responding, "That is great!" Yet, this arouses an awkward smile on Nana's face. She quickly turns to another topic, telling the interviewer that a foreigner she met aboard an airplane expected to run a rotating restaurant and invited her to be the manager. She admits that she is a stranger to this industry but wants to have a try. "Maybe I can become a professional woman. Don't you think so?" With the firm endorsement from the interviewer once more, she attempts to disguise her motives for buying a car and showing off her wealth by arguing that, "I just want to have a platform for myself. It would be better for my business with those rich ladies if I could buy a car." Obviously, she is not a representative of contemporary workers. But it is not negligent of the director to prefer a lazy person like her to a regular worker in the enclosed workshop at Foxconn, or any other factory in South China, as the "representative" of factory beauty. As with the narcissists selected by the movie as the paragons of workers in Mao's era, she signifies the unconscious sense of superiority of a certain class in present society.

Without any cue for the transition, she then starts to talk about her mother, who was a state worker laid off in 1995. Her husband—Nana's father—was the factory manager then; but he refused to arrange a job for his wife simply because of his adherence to certain principles. Thereafter, Nana's mother finds a temporary job at a wire factory and has continued working there till now. Nana then goes on to talk about her understanding of her father. In her eyes, her father was at a total loss in the early days after retirement, and he could not help smoking every day when he got up in the morning. For her, this is because he was not used to days without exerting his power of supervision. What he considered is surely beyond her understanding, for she believes that he is listless simply because it is a long time since visitors came to their home.

What Nana is discussing is the gigantic societal-political transformation since the middle of 1990s when pro-capitalist reform decidedly changed the direction of the state. Her father was apparently a Maoist model leader, who followed the revolutionary or socialist ethics and refused to exploit his public office for private gain. This, together with his misgivings and anxiety towards the national politics (in particular, the pro-capitalist reform policy), is beyond her intellectual appreciation. Being oblivious to these subtle details, which remain unexplained throughout, the movie unfortunately sanctions this de-politicized narration (Fig. 6.5).

Despite her failure to understand the choices of her parents due to her lack of the ideas and concepts of that generation, Nana then unashamedly mentions her previous cohabitation with three boyfriends. She is reluctant to go home because of the dejection she feels whenever she goes back. However, during one incident she was forced to return home to retrieve her residence registration. When she realizes that her house key is missing, she has to visit the factory and ask her mother for it. What follows is the first, and only, narration about physical labor in the movie. "The moment I walked into the workshop, I found I had to yell and shout to make myself heard because of the roaring machines. I could not find my mother inside. Everyone was wearing a blue uniform and working attentively." This is a typical scene of labor in a large factory in the industrialized era: on the surface, there is virtually no difference

Fig. 6.5   Nana appears to be melancholic when watching the fast-changing cityscape

between a socialist factory and a capitalist one (there was little difference, if the spiritual conditions—the class consciousness—of workers were ignored). On finally identifying her mother by means a "face-by-face" search, finding her working and carrying a heavy steel ingot robotically like a man at the corner of the workshop, she cries out in pain. That night she sleeps at her home and sighs, "I have grown up while lying in bed. I genuinely feel sorry for my parents."

Such a tearful narration could be heartfelt; however, it is also a kind of disguise. It is particularly worthy of note that she is an emblem of the fall of the working class together with their (socialist) mindsets, rather than a "flower of factory" or the "daughter of a worker" as the publicity for the movie would have us believe.[44] In conclusion, through the representation of the three generations of "Flowers of Factory," the movie unwittingly shows their vanities, affectations and self-conceited. This unconscious lapse on the directorial side is politically over-determined.

Empty Memories of the Working Class

The question remains whether the memories of the "real" workers be more "authentic." In reality, the film project originated from the director's feeling that "Memories were lost. That's why when I read the news, I thought to myself: Wow, in the end, even memories had to be sacrificed."[45] So, did he successfully recreate the "sacrificed" memory of historical experience?

The first female worker that appears in the film is Hou Lijun. But neither her appearance nor her narration impresses the audience as a "factory beauty." In other words, she is an ordinary staff worker. Born in 1953, this repair woman sits inside a large, empty commuter bus, narrating emotively about her long-term separation from her mother, who has worked in the Chengdu factory, and her maternal grandparents in the Northeast of China. They have only had one opportunity for a family reunion in 14 years. Even though this family has worked for the factory for several decades, she was still laid off during market-oriented economic reform at the age of 41, when her son was a sixth grader. This comparison demonstrates the different political preferences between the two eras. "The mother sacrificed her 'small family' for the 'bigger family.' Yet when Hou Lijun became a mother, the 'big family' no longer needed her anymore."[46] However, she apparently accepts the official rhetoric of downsizing the workforce for higher productivity and happily recalls the farewell party that the factory held for the first group of laid-off workers. They were all in tears and held hands with the leader, asking him, "Was I ever late for work in these years? Was I ever absent-minded at work? Did I ever make a mistake?" The leader replies, "Not at all," but the factory just "doesn't need so many people now" because it "has to become a responsible business for its losses and gains." As a result, the tuition of her child and the living expenses of all three family members were dependent on a monthly maintenance fee of 200 *yuan*.

What she narrates is the history of the compulsory layoff of state-owned enterprise workers with nominal compensation justified with the excuse of downsizing staff to increase efficiency in the neoliberal reform agenda of the late 1990s. This process is frequently associated with authoritarian privatization, the cheap sale of state-owned assets and governmental corruption. Yet, she does not express any doubt or criticism. What she shows is merely the pathos of workers, and she often displays her willingness to "share the hardship of the state," as called for by the government. Worse, this suffering is soon replaced by an inspirational story of "becoming successful out of personal diligence," a tale favored by the official propaganda. She posts her maxim "Go ahead courageously regardless of any obstacle," which she repeats a couple of times before going out to look for work. To earn a living, she had worked as a peddler selling Michelia champaca, but she gave up as the police would confiscate her stall as she has no license. Now, she works as a tailor at home. She believes that, "One grows older slowly when keeping busy." The last scene switches to two middle-aged women standing together and singing a happy song, "We have an appointment tonight, a sleepless night; when the bell rings for the new millennium, come on, my dear friends! Come on, my dear friends…" The unfairness taking place during economic transformation is hidden and overlooked in this narrative. Apparently, it is her historical experience of education by the Communist Party that facilitated her acceptance of the official rhetoric. To be sure, other staff workers engage in protests, and the director admits that he has omitted many "extreme" personal memories, instead selecting only those he believes to be "representative" cases. His political stance determines what is to be represented and what is to be left out (Fig. 6.6).

Doubtless, the personal narration of this worker unwittingly shows the style of an official narrative. What about the narrative made by the real worker "acting" as himself? This male worker, He Xikun, is the first to appear in the interviews. Sitting in an empty and dilapidated

Fig. 6.6   Old worker He Xikun tells his story in a decrepit, spacious room without decoration

workshop, he does not tell us his own story. From the caption, we know that he was born in Chengdu in 1948 and became the apprentice of a locksmith in 1964 before joining the PLA. Strangely, we do not know his present identity, either through the caption or his personal narration. He begins to recollect the past and then visits his master, who is the leader of the work team that migrated from Shenyang to Chengdu in the 1950s. However, the story, which is taking place between him and his master, is merely about the master's instructions to take care of working tools and recycle those that would typically be deemed useless but are still usable. The work ethic of this master inspired his disciple to stay in the workplace even during the Cultural Revolution, when there were few if any workers who remained in the factory. From this portrayal, the master merely appears to be stubbornly and unreasonably devoted wholeheartedly, yet also blindly, to his job. One particular case is noteworthy. The master recalls himself working overtime, even during Chinese festivals in 1959, when he came to the factory. This is because the schedule was tight as the Korean War was taking place. Apparently, the master's memory has a problem (the Korean War ended in 1954); He Xikun, who is listening does, not correct it. Such a confused memory adds complexity to the simplistic labor scene, and renders it impossible to recall.

He Xikun attempts to tell something about his master, but his recollection is actually very simple; apart from talking about the conceptualized details of treasuring tools, he merely mutters some vacuous concepts such as "You have made great contribution to the factory!"[47] Possibly, because he soon left the factory and joined the army, he had very limited work experience and knowledge about industrial production. Consequently, "the long-separated two generations actually could only communicate through silence, with the disciple stroking the forehead of his master, while the latter uttering some meaningless groans from his throat, as if he had lost his memory and ability of oral communication."[48] Regarding the scene where he remains silent over what his master says, the following comment is convincing:

> It is noteworthy that the role of He Xikun as an interviewer in the master-disciple meeting is exactly the role that the director Jia Zhangke plays in all the subsequent interview scenes. They used to share the same history as interviewees. As the lucky "escapees," however, they have lost the continuous association and experience with such a history and therefore, can only rebuild their memories through the interviewee's narrations. The narration of the movie starts in silence or lapse of memory, and it may be interpreted in a Lacanian way: Memory only works in vain to fill up the vacancy left by the missing objects; and language could never reach reality by its nature. However, the place where silence resides is not a pure gap. Instead, it is a specific identity. When the narrator is a mother, a daughter, a single woman or a successful figure inside/outside the system, he/she has his/her own story to tell. Why can't a worker tell his or her story?... How shall we look historically at the speechless old worker? What other messages does it convey other than an aging life and a profession in a desperate position? [49]

Apparently, He Xikun's visit to the amnesiac and deaf master is simply to pay his last tribute, a ritualistic mourning of the good, old days.

Another incompetent former worker the director presents is a retired manager, Guan Fengjiu, who was the vice secretary of the factory's Party Committee. Although the senior manager was also considered a member of the working class, no relevant narration is provided here regarding his job, either relating to physical work or about ideological supervision. His role is almost non-existent in the movie. According to the caption, he was born in Haicheng in the Liaoning Province in 1935 and used to be the head of the Security Department of the Chengfa Group.

The director only permits him to tell one story—the relocation of the factory. He appears intermittently later on, patrolling the factory premises, flashlight in hand, seemingly reviewing the sites where he used to work diligently. Interestingly, his interview is arranged in a venue like a worker's theatre, where he sits in the auditorium close to the camera. The movie gives a close-up of the remote stage, where two youngsters are playing badminton; the stage curtain is decorated with an image of the meandering Great Wall. It seems to imply that the era of defending the country and homestead is gone forever; the familiar place has now become a venue for fitness and entertainment.

The account of Secretary Guan relates to the first half of the factory's history; whereas the "recollection" of Song Weidong, played by renowned actor Chen Jianbin, consists of the second half of the story. Born in 1996, he was set to be a successor to his father's career, and is now vice manager of the GM Office. He smokes and talks in an eloquent manner. Proudly, he is designing the blueprint for the future: the proceeds from land transfers will be used to build a new industrial zone, and the plot of land where his office is located will become a five-star hotel in the future. This narration is obviously recognition of the achievement brought by the official policies of "reducing workforce for higher productivity" and privatization of land. The audience would easily forget the laid-off Hou Lijun upon seeing his excitement and optimism, for the two are separated by Hao Dali.

Weidong continues to introduce the "cradle to grave" educational, working and welfare system, which was one enjoyed by any large-scale state-owned factory in the Maoist era. In the neoliberal rhetoric of the present time, such a system is chastised as bringing a burden upon the people, resulting in financial loss and low productivity within the enterprise. But Weidong proudly claims an independent factory like this to be *great* and there was no need to "have a contact with the local community." The only tie, according to him, was the fighting with local youths. He recalls that, on one occasion, he was caught up by those youths in a fight simply because it was the day of Premier Zhou Enlai's death. Through this incident, his narration skips smoothly to 1976.

Thereafter, the changes occurring in society are indirectly reflected by his lost love. Due to the profitability of the factory upon his graduation from high school, he stayed in the factory instead of going to college, while his girlfriend left there for college. When the factory became less profitable a few years later, his girlfriend broke up with him at the request of her parents. He remembers a famous Japanese TV series being broadcast then. With the sound of the interlude piece, his juvenile trauma becomes another type of "sacrifice," though it has a poetic sentiment.

However, in this poetic recall, not only are the scenes of the workers' past labor being narrated, the feelings of workers of the "new era" are also absent. Other than Su Na, who abandons her worker's job and runs her own businesses, we only see one other former worker who left his job to enter the world of entertainment. Zhao Gang, born in 1974, then starts speaking of his experience. He narrates his excitement about the outside world when he traveled from Chengdu to the Northeast province Jilin by train after receiving notification of his admission to a vocational school in 1990, and the new feelings of wearing a uniform and acting as an intern in a factory. However, he soon got bored with the mechanical grinding work. The dull and insipid work killed his passion, and he made up his mind to adventure in the new world. This choice made at that time is more of a demonstration of the fall of the working class and the multitude of new opportunities in the outside world on the eve of China's market-oriented economic reform, than the youngster's initial discovery of the dullness and repetitiveness of industrial labor. After the interview, Zhao Gang and his father have a photo taken of them together in front of a fighter jet. The screen then shifts to another scene, where a group of farmers holding a steel drill each take a group photo in front of the camera with stern expressions on their faces. Skilled technicians were hardly available then, and the role of the new generation of workers had to be taken up by the farming sector. Apparently, this narration is "the personal expression of the changed identity of the community. The factory is no longer a token of national modernization but a marginalized space in the fast-changing Chinese society."[50]

Cultural Politics of "Oral History"

Jia Zhangke has admitted that he gave up filming his original script; instead, he prefers personal stories because he believes Chinese films or literature "used to conform to the mainstream stance and ideology;" and he "hope[s] that our relation to history can have a personal – and genuine – starting point."[51] Does his "personal" view of history become more "genuine" than the "mainstream stance and ideology"? In any case, in addition to any reservation about putting real people and actors together, film reviewers have also had other concerns, which show that the ultimate product did not necessarily meet the director's expectation:

> Is the filmmaker bemused or amused by a factory bureaucrat's earnest remark that "our offices will become a five-star hotel"? And what is one to make of the casually revealed information that the movie itself was partially financed by *24 City*'s developer? Have we been watching a kind of infomercial? Is there irony or pathos in the juxtaposition of retired workers enthusiastically singing "The International" as their factory collapses?[52]

Indeed, we can find many ambiguities or contradictory elements in the cinematic space. In this oral recount, the order of the characters is as follows:

1. He Xiku (1948–): Senior worker.
2. Guan Fengjiu (1935–): Senior manager.
3. Hou Lijun (1953–): A female worker sacrificing her family life for the factory and making a living independently after her layoff.
4. Hao Dali (1937–): A first-generation representative of the "factory flowers" who sacrificed being together with her family for the sake of the factory.
5. Song Weidong (1966–): The present manager.
6. Gu Minhua (1958–): A second-generation factory woman who sacrifices her youth for the factory.
7. Zhao Gang (1974–): A new-generation youth who puts an end to the traditional worker's family.
8. Su Na (1982–): A new-generation broker.

If we re-order the positions of the fifth and sixth narrators, then the chronological order would fit in with the evolution of the factory. In this chain of recollection, "the narrative from the roles of mother, daughter, or single woman normally illustrates their experiences of separation between private and public life," while the males' narrations of father and son stories tend to demonstrate a more complicated meaning of country and family. Moreover, "the close ties of consanguinity squeezed together within factory dorms seem to be the only thing that people can identify with" in the 50-year evolution of the factory.[53]

Applying the dichotomies between planned economy and market-oriented economy, and between collectivism and individualism, the movie follows a rigid and dogmatic mentality in which market economy and individualism prevails. Thus, abiding by the rule, it chooses the characters according to the content of their narrations. Besides, the director, who did not share the characters' experiences, relies on the impersonations of these characters to establish his imagination and perception. He admits, "I thought I could only fully comprehend these real people's feelings through imagination. I'm not a historian writing history. I'm a film director reconstructing experiences incurred in history."[54] This confession nonetheless shows the fictional nature of this documentary-style film.

Jia believes that, when finding professional performers to act as real people while let most people do not know that it is a performance, it would only turns the movie into a fake documentary. He thus suggests that:

> If there is any fictitious part, it is necessary to tell the audience, which part is rehearsed with an actor or intervened by the director's imagination. I believe all productions have been plotted and interfered with by the director. From this perspective, (to make) a movie, which tells a 50-year history with the hues of recalls and retrospections, there would be many factors that have contributed to this method. In this sense, the spectators should be told directly that it is a performance.[55]

The statement seems to be in line with Bertolt Brecht's theory of estrangement. However, Brecht expects the spectators to understand the ridiculousness of routine phenomena and behaviors and, hence, to mount criticism against the capitalist world and unveil their imaginings of alternative life. Jia's intention of notifying the spectators that what is being shown is merely a play, by contrast, displays his strong distrust of the (recalled and written) history. In other words, it is a subversion of the original concept of documentary under a neohistoricist concept; and it is also a deviation from the initial intention of the Sixth Generation directors whose aim is to reveal the reality under the slogan "my camera does not lie."

In China, the opinion that historical truth can only be imagined, rather than demonstrated, originated in the mid-1980s and was highly popular among the so-called "avant-garde fiction." It shows the distrust with and the abandonment of the official, grand narrative. In this movie, we find some style traits similar to that particular brand of fiction. For instance, when Dali loses her child, the screen displays a caption which reads: "The Fengji government immediately organized the public to search for the child along the Yangtze river, and the factory had also dispatched people to do the same thereafter. But the child was never found (excerpts from *The History of the Chengfa Group*)." Considering it is highly unlikely that such a personal experience to be kept in an official record, it spontaneously reminds us of the fabrication of history in the famed avant-garde novelist Gefei's story "Qinghuang."

Let us go deeper into the messages that the director intends to convey. Through showing the sacrifice of the female characters, he is particularly keen to demonstrate that country and society are alien to individuals. A revival of the past from the perspective of a common, universal human nature indicates that, while on the surface the movie displays their experiences vis-à-vis the background of that era, in truth, it only displays the director's understanding of them—and he is oblivious to the ideology of the time which constructed the thinking of the people. Their pain is expressed in the present age of the post-socialist era, when the original purpose for their sacrifice no longer exists (although they might not realize it; and this does not mean that such sacrifices were not painful then). What is more, their pain is now accentuated by the de-politicized atmosphere in which they acquire certain psychological compensation through this cathartic release. They believe that they have sacrificed for the state, yet the state of today is different from that of the past. In this light, their experiences actually become a critique of a de-politicized country. On the surface, however, their narration seems to be oriented towards a criticism of the mechanism of the erstwhile socialist state, in which the personal traumas of different eras are lumped together to show the costs of the inhuman, planned economy.

What is particularly worthy of analysis is the appearance of female characters in the movie. All the female workers active in the Maoist era now appear aggressive, offensive and narcissistic. While ostensibly they are continually engaging in nostalgic remembrance of the past, in reality they only recall their honorable "sacrifice" in a rather self-conceited manner. On the other hand, the young ladies of the post-socialist period are shown to be fashionistas putting on makeup all days, such as Minhua and Nana, who nevertheless are presented as more "human" and normal than their elders. Even the broker Nana is flattered by the interviewer. In this way, through the naturalization of the traditional concept of female gender, the mainstream concept that it is better for women to return to their proper place in the home (rather than serving the socialist enterprise in the same way as men) is once again subtly confirmed.

While the female characters are foregrounded, we need to notice the silent and amnesiac-like part of the movie. At the end, when the camera is presenting a panorama of the city, the screen displays a poem that reads "Chengdu/even only your missing part/is enough to give me a lifetime glory." Doubtlessly, the director intends to display this missing element. However, he covers up more than he reveals. In any case, such "missing part," whatever it may be, bears little relation to the present prosperity of the city, as demonstrated by the skyscrapers seen in the panorama. In the cinematic space, the "missing part" seems merely to be the abandoned factory, a product of a special system and era. It can only be so because the past here is objectified to be a special space and profession.[56] We can infer that this missing part refers to nothing but labor.

A poem appears in the movie as follows: "The entire factory is like a giant eyeball, and labor the darkest part of all." Nevertheless, the portrayal of labor in the movie, if any, is flat and lacks life. Surely, the high intensity of labor in the socialist days for the purpose of industrialization was also conducted in the manufacturing mode of Fordism. However, the movie's approach of de-politicization does not allow real senior workers to express their feelings regarding labor; and none of them is permitted to talk about the class awareness that used to have an impact on their passions for work as well as their political life in the past. Obviously, to the director, labor is labor, which has no difference physically and psychologically, or in terms of its appearance in socialism or capitalism. However, this is merely a metaphysical and non-historical understanding.

This mistake can be examined through another perspective concerning the geological relationship between Shenyang and Chengdu, which is "metonymically displaced to be the antithesis between factory and city; and such an antithesis is denoted not merely spatially, but also temporally signifying 'the Subject' and its 'Other'."[57] Nevertheless, while the movie fully utilizes this city as a token—a city of poem and leisurely life, Chengdu as a city is virtually invisible here—until the last moment, when it is shown in a panoramic shot at the end of the movie. It is reminiscent of what the manager Weidong says to the interviewer: the folks felt that the factory was a self-sustaining world and did not need to have relations with the outside world. From an isolated perspective, it is a fair assessment. Yet, it is actually an extended metaphor of the atomic individual which severs its ties from society and interpersonal relations.

This means that the film cannot provide a concrete context of the various eras; by contrast, labor is only significant in such a concrete social, political and interpersonal milieu.

Consequently, the factory and city form a binary contradiction spatially: "The former is a fully-closed or semi-closed workshop of heavy industry and the zone of worker's dorms, while the latter is represented by alleys, *hutongs*, courtyard houses, and other traditional citizen spaces, or the more abstract 'poems' and arts."[58] But this is simply a projection of the present knowledge, which is deemed "common and natural." However, the "vast median between the binary spaces – the city of the working class" is invisible here. This is a problem because "a city in the era of the planned economy was organized and constructed on the basis of (the needs of) the working class. The central position of the working class in the city corresponds to the national identity of socialist China, i.e. a class-nation. Specifically, (China's) national identity was established through identification among the leading class."[59] As such, the "invisibility of the working class in a city signifies the elapse of a national identity." [60]

As said, this setting is simultaneously a projection. It projects the feelings of laborers in the capitalist era (e.g. workers isolated from each other in Foxconn-like factory settings) into the past era. These interviewees, including the real workers, are already strangers to the political feelings of that era. At the instigation of the interviewer, they are actually encouraged to express their sense of sacrifice and trauma: they are the people "who were often treated high-handedly and whose work often separated them brutally from their families."[61] It is worth noting that none of them talks about the glory and pride they had in the past, or mention the various privileges they enjoyed as the leading class (at most, they only mention their relatively high salaries and welfare). The resulting effect can be anticipated: the film is "clouded by desolation that it's all gone and they are on the scrapheap and a sense that there has not been sufficient gratitude for this work." What is often neglected, however, is the post-socialist transformation that has brought out or preconditioned this pitiable atmosphere: "the state that should be expressing it, and for which they sacrificed their lives and happiness, has disappeared and been replaced by a capitalist agency devoted to a new economy."[62] In light of this fact, the following observation is insightful, "the working-class acquires the patents of industrial labor, but it loses the totality of their own city and life…History is thus recalled in such an aesthetic way. However, such an art of recollection is completely unable to imagine the history of an alternative type of factory, a history of a production space that was closely linked to the fate of the general life of a metropolis."[63]

The name of a new real estate project, 24 City, is simultaneously a reference to Chengdu, which originates from an ancient Chinese poem. Just like "the poetic, upscale real estate project 24 City replaces the remains of the factory," the poets from Chengdu, whose poems continually appear throughout the movie, also "use their poems to cover the interviews of Northeastern Chinese Working Class."[64] However, those interviews being shown onscreen are not randomly chosen from the archives; rather, they are selected on the basis of the director's preemptive concept: "We need to face the fifty-year industrial memories of the People's Republic of China. In the past, we have chosen the planned economy for national prosperity and individual well-being. But what have we paid for such a trial in the past 50 years?"[65] In other words, what he intends to record is the cost—the painful sacrifices. On the surface, this selection has been made out of the appreciation of the workers' lofty spirits. But, in actuality, it is more of an exposure (in order to indict the inhuman experience). With this motivation, the Chinese working class, which was the historic subject, is dissolved in a mechanism of displacement and projection:

> From the eulogy of the "contributions" of collectivism to the accusations of "suppression" of individualism, from the accumulation theory from the perspective of national modernization to the theory of sacrifice premised on the position of a universal value, from the "whitewashing" of the mainstream propaganda to the "exposure" of avant-garde arts, the stereotyping of the same history always persists regardless of their differences in value judgment. What is supplementary to such an external production space is only the family life of the workers. Factory and family seem to be the entire life of the working class…"The elder son of the Republic" (namely the working class) has owned only factories but no cities, and only has its labor and family-life being examined; but there is none of an organic and vivid representation of its organic life and historical subjectivity.[66]

Indeed, Jia Zhangke himself has admitted that he "keeps wondering how many startling memories remain concealed…when the workers stop talking and remain silent. Perhaps those silences are the most important."[67]

Apparently, while he indicts the "inhuman" cost or sacrifice of the socialist period in the name of progress, he does not yet touch the hidden secrets within this silence, which runs throughout the movie.

CONTRADICTIONS OF CONTEMPORARY CHINA FROM AN ELITE'S PERSPECTIVE

A Touch of Sin has received an enormous amount of attention and has been shown in many countries (including the U.S.A., France, the U.K., Germany), winning the 66th annual Cannes International Film Festival's award for best screenplay, as well as other notable international awards. In comparison with the director's other prize-winning works, the uniqueness of *A Touch of Sin* lies in its content as well as its form. For example, Isabelle Regnier expresses her surprise: "Who would have predicted the genial Jia Zhangke could produce such a violent film? Who could have believed Jia would express such unconcealed violence on the silver screen in such a delightful manner?"[68] Marie-Pierre Duhamel also enthusiastically recommends, "Many comments will no doubt be made about a 'new' trend in Jia Zhangke's cinema. As he himself puts it, *Tian zhu ding* is a 'martial arts film for contemporary China,' paying direct homage to director Hu Jinquan (King Hu, as he was known in the West) and nourished by the vision of martial arts films like those of Chang Cheh."[69]

Indeed, the film's content is gory and violent, making very controversial. Nevertheless, Jia has argued that his film is one about "modern chivalry" that follows the examples of the classics of "Wuxia" works (the Chinese martial art filmic genre). Does this mean that the film develops upon the traditional concept of "chivalrous spirit?" How does Jia judge societal conflicts? Since the film shows the desperation faced by people enduring humiliation and their final retaliation, considering Jia's other films thus far, which sympathetically portray the lamentable lives of the lower classes in the spirit of critical realism, we could wonder whether this film reaches a new critical stage of revolutionary realism? Against many popular opinions, I suggest that, although the film focuses on acts of rebellion, it takes a reactionary stance against the age-old Chinese tradition of chivalry, which shows the elite's viewpoint on social contradiction at odds with the ordinary populace.

Critical Realism or Revolutionary Realism?

The film is roughly divided into 4 parts, based on four real-life stories that had caused a sensation across society. The audience can easily identify the four cases: the 2001 Hu Wenhai incident, the 2009 Deng Yujiao incident, the 2012 Zhou Kehua incident, and the Foxconn labor workers suicides that have taken place since 2010. But we should analyze how this film has adapted these incidents, in particular from which points of view, and how it attempts to communicate this to us. The four sections of the film are the stories of Dahai, San'er, Xiaoyu and Xiaohui.

Dahai, who is from a Chinese village, holds great animosity towards the village leader as well as his former classmate Jiao Shengli, who collude with each other in monopolizing the village mines. After arguing numerous times with them and trying to appeal to a higher authority, not only never getting a satisfactory explanation but also even being bitterly humiliated, he is infuriated to the extreme. One day, he murders the village head as well as the village accountant, and even carelessly kills a carriage driver who is mistreating his horse. He becomes so enraged that even the doorman is not spared.

Wandering from place to place, San'er rushes home before the Spring Festival begins in order to celebrate it with his seventy-year-old mother. However, he purchases a gun from an unknown source and kills three hooligans who try to rob him in the street. After staying at home for a few days, he sets out again. Following a couple after they exit a bank, he murders both of them to steal their money. In a cold and cruel manner, he rides off on his motorcycle.

Working at a massage parlor, Xiaoyu hopes that she can establish a stable relationship with her lover, a private entrepreneur. However, the businessman offers various excuses to avoid the commitment. After she sends him away, the man's wife shows up to humiliate her for what she is doing. Shortly after, a domineering client who wants more than just a massage curses and beats her; in a fit of rage, Xiaoyu stabs this pig-headed patron to death in the manner of a classical chivalrous knight.

A migrant laborer, Xiaohui, strikes up a conversation with his fellow worker, which leads to this workmate inadvertently being injured and having to rely on disability allowance. To avoid shouldering the responsibility, Xiaohui flees to Dongguan, a famed "sex capital" in southern China, to work in a night club. He unexpectedly meets a beautiful girl from his hometown there. But, when love cannot override the cruel reality, he jumps to his death without any forewarning.

The four stories are seemingly unrelated to each other but, in effect, are subtly connected. The relationship between time and space in the four sections is also ingeniously constructed. The director has explained his scheme:

> The relationship of space: (in terms of the four locations) Shanxi, Chongqing, Hubei, Guangdong...(they are) exactly running through China's North to South. Whereas (in terms of) the relationship of time: The four stories revolve around the Spring Festival. The first takes place prior to the Spring Festival, centering on the atmosphere of returning home; the second occurs during the middle of Spring Festival; the third happens after the festival, showing the character returning back to work; and the fourth occurs outside of this time interval. I have studied the narrative skill of many Chinese classical novels; therefore (the movie) follows rigorously the structure of "four steps of composing an essay."[70] Thus, I have written the film into one story instead of four separate and unrelated small ones. The first story is the one that shows the setting (the unequal dispersion of wealth); the second story reveals the lives of the characters (including that of husband's and wife's, brother's, and family's): (there is an absolute equalitarianism that) the remaining cigarettes needs to be divided into three parts; the third story discusses the issue of dignity in detail; the fourth story displays an omnipresent, implicit violence. While all the three stories are about killing, the last one deals with self-annihilation.[71]

This explanation provides us the directorial scenario. The first story introduces the great divide between the wealthy and the poor, and the collusion between officials and merchants. This lays out the backdrop of the era and society in which the film is set. The second story reveals the lives of the average person, as well as their relationships in society in this atmosphere. Afterwards, it shows Chinese peoples' social customs, and what can happen when one's honor and dignity are violated. Finally, under this inescapable net of circumstances, the film reveals how a normal person can resort to self-destruction when ubiquitous violence envelops him.

On the surface, the director aims to disclose the existing social contradictions from the perspective of the ordinary population. For example, he has explained his concern in the first story. The prototypical incident "takes place in my home province of Shanxi, where the village government's corruption and the increasingly unequal allocation of wealth have forced farmers to take up arms. The focus of the contradiction is the coal mine's privatization and the unfair distribution of wealth."[72] Corresponding to this theme, the film's use of the three traditional Shanxi opera arias also makes the audience recall classical Chinese stories such as "Tragedy of Dou'e" and "the rebellious Lin Chong forced to raise the standard of revolt." Jia has admitted his source of inspiration:

> I have come to realize that the plights of the characters in the film are very similar to stories found in martial art movies. I'm very happy to have found a suitable cinematic language to describe contemporary China... I have discovered that these events are one and the same as those found in *Water Margin* of the Song Dynasty and Hu Jinquan's works of the Ming dynasty (here the director makes a mistake by taking the famed Taiwan auteur Hu Jinquan as one living in the Ming dynasty). In the transformation of society, a single person can only take up violence when facing a crisis."

Jia adds, "However, these are all tragedies."[73] For the sake of showing this timeless condition, he spends a lot of time developing the characters. For example, Dahai is modeled on Lu Zhishen, while San'er is created according to the image of Wu Song. Both characters are heroes found in the Chinese classic *The Water Margin*. Additionally, the feature of Xiaoyu mixes the image from Hu Jinquan's *A Martial Woman* with the image of Lin Chong in his red trial clothes in *Ye Zhu Lin (Wild Bear Forest)*, which is a famed piece from the Beiing opera. Besides, the film also directly uses some particular scenes from classical Chinese dramas to arouse intertextual associations. When the climax scene of the opera *Lin Chong Escapes to Liangshan at Night* is performed on stage, the camera cuts to Dahai, who is holding his hunting rifle aloft and beginning his journey on the violent road to revenge. Before Xiaoyu surrenders herself to the police, she is watching *Su San in Chains (Su San qi jie)*, a famed segment in the traditional opera piece *Yu Tangchun*, which narrates how a courtesan, Su San, is wrongly accused of murder and subsequently becomes a helpless victim of the corrupt judicial system. On the stage, Su San is weeping, while the corrupt official behind her shows his shameless, sinister face, the image of which provides a striking contrast to that of Xiaoyu's tragic experience. Critics thus are inclined to believe that:

> this repertoire plays the exact part it plays in real life: it provides expression, postures and moves to the victims of injustice to whom expression and action have been denied. A heroic posture for the humblest, a

dignified image for those who do not count. It goes for Dahai and his "Water Margin" move, for Xiaoyu's *wuxia* killing gesture, and even for San'er's use of the gun in the opening sequence.[74]

Jia emphasizes that, if "we examine case by case, all the incidents are incidental. However, as these incidents occur one after the other, they become non-accidental. I feel that I must use the multiple narratives to present this 'accidentalness'."[75] The process through which Dahai's violent tendencies erupt is comparable to the stories from *Water Margin*, which shows the inevitability of his being forced to rebel. Dahai tries to expose the corrupt behaviors by every means possible, yet he receives scant attention. Even when he goes to the post office to mail a complaint letter to the disciplinary committee of the Party, he is kicked out because he is incapable of writing the address clearly enough. In light of this, the director's rhetoric of the "inevitability of accidentalness" is much like the logic taken by those works of revolutionary realism—the irreconcilable nature of social contradictions leads to the eruption of revolution.

However, what is peculiar is that, besides these associations, we can see no more comparable reasons for Dahai's revolt—and even fewer for other characters in the film. For San'er, we are completely left with no clue as to why he would decide to murder someone and steal from them. Xiaoyu also only acts out in a moment of impulse when the customer looking for more than a massage humiliates her. Xiaohui is much like the other Foxconn factory workers in the daily news, who do not take resistance as an option but blindly annihilate themselves. Therefore, although the film uses images of small animals as metaphors for the conditions in society,[76] in comparison with the resolute attitudes of the heroic characters in *Water Margin*, the characters here appear irrational and abnormal.

We need to note that the film's inspiration in no way arises from the rebellious spirit represented by the heroes from *Water Margin*, which has been often rejected by China's "public intellectuals," who regard the revolts as nothing but unlawful riots against the modern spirit of civil society. The director himself, greatly influenced by this trend of thought, clearly explains that he opposes using violence to combat violence:

Reading Weibo, Mr. Jia said, made him realize that violence wasn't an occasional misfortune visited on an unlucky few, but a fundamental thread running through Chinese society and culture. "In Chinese culture, violence is always used to solve problems," he said, citing Mao Zedong's famous adage that "political power grows out of the barrel of a gun."

"The potential for violence lurks in everyone. It's just that people manage to control themselves," he added.[77]

Then, where does the inspiration come from? Upon scrutiny, it comes from the director's understanding of the Chinese chivalrous spirit (*Xiayi*). As he says, the movie "focuses on establishing a relationship between ancient and contemporary people, whereas the tie for this relationship is this chivalry."[78]

It is well-known that the Chinese tradition of chivalry opposes tyrannical rule, fights crime and addresses injustice, while simultaneously helping the innocent. Do the characters in the movie measure up to these standards? Jia has made comments on this matter:

> As for the definition of Xia (martial or chivalrous man, [侠]), because they have superb martial arts, so they fight injustices and stand up for the innocent. In the film, I have taken the four characters to represent these type of person, but they have trouble even in taking care of themselves. From the perspective of human nature, I feel that they are fighting for their dignity and self-respect... In the movie, these characters are the surviving "Xia," or the residual Xia. This is because from the perspective of our cultural background, in the past, underneath the long-time reigns of authoritative regimes, we have fundamentally lacked the spirit of self-protection and dignity. However, this movie's four leading characters seek to reaffirm their honor in the last moment. When ordinary people find themselves in a crisis, in the end they will become a Xia.[79]

Here, the director substitutes one concept for another, or re-defines the original meaning. What he does is replace the chivalrous spirit, which resists oppression and thus is compatible with the modern revolutionary spirit, with the liberal concept of self-preservation and safeguarding one's honor.

Although peasant rebellion was highly praised in Mao's era for its pursuit of justice and its revolutionary qualities, Mao also stresses its historical limitations for its shortage of political vision. Moreover, *Water Margins*, and traditional novels like it, were never extolled as works of "revolutionary realism." We have also noted the director opposes any violence, "I feel that using violence to fight violence is not a good way, including those martial art films which idealize heroism, because tragedy and injury is unavoidable [in the process]."[80] This viewpoint echoes Chinese public intellectuals' position of anti-revolution, a conservative stance particularly targeted towards the socialist revolution. It is in light of this knowledge that we can understand that not only does the movie not follow the spirit of revolt of *Water Margin*, but is also in direct opposition to the political message of "revolutionary realism." Consequently, we can comprehend the paradox: on one hand, the movie seemingly shows the despair and reluctance of the characters at the last moment when they have no alternative option; on the other hand, what it highlights is the senselessness and cruelty of the violence to which they resort.

The Origin of Tragedies

So, what, essentially, is the ultimate cause of the various tragedies portrayed in the film? After carefully examining the narrative strategy of the movie, we would find that every example comes from the idiosyncrasies and perversities of the protagonists.

First and foremost, the indirect cause of Dahai's deadly violence is introduced by presenting his interrogation of the accountant and the chairman of the board, as well as by showing his fury towards the village head. Through this the film reveals that the privatization of public property and monopolizing of local coal mines are the result of a collaboration between officials and the businessman. However, there is simultaneously an implicit narrative thread. It meant to foreground his personality and character in order to tell another story. In this less obvious line of narration, Dahai appears to be well-known in the village as a reckless man. After he loses the battle over ownership of the mine, he becomes jealous of the boss and spiteful towards the village cadres who are depriving him of opportunity; finally, he decides to appeal to a higher authority. However, after he is beaten and humiliated by the rival party, he begins ranting about how these men are stealing his fortune and proclaims, "I can be 10 thousand-times more evil than them."

Thus, his behavior is atypical—he cannot be viewed as a representative of ordinary villagers in China. The unspoken reason for his exposure of the collaboration is implied to be his own selfish interests. Although on the surface, he continuously poses the question, "What happened to the item in the original contract which stipulates that 40 percent of the royalties should belong to the villagers?," we never see any other villagers express the same discontent as him. Conversely, as he is going from place to place explaining how he is going to spill the beans about the village leader's corruption, the other villagers simply ridicule him. In addition, we are not shown one piece of evidence to indicate that he is suffering in any way. On the contrary, he parades around in his army greatcoat, appearing robust and energetic. We can only conclude that he is merely vengeful out of jealousy. After he makes the chairman of the board (who was his classmate in elementary school) lose face, as expected, he is taught a lesson by the man's lackey when he is hit over the head with a golf club, which earns him the nickname "golf ball." Due to this, he becomes a buffoon in the eyes of the entire village. Since he loses control of the mine as well as the opportunity to share the profits, he vengefully makes his wicked pledge. Thus, his horrendous murders are nothing more than a personal vendetta—or a murderous ploy between businessmen with interests in conflict.

Besides, the movie also hints that the other cause for Dahai's deadly action comes from the vicious spirit and influence of Chinese traditional chivalrous fiction such as *Water Margins*. In addition, it is also subject to the (bad) influence of the extreme Maoist ideology. The latter is less noticable; only traces can be detected. Dahai wears an army greatcoat, the style of which was often seen in the Maoist era. When he opens his cabinet before he sets out, we see a row of similar greatcoats, which confirms his identity as retired military personnel ready to return to combat. When he holds his weapon as he crosses the plaza, there is a statue of Mao in the background gesturing to go forward, which hints at the fact that Maoist ideology is still present in Chinese society and Dahai is deeply affected by the "ultra-leftism" which promotes violence.

Therefore, Dahai, a murderous villain, is subject to the impingement of Maoist education from the "extremist era"—at least this is the message we get from the movie. Also, from what his past lover has criticized him about, we learn that he has been viewed by others as unimportant and a "nobody" ever since he was a child. This older lover, who has already married someone else, blames him for not taking the initiative to find a wife and a proper job: "If you have so much free time, why do you not open up a small restaurant or a store? You can earn more cash in this way so as to get yourself a wife, and be in control of your own life. Why bother with taking care of what they are doing?" Dahai has no response to this. Put another way, he is indolent and makes a fuss over nothing, which arises from his jealousy of the rich, as well as his frustrations over the loss of monopoly.

For San'er, why does he commit the brutal murders? We barely see any cues. While he seems to be a dutiful son to his mother, he curiously does not pay her a courtesy call. When his mother sees him, she does not show any expression of happiness. Even his son avoids touching him (probably because of the unfamiliarity, or his cruelty). When he is with his two elder brothers, they have to share three cigarettes together. In other words, we do not see much genuine interpersonal affection between him and his close relatives. During his mother's seventieth birthday, all he does is stare coldly at his mother. His conversation with his wife is also devoid of emotion, and he even goes as far as to allow her to go and find another man. His wife does not know where her husband has gone, neither does she know where he will be going. Apparently, being an adult, he cannot realize his self-worth. Finally, hearing the sound of a gunshot, he finds something to catch his interest. Being a loser, just like Dahai, he takes his son outdoors during New Year's Eve. During the magnificent fireworks display, he says to his son, "Let me give you a firework to see!" Then he shoots his gun in the air. This scene gives the audience a hint: he has already taken firing a gun as a kind of entertainment. As his feelings towards his mother and brothers have gradually become indifferent, his tragedy has become rooted in this insipidness. In other words, a desperate man loving ease and detesting work, he is merely searching for stimulation in life. To make money, he could do anything, fair or foul. After coldly and indifferently killing a couple who are withdrawing money from an ATM, his at running away and evading the police betrays him to be a habitual recidivist (Fig. 6.7).

Fig. 6.7 A low-angle shot highlighting San'er's supercilious nonchalance showing his firing like setting off fireworks

On the other hand, why does Xiaoyu, who appears soft and agreeable, become so violent as to kill the whoremonger? Discovering the cause will explain why the representation of her experience must be divided into two parts. The prior section shows her relationship with her lover; and the later section presents us her encounter at the nightclub. Xiaoyu and her paramour, a factory owner, have passionate feelings. Yet, there is no alternative and the businessman cannot escape from his wife's control and get a divorce. This makes her feel very disappointed. After the owner leaves, Xiaoyu is beaten up on the landlady's instructions and loses her face in public. It is obvious that she feels humiliated, which brings out her distorted psychological state. The next section then turns to her work environment. As a receptionist at the sauna, two clients mistake her for a prostitute and insist that she gives them a massage. She firmly refuses their demands, but is beaten by the crazy clients. In a moment of hysteria, she takes a fruit knife that is close by and kills the man insulting her. Wandering around in the night aimlessly, she soon makes a phone call to turn herself in. Apparently, the accumulated sense of humiliation has reached its point of no return, causing her psychological state to become distorted. In conclusion, it is not the oppression of some evil forces that push her to take a path of no return; on the contrary, the movie shows that it is her doubtful morality and her loss of her self-respect that result in her frantic state, in which her own paranoiac character plays a significant role.

Lastly, why does the worker, Xiaohui, decide to kill himself? On the surface, he is very different from the previous three characters; they killed to vent their sense of infuriation and frustration. Yet, Xiaohui is similar to the others, for they all bear feelings of desperation and self-annihilation; they all behave suicidally, rather than take any action of chivalry. When Xiaohui works in a workshop, his trivial talk causes his co-worker to injure his hand, and Xiaohui runs away to Guangdong to avoid paying the absence fee for the boy. This makes him seem to be a person who is accustomed to retreating from responsibility. Like San'er, he loves leisure and hates work. Upon hearing that working at the nightclub in the sex capital Dongguan makes more money and is easier to do, he decides to travel there. During this time he meets a girl who is also a fellow villager, and they develop feelings for each other. Xiaohui thus proposes that they elope together, which nevertheless violates professional ethics. However, the innocent looking lover—or his mistress—turns out to have a three-year-old child and thus cannot leave with him. Unable to endure the fact that the girl he loves works as a prostitute (an ambiguous scene reveals this secret), Xiaohui changes his job again and goes to a restaurant to work. However, his measly salary at this time is unable satisfy his family's demands; a particular close-up scene delivers this message. In a phone call he receives, Xiaohui's stern face implies that he is being interrogated: Why haven't you sent any money back? Is it because you are spending money wastefully outside? The incessant complaints cause Xiaohui to collapse psychologically. At that time, the co-worker to whom he caused the hand injury comes to him to take revenge, which is the final straw. Without leaving any note behind, he climbs on top of the balcony and jumps off.

This is the reason that the movie offers to account for the workers' suicides in the Foxconn factories. It is nothing other than their own failure in terms of their personal affections and professional careers. Therefore, the responsibly lies not in the exploitation and inhuman management of the capitalist entrepreneurs; rather, it is in the callousness of the worker himself and his moral laxity. The responsibility even extends to his family education: his mother's phone call shows no care for her son's life, instead, he is blamed for sending such a small amount of money and spending it carelessly, which is an act of violence in itself. Overall, it is the personal (and familial) problems of the lower class themselves that lead to the tragedy. This kind of diagnosis typically reflects the elites' understanding of the under-classes.

Some may probably protest in this regard: is it not that the film shows these people being forced onto a desperate life path? Actually, this is where the film pretends to advance along one path but secretly takes another. Let us first look at how it lays out the villains and evil forces. Dahai's opponent is the village head, as well as the businessman Jiao Shengli, who was also his elementary school classmate. The village head does not show up until towards the end of the movie; facing Dahai's long barrel rifle, this upright-looking leader (by his dress he even looks like Jiao Yulu, the model cadre the Party has promoted for a long time) appears very calm and instructs him: "Calm down. Is there anything that we cannot sit down and discuss?" But Dahai completely loses his reason and goes mad. Moreover, how much evil intent caused by inflated selfish desires would it take for Dahai to unexpectedly commit this act on his elementary school classmate? When we see Jiao Shengli the first time, he is wearing a pair of sunglasses and a black cloak, taking an airplane and arriving in the village. He looks handsome and is reminiscent of the appearance of film star Chow Yun-fat in the film *A Better Tomorrow* (1985). He is, indeed, a hero of contemporary society, with an ambitious will in this era's surge of market economy. He obviously cannot help having his subordinates teach Dahai a lesson; afterwards, he provides Dahai handsome compensation. Facing Dahai's gun barrel, he shows no sense of panic, but just calmly informs Dahai, "Whatever you demand, just speak up."[81] In sum, we are unable to see how these "evil people" would engage in collusion to embezzle state-owned resources, and we are unable to feel any sense of disgust with them. Neither can we find this action to have caused the ordinary villagers any loss. As for those less important characters such as the apparently honest accountant, he always appears helpless in front of Dahai, which reminds us that he is passive and reluctant, even though he may have to prepare false accounts on the orders of the authority. When Dahai comes to his house for the last time wanting to take his life, under the threat of the gun barrel he has to write down the confessions Dahai says, just like as he has to do to appease the higher authority. Yet, while his wife attends to Dahai in a friendly manner, Dahai, who has been filled with hatred, brutally kills both of them.

The three bandits San'er encounters in the street look just like him. As soon as he pulls out his gun, they all begin to panic; but even though they run away, San'er is mercilessly determined to take their lives. Obviously, he is not doing this for the sake of justice but, rather, for a certain idiosyncratic addiction to and fetish for murder. The identity of the couple that San'er subsequently kills is unclear; judging by their ordinary dress, they are probably normal citizens. Thus, the audience can only suppose that his action arises from his absurd hatred of the rich. When the man sees his wife being killed, he courageously faces the barrel of San'er's gun, which gives the audience a feeling that he is the one who is truly righteous and courageous. It is evident that San'er's cruelty has caused him to appear inhuman.

How about the evil forces that push Xiaoyu to revolt? She is the mistress of a factory owner played by the well-known Chinese actor Zhang Jiayi, who is famous for his guileless face, being solemn, and looking tall and strong. Facing Xiaoyu's pressure, he appears helpless, and tells her that he has already informed his wife of the situation, although he has not explained to her everything; thus, all he can do is to plead for Xiao Yu to wait for some time. But Xiaoyu resists his pleas, claiming that, at her age, she cannot wait any longer and will only give him six months to think over clearly who he really wants to be with.

This pitiable businessman later appears in Xiaohui's factory. He is so busy and devoted that, even when he is having lunch, he is simultaneously teaching Xiaohui to be an upright man. Not only does he not fire the worker who has been crippled, but also negotiates with Xiaohui—the reason being that, since Xiaohui is responsible for the injury, he should give the injured worker his salary as compensation. This penalty—if there is any—is reasonable, and shows the owner's unbiased and excellent management talents. Even the man bullying Xiaoyu is excusable, because it is caused by a misunderstanding: he does this simply because he feels that she looks down upon him. It is her own idiosyncratic personality which, out of a freakish sense of self-respect, brings out the inexorable consequences. This causes her to endure suffering unnecessarily. Moreover, the person hitting her is "Xiao Wu," a protagonist in one of the director's earlier movies; he is a man that, although he has many defects, is ultimately still a kind-hearted person (Fig. 6.8).[82]

Indeed, the powerful and rich, who in the classical works of revolutionary realism appear as an oppressive evil force, take on a new appearance here. Regardless whether one considers them to be lacking empathy or sincerity, they are also just ordinary people like you and me, and thus do not deserve the violent reaction taken to them. This presents a sharp contrast to the archetypal characters in both the classical work *Water Margin* and the modern revolutionary novels. The movie thus presents its own understanding of the contemporary Chinese upper class. In

Fig. 6.8 Displayed in a medium shot, Ladies in opera dress perform pornographic shows to entertain the nouveau riche

another scene, which lasts two minutes or so and shows the extravagant lifestyles of the Chinese new rich, the director Jia Zhangke himself makes a guest appearance as a member of the nouveaux riches from Shanxi going to Dongguan's well-known nightclub "World Paradise" looking for happiness. He passes a group of young girls wearing Chinese Red Army uniforms, which apparently is a satire on the changed nature of the ruling class. The uniform is a symbol of revolutionary passion past and present; however, here it works to stimulate sexual desire. In less than one minute, Jia the businessman does three things: buys a painting by the Chinese artist Xu Beihong (1895–1953), makes an appointment with friends to go to Macau gambling and orders the service of a bargirl. However, this glance at the life of the nouveaux riches does not truthfully portray the era. When Xiaohui's girlfriend provides sexual services, the customer does not force her, neither does she show any unhappiness. Instead, we just witness that she closes her eyes, smiling in the face of adversity. This is the "professional spirit" that Chinese "public intellectuals" advocate, which also displays their dictum of freedom: if a girl cannot resist the destiny of being raped, then it is better to just close her eyes and enjoy the pleasure.

In all the characters' encounters, we cannot see any reduction of wages, exploitation, and inhuman disciplines and regulations put in place by the capitalists; thus, all the tragedies seemingly come from the characters' own troubles in terms of their personal failure in forming friendships, finding affection and suffering family stress. When we see that Xiaohui picks the iron club as a weapon looking confused as to where his enemies are, we know that the movie is, indeed, unable to find who is responsible for their tragedies.

Politics of Dignity or Class Polarization?

Therefore, while the movie ostensibly demonstrates the "forced rebellion" of the lower classes, what it actually shows is the humiliation of their sense of dignity. Moreover, this humiliation is closely related to their own moral flaws. Thus, we can understand why the director contends that "the cause of violence lies in the society, but it is also related to psychological problems. Violence is all related to dignity; it occurs at the moment when one feels deprived of dignity."[83] But this is a deceptive rationale that bypasses, if not deliberately glosses over, the economic stratification, which brings out class polarization. As in the earlier films,

Jia is trying to express the voice of the oppressed; or, rather, he intends to represent the society's under-classes who are often subjected to humiliation. But his way of doing this is to disclose their privacy and their tendency toward egalitarianism, which is due to their poverty. By exposing their weaknesses in terms of personality and their defects in morality, the movie essentially holds that the underprivileged should, to a large extent, be responsible for their miserable lives. For instance, as one critic aptly observes:

> We have a deeper understanding of poverty from San'er…The elderly brother of San'er introduces the detailed expenses of the birthday feast to his two younger brothers and distributes the remaining money to them accordingly. He even divides the nine cigarettes into three parts (reflecting the humbleness of people from the countryside and their yearning for equality and justice…). Such emphasis on equality arises from extreme poverty while extreme egalitarianism only leads to greater poverty. Poverty is sometimes not the problem. What really matters is the frustration arising from poverty. On the eve of the Chinese New Year, a group of people get together for Mahjong and make fun of each other and their wives, indicating the latter's pornographic services under the disguise of work. They seem to find superiority by disparaging each other and even engage in a physical fight. Poverty has successfully eroded the innocence of the countryside and the pitiful dignity of all.[84]

Consequently, the movie also hints numerous times at the "sins" of these lower-class people. In one of these scenes, San'er's girlfriend believes that she is committing sins in her present life and therefore needs to set fish free to compensate for her wrongdoings or "sins,"—this practice is based on the traditional faiths of Buddhism in China. At the end of the movie, the lyrics of the traditional Chinese opera are, "Do you plead guilty?" This then leads to the camera shifting to a group of observers. The implication is more than clear. It is interrogating whether these violence-oriented, lower classes know that they should "plead guilty." At this point, we also come to know why the English name of the movie is taken to be "A Touch of Sin." To the director, sin resides in these people and forms their inexorable burdens, which belief, nevertheless, only reflects the class-based nature of this portrayal and narration. In other words, while the movie ostensibly shows the oppression of the lower class, it is from the perspective of the bourgeois elites and actually purges the oppressors of their "sins."

This said, let us examine the story arcs from the perspective of realism, through which we find that it is based on certain postmodern, "imaginative" poetics. In the introduction to an interview, the director discusses how he created the plot-line. He asks, "How violence is bred in the mundane life? Why a rule-abiding person would become a gunner? It is impossible for us to document the exact process of how violence is bred. The process can only be grasped when we imagine it as a whole, when we delve into imagining the influences of and frustration in the character's interpersonal relations."[85] If this is the case, how does the director imagine the actual events the film portrays?

In the first story, Dahai is the only person in the village who suspects the village head is a corrupt official conspiring with merchants. However, although the villagers cannot benefit from the privatization of the coalmine, neither are their interests undermined. Therefore, Dahai is merely an extremist who cannot win the support of the other villagers. But, if we looked at the real events that have occurred in recent years—e.g. the Qian Yunhui case—we would know that the embezzlement of state-owned assets and interests has always done great harm to the interests of villagers. For instance, in Qian's case, the farming mudflats, which are essential to the living of villagers, were leveled out by real estate developers; the villagers consequently lost their livelihoods. Those who dare to challenge authority on the behalf of villagers normally die in some mysterious incident, just like Qian.

In the second story, because of people's hatred towards murderers such as Zhou Kehua and the unilateral report by the media, we can neither know how a man such as Zhou has become what he is, nor can we understand his inner self. So, in terms of the issue regarding how San'er commits his crimes, we can only infer that "the less distinguished San'er, who is abandoned by modern culture, finally feels a sense of value by controlling the life of others when he hears the gunfire."[86]

In the third story, Xiaoyu is a mistress despised by all, and she kills others due to a misunderstanding. In this portrayal, girls in real life such as Deng Yujiao who stand up against oppression and exploitation become eccentric and morally defective. In the fourth incident, we only see the betrayal of workers to their workmates, their laziness, their frustrations at their failure to satisfy family demands, ignorance and pretense of indignance at social corruptions.[87] On the other hand, the audience does not witness any inhumane behavior in the "blood factories" such as Foxconn, or the physical and mental traumas caused by it (Fig. 6.9).

Fig. 6.9 The closeup shows Xiaoyu turning chivalrous

This pretension of understanding the life of the oppressed and assuming the role of its spokesperson typically shows the ability of contemporary Chinese cultural elites to comprehend. Keep this in mind, we can further appreciate the features of the movie's aesthetics—i.e. the alleged modeling of characters after the ancient chivalrous heroes. For example, why does Xiaoyu suddenly turn herself into a chivalrous knight, which is accompanied by exaggerated, "heroic" actions and music? While critics easily find the real absence of chivalrous spirit in the movie, they generally fail to perceive the deconstruction of the spirit of chivalry in the name of humanism and anti-violence. That is to say, the film takes the lower class's last resort as the spontaneous eruption of their original sinful ideas, which are subject to the poisonous influence of ancient Chinese novels and the pollution of Maoist "extremist" doctrines. And although the oppression of the lower classes is revealed to a certain extent through various metaphors, it distorts and defames the images of the lower classes due to its bias. As a result, the audience cannot infer the causes for the characters' desperation from a social-economic-political perspective; the audience merely experiences their coldness and cruelty. In addition, as the director does not show their pain (e.g. the reluctance to become a prostitute), we are unable to understand why they feel they have to commit suicide, or why they have to kill others, for the director does not show their pain.

To understand why the director adapts the real-life events in this way, we need to analyze his attitude towards reality. In other words, his adaptation corresponds to his ideological concepts. Jia believes that the changes in China behind these events are "pains occurred during China's

Fig. 6.10 Presented in a long shot, Dahai kills the head of the village in front of the magnificent, ancient temple

modernization process."[88] That is to say, this is the unavoidable cost of the objective of modernization. On the surface, this is a cliché associated with the discourse of modernization since the 1980s. But, in essence, it is nothing but the official's version of "mainstream melody," which calls for people to understand and accept the "birth pains" by upholding the socialist spirit of sacrifice. This meant, to "take the general situations into consideration," in order to accommodate the neoliberal reforms that have taken place since the 1990s. The director not only advocates this neoliberal creed, but also aligns his views with those of public intellectuals: i.e. what is lost in this process is traditional morality and the awe of authority. Hence, we witness the scene in which the village head solemnly maintains his dignity before being killed by Dahai, which takes place in front of the magnificent, ancestral temple (Fig. 6.10).

When producing the movie *Xiaowu*, Jia Zhangke used to say that, "When a society is moving ahead rapidly do not ignore those who are knocked over by you simply because you want to get ahead."[89] Many people quote it as a comment on this movie. It sounds similar to a comment made by public intellectuals during the high-speed train accident that took place in 2012. This reads: "Oh, China, please slow down the pace of your development! Please take care of the lives of your citizens!" The problematic of political line and the economic orientation of China's neoliberal reform is simplified as a problem of speed and, therefore, the issue of class stratification is converted into cheap, humanistic care, although such care seems to be in the disguise of a criticism of capitalism:

Economic development is not equivalent to the development of civilization. Instead, it widens the gap between economic activities and value concepts. Rapid development of the economy and continuous expansion of living space offer people more opportunities to enjoy life. However, the Chinese who used to emphasize family life and lack ultimate care and a sense of social justice are increasingly staying away from the normal social practices' or are occupied by money worship with the encroachment of capitalism. These fully tragic images [of the movie] constitute a mosaic portrait of China and display the loss in connection with defected personality and missing morality.[90]

Apparently, in such a spirit of critical realism, a fundamental social issue is displaced to become an issue of defective personality and lost morality. The exploitation and oppression, in the plutonomic sense, is substituted with a pseudo proposition that the Chinese should embrace the "ultimate care and a sense of social justice." Money worship is believed to be a negative phenomenon unavoidable in the process of economic development. Under the guise of a sympathetic portraiture, the "sins and faults" of the "criminals" are hinted at being the consequences of their greediness, desire and other "original sins;" and their forced but unwilling outburst is taken as a spectacle (Fig. 6.11).

The original Chinese title of the movie is *Tianzhuding*, which means "Decided by Fate." This "fate" is not the implication of destiny in any religious sense; it "evidently refers to the dramatic impulse that moves

Fig. 6.11 A wide-angle, medium shot displays a pornographic show in an entertainment bar

tragedy," which is not caused by the "pitiless authority that makes the characters...be subjected to unfair powers and rebel against their evil sentences"[91] Rather, their plights are caused, to a large extent, by these social outcasts' own weak human nature. It is in this light that Jia claims that "this film represents part of the missing picture to these (real) events," and "I wanted to explore a deep contemplation of two factors. One is the social roots of violence and the second is violence that has its roots in a very human level."[92] Apparently, the "second level" is taken by him to be what is "missing" in the general picture.

Compared with his previous works, Jia does not completely change his style in the movie. Instead, he only incorporates elements of gang movies, Kungfu movies and comedies, which bring out a sense of nervousness that we have never seen in him before. It interrogates those that have been humiliated and defamed "Do you plead guilty?" and does not concern itself with how they could attain justice. Instead, it uses a series of religious images to insinuate how the sinful souls of the lower class can be "purged."[93] To the director, who originates from the lower class but has ascended to the elitist circle through personal effort, these disoriented murderers are pitiful; also, those ordinary people that used to be pillars of Mao's socialist era appear foolish and numb, as the apathetic faces of the people watching folk opera performances demonstrate. As a matter of fact, Xiaoyu, who loiters in the numb crowd and has seemingly deep thoughts like an intellectual featured at the end of the movie, could be taken an incarnation of the director himself with the mindset of elitism.[94]

However, self-contradiction is unavoidable if the movie meant to distort social conflicts in this way. It is noteworthy that "sin" has a totally different meaning from "罪 (crime)" in Chinese. In Christianity, it refers to the "antagonism of human beings towards the will of god, and is inherited through generations." Jia "accepts such a Christian definition in an ambiguous way and believes that the human beings are destined to be sinful in nature and that such sins are inherited through generations."[95] This is witnessed in the director's attempt to attribute the faults of the under-classes to their "original sin." However, Jia also seems to be endorsing their "claims for justice and antagonism against violent authority" when he says that, "I feel that all the four characters have a rebellious personality, which I value very much. It is a quality that China is losing gradually, for all of us have been conditioned to submit to authority...[yet] such a personality needs to be preserved."[96]

In reality, such recognition of the "rebellious personality" originates from the Maoist revolutionary concept, which holds that "wherever there is oppression, there is resistance." However, since Chinese elites are antipathetic to the socialist idea of revolts against the oppressive ruling class, they have to treat the rebellions of the under-classes as nothing but ignorant, destructive and worthless behavior.

NOTES

1. Peter Hitchcock, "The Paradox of Moving Labor: Workers in the Films of Jia ZhangKe."
2. Hubert Vigilla, "The Director and Star of A Touch of Sin Discuss the Changing Face of China."
3. Jason McGrath, *Postsocialist Modernity*, 10.
4. Ibid., 11.
5. Sebastian Veg, "Introduction: Opening Public Spaces," 7.
6. Kin-Yan Szeto, "A Moist Heart," 102.
7. Hubert Vigilla, "The Director and Star of A Touch of Sin Discuss the Changing Face of China."
8. Fredric Jameson, "Globalization and Political Strategy," 56.
9. Shuqin Cui, "Negotiating In-Between," 112.
10. Kin-Yan Szeto, "A Moist Heart," 102.
11. Shuqin Cui, "Negotiating In-Between," 115.
12. Kin-Yan Szeto, "A Moist Heart," 103.
13. Ma Ning, Ni Zhen, et al., "Xuezhe Shanghai duihua *Shijie*."
14. The Soviet Union was regarded as the epitome of "social Imperialism" in the Maoist era through the 1960s–1970s. Mongolia was the ally of the Soviet Union at the time.
15. Shi Xiaoling, "Between Illusion and Reality: Jia Zhangke's Vision of Present-Day China in *The World*," 221.
16. Ibid., 227.
17. Shuqin Cui, "Negotiating In-Between," 114.
18. Manohla Dargis, "Caged in Disney in Beijing, Yearning for a Better Life," 11.
19. Shuqin Cui, "Negotiating In-Between," 116.
20. Kin-Yan Szeto, "A Moist Heart," 103.
21. Xiaoling Shi. "Between Illusion and Reality: Jia Zhangke's Vision of Present-Day China in *The World*," 220.
22. Walter Benjamin, *Illuminations*, 257–258.
23. Robert Koehler, "The World," 57.
24. Charles Pierre Baudelaire, *Artificial Paradises*, 7.

25. Modris Eksteins, "Ragpicker: Siegfried Kracauer and the Mass Ornament," 609.
26. Zhangke Jia, *Zhongguo Gongren Fangtanlu*, 3.
27. Edmund Lee, "Invisible Cities: An Interview with Jia Zhangke."
28. Reuters/Hollywood Reporter, "'24 City'—A Moving Elegy to Modern-Day China."
29. Yan Liu, "'Gongren Laodage' Zuihoude Jiaguo Shenying."
30. Reuters/Hollywood Reporter, "'24 City'—A Moving Elegy to Modern-Day China."
31. A.O. Scott and Manohla Dargis, "Reality Rudely Intrudes in the Screening Rooms."
32. Richard Corliss, "Cannes Gets Real."
33. Jim Hoberman, "The Cannes Film Festival Thus Far."
34. Scott Tobias, "Movie Review: *24 City*."
35. Edmund Lee, "Invisible Cities: An Interview with Jia Zhangke."
36. Peter Bradshaw, "Review: *24 City*."
37. Hsiu-Chuang Deppmana, "Reading Docufiction: Jia Zhangke's *24 City*," 188.
38. Peter Bradshaw, "Review: *24 City*."
39. Ibid.
40. Critic Jim Hoberman notes that this is an "offbeat, vaguely absurd" detail: "an elderly worker walking past the doomed plant holding aloft her bag of IV fluid as if it were a torch of freedom." See Jim Hoberman, "A Chinese Factory Reborn as Condo Heaven in *24 City*."
41. Born in 1958, we might surmise that Minhua did not receive the official and orthodox teaching of national history, and thus is susceptible to the popular, revisionist historical narrative nowadays, i.e. flattering the contributions of the Nationalist Party during the Anti-Japanese War.
42. Yan Liu, "'Gongren Laodage' Zuihoude Jiaguo Shenying."
43. Ibid. Excerpt from Jinhua Dai, *Yinxing Shuxie*, 217.
44. According to an online report, we are justified in believing that there was a scene in the domestic version that was deleted for a particular reason (possibly the over-long running time of the movie). In this episode, Nana confesses that her greatest wish is to "make lots of money" and to "buy an apartment for my parents at the 24 City." Workers living an arduous life like her parents could not afford such good accommodation. But an agent such as Nana could become financially sound enough to afford a much better life. The socialist concept of "labor is the greatest honor in life" cherished by her parents became mindless, if not thoroughly abandoned, in the post-socialist era. Thus, when watching the scene in the foreign version in which the heroine declares that she would buy an apartment for her parent because "I'm the daughter of a worker!," critic

Jim Hoberman notes that the "apparent hollowness of this proletarian pride…is accentuated by a burst of ambient technopop." Jim Hoberman, "A Chinese Factory Reborn as Condo Heaven in *24 City*."

45. Edmund Lee, "Invisible Cities: An Interview with Jia Zhangke."
46. Yan Liu, "'Gongren Laodage' Zuihoude Jiaguo Shenying."
47. Ibid.
48. Ibid.
49. Ibid.
50. Ibid.
51. Edmund Lee, "Invisible Cities: An Interview with Jia Zhangke."
52. Jim Hoberman, "A Chinese Factory Reborn as Condo Heaven in *24 City*."
53. Yan Liu, "'Gongren Laodage' Zuihoude Jiaguo Shenying."
54. Edmund Lee, "Invisible Cities: An Interview with Jia Zhangke."
55. Zhiyuan Xu and Zhangke Jia, "Duihua: Lish yu Shidai."
56. Yan Liu, "'Gongren Laodage' Zuihoude Jiaguo Shenying."
57. Ibid.
58. Ibid.
59. Ibid.
60. Ibid.
61. Peter Bradshaw, "Review: *24 City*."
62. Ibid.
63. Yan Liu, "'Gongren Laodage' Zuihoude Jiaguo Shenying."
64. Ibid.
65. Zhangke Jia, *Zhongguo Gongren Fangtanlu*, 3.
66. Yan Liu, 'Gongren Laodage' Zuihoude Jiaguo Shenying."
67. Zhangke Jia, "What Remains Is Silence," 57.
68. See Isabelle Regnier, "A Touch of Sin": et le doux Jia Zhangke dégaina son sabre."
69. Marie-Pierre Duhamel, "Cannes 2013. Consistency in a Filmmaker's World: Jia Zhangke's 'A Touch of Sin.'"
70. It is a classical technique with which to compose an article, and comprises four parts: an introduction, elucidation of the theme, transition to another viewpoint and summary.
71. Anonymous, "Jia Zhangke Niuyue tan tianzuding."
72. Ibid.
73. Ibid.
74. Marie-Pierre Duhamel, "Cannes 2013."
75. Ibid.
76. It is implied that, in society, the weaker and underprivileged are tortured and waiting to be slaughtered, whereas evil forces are like leopards and tigers unsheathing their claws, and snakes and rats crossing the street.

77. Olivia Geng, "Jia Zhangke Explains Why Censors Are Scared of His Award-Winning Film." Weibo is a Chinese microblogging and social media website, just like Twitter in the West.
78. MTime Cannes Report Team, "Jia Zhangke Reveals His New Work 'A Touch of Sin'."
79. See Anonymous, "Jia Zhangke Niuyue tan tianzuding."
80. Ibid.
81. Moreover, when his wife reappears in the fourth section of the movie, this attractive woman, in her face full of sadness, is kind Xiaoyu, who is just seeking employment. Apparently, the episode is meant to deliver the message that it this kind-hearted businesswoman is handing the under-class a life-line.
82. Critics note this contextual message, e.g. Marie-Pierre Duhamel points out, "Xiao Wu has a filmic biography that made him a small town crook again in *Ren xiao yao*. In *Tian zhu ding*, Wang/Wu dies under the blade of the film's lady knight... He did not make a big fortune, his money came from local corruption. The banknotes he slaps Zhao Tao's Xiaoyu with are somehow archaic." Marie-Pierre Duhamel, "Cannes 2013."
83. See Anonymous, "Jia Zhangke Niuyue tan tianzuding."
84. See Haiyan Xu, "Jingyin shenjiao xia shehui wenti de chengxian jiqi Juxianxing."
85. CineVue, "Look Back in Anger." Interview with Jia Zhangke and Zhao Tao on *A Touch of Sin*, 2013.
86. See Haiyan Xu, "Jingyin shenjiao xia shehui wenti de chengxian jiqi Juxianxing."
87. The film shows Xiaohui and his girlfriend reading news via an ipad and posting a rubbish message for each piece of news, which is meant to show that the lower classes do not understand social injustice at all, but simply pretend to have a sense of justice.
88. See Anonymous, "Jia Zhangke Niuyue tan tianzuding."
89. Zhang Yaxuan, Jian Ning, and Jia Zhangke, "Fangtan: Ba Jia Zhangke gao qingchu."
90. See Haiyan Xu, "Jingyin shenjiao xia shehui wenti de chengxian jiqi Juxianxing."
91. Marie-Pierre Duhamel, "Cannes 2013."
92. Hubert Vigilla, "The Director and Star of A Touch of Sin Discuss the Changing Face of China."
93. For example, "Two Catholic nuns next to a martyr horse in Dahai's story, magical snakes around Xiaoyu and buffalos watching over her desperate night flight, a duck promised to sacrifice in San'er story, a few fishes 'liberated' by Lianrong to please Buddha...." Marie-Pierre Duhamel, "Cannes 2013. Consistency in a Filmmaker's World: Jia Zhangke's 'A Touch of Sin.'"

94. It is noted that "Zhao Tao's expressive face and focused talent inspire the filmmaker's figure of womanhood. A wanderer in cities, a melancholic image of an endless quest and of a hard to tell grief." Marie-Pierre Duhamel, "Cannes 2013."
95. See Haiyan Xu, "Jingyin shenjiao xia shehui wenti de chengxian jiqi Juxianxing."
96. See Meng Pan, "Meiyou Yinyu, Zhiyou Xianshi: New York Tianzhuding Jia Zhangke Zhuanfang."

REFERENCES

Anonymous. "Jia Zhangke Niuyue tan tianzuding." (2013, September 30). http://blog.sina.com.cn/s/blog_6a1894c10101ly9d.html. Accessed May 6, 2016.

Baudelaire, Charles Pierre. *Artificial Paradises*, trans. Stacy Diamond. New York: Citadel Press, 1996.

Benjamin, Walter. *Illuminations: Essays and Reflections*. New York: Schocken Books, 1969.

Bradshaw, Peter. "Review: *24 City*." *The Guardian*, April 29, 2010. http://www.theguardian.com/film/2010/apr/29/24-city-review. Accessed April 11, 2016.

CineVue. "Look Back in Anger." Interview with Jia Zhangke and Zhao Tao on *A Touch of Sin*, 2013.

Corliss, Richard. "Cannes Gets Real." *Time*, May 17, 2008. http://www.time.com/time/arts/article/0,8599,1807446-2,00.html. Accessed April 10, 2016.

Cui, Shuqin. "Negotiating In-Between: On New-Generation Filmmaking and Jia Zhangke's Films." *Modern Chinese Literature and Culture* 18 (2) (2006): 98–130.

Dai, Jinhua (戴锦华). *Yinxing Shuxie* (隐形书写) [*Invisible Writings*]. Nanjing: Jiangsu Renmin chubanshe, 1999.

Dargis, Manohla. "Caged in Disney in Beijing, Yearning for a Better Life." *New York Times*, October 11, 2004, p. B5.

Deppmana, Hsiu-Chuang. "Reading docufiction: Jia Zhangke's *24 City*." *Journal of Chinese Cinemas* 8 (3) (2014): 188–208.

Duhamel, Marie-Pierre. "Cannes 2013. Consistency in a Filmmaker's World: Jia Zhangke's 'A Touch of Sin'." *Notebook*, May 17, 2013. http://mubi.com/notebook/posts/cannes-2013-consistency-in-a-filmmakers-world-jia-zhangkes-a-touch-of-sin. Accessed January 29, 2016.

Eksteins, Modris. "Ragpicker: Siegfried Kracauer and the Mass Ornament." *International Journal of Politics Culture and Society* 10 (4) (1997): 609–613.

Geng, Olivia. "Jia Zhangke Explains Why Censors Are Scared of His Award-Winning Film." http://blogs.wsj.com/chinarealtime/2014/03/14/jia-zhangke-explains-why-censors-are-scared-of-his-award-winning-film/. Accessed November 12, 2015.

Hitchcock, Peter. "The Paradox of Moving Labor: Workers in the Films of Jia ZhangKe." https://cinemastudies.sas.upenn.edu/events/2013/October/ColloquiumPeterHitchcock. Accessed May 17, 2016.

Hoberman, Jim. "The Cannes Film Festival Thus Far." *The Village Voice*, May 20, 2008. http://www.villagevoice.com/film/the-cannes-film-festival-thus-far-6388296. Accessed April 16, 2016.

Hoberman, Jim. "A Chinese Factory Reborn as Condo Heaven in *24 City*." *The Village Voice*, July 29, 2009.

Jameson, Fredric. "Globalization and Political Strategy." *New Left Review* 4 (2000): 49–68.

Jia, Zhangke (贾樟柯). *Zhongguo Gongren Fangtanlu* (中国工人访谈录) [*Interviews of Chinese Workers*]. Jinan: Shandong Huabao Chubanshe, 2008.

Jia, Zhangke. "What Remains Is Silence." *China Perspectives* 1 (2010): 54–57.

Koehler, Robert. "The World." *Cineaste* 30 (4) (2005): 56–57.

Lee, Edmund. "Invisible Cities: An Interview with Jia Zhangke." *Time Out*, June 19, 2009. https://www.timeout.com/london/film/invisible-cities-an-interview-with-jia-zhangke-1. Accessed April 11, 2016.

Liu, Yan (刘岩). "'Gongren Laodage' Zuihoude Jiaguo Shenying" ("工人老大哥"最后的家国身影) [The Last Image of Chinese Working Class Brothers]. *Zhongguo Jingji* (中国经济) [*Chinese Economics*] 7 (2009).

Ma, Ning (马宁), Ni, Zhen (倪震), et al. "Xuezhe Shanghai duihua *Shijie*' (学者上海对话世界) [Scholars from Shanghai Are Discussing *The World*]. *Dongfang Zaobao* (东方早报) [*Oriental Morning Post*]. 2005, April 7.

McGrath, Jason. *Postsocialist Modernity: Chinese Cinema, Literature, and Criticism in the Market Age*. Stanford, CA: Stanford University Press, 2008.

MTime Cannes Report Team. "Jia Zhangke Reveals His New Work 'A Touch of Sin'." http://news.mtime.com/2013/04/18/1510504.html. Accessed May 6, 2016.

Pan, Meng (潘萌). "Meiyou Yinyu, Zhiyou Xianshi: New York Tianzhuding Jia Zhangke Zhuanfang" (没有隐喻, 只有现实——纽约《天注定》贾樟柯专访) [No Metaphor, Only Reality—Interview of Jia Zhangke on *A Touch of Sin* in New York]. http://cinephilia.net/archives/21539. Accessed December 1, 2015.

Regnier, Isabelle. "'A Touch of Sin': et le doux Jia Zhangke dégaina son sabre." *Le Monde*, May 13, 2013.

Reuters/Hollywood Reporter. "'24 City' a Moving Elegy to Modern-Day China." (2008, May 18). http://www.reuters.com/article/review-film-24city-dc-idUSN1846231420080519. Accessed April 10, 2016.

Scott, A.O., and Manohla Dargis. "Reality Rudely Intrudes in the Screening Rooms." *New York Times*, May 19, 2008. http://www.nytimes. com/2008/05/19/movies/19cann.html?_r=2&scp=13&sq=Cannes+-Film+Festival&st=nyt&oref=slogin#. Accessed April 10, 2016.

Shi, Xiaoling. "Between Illusion and Reality: Jia Zhangke's Vision of Present-Day China in *The World*." *Asian Cinema* 18 (2) (2007): 220–231.

Szeto, Kin-Yan. "A Moist Heart: Love, Politics and China's Neoliberal Transition in the Films of Jia Zhangke." *Visual Anthropology* 22 (2009): 95–109.

Tobias, Scott. "Movie Review: *24 City*." http://www.avclub.com/review/24-city-28819. Accessed April 13, 2016.

Veg, Sebastian. "Introduction: Opening Public Spaces," *China Perspectives* 81 (2010): 4–10.

Vigilla, Hubert. "The Director and Star of A Touch of Sin Discuss the Changing Face of China." (2013, October 9). http://www.flixist.com/interview-jia-zhangke-zhao-tao-a-touch-of-sin-216577.phtml. Accessed January 15, 2016.

Xu, Haiyan (徐海燕). "Jingyin shenjiao xia shehui wenti de chengxian jiqi Juxianxing" (精英视下社会问题的呈现及其局限性) [Displaying Social Problems from an Elites Perspective and Their Limits]. Bachelor's thesis, Xiamen University, 2015.

Xu, Zhiyuan (许知远), and Jia Zhangke (贾樟柯). "Duihua: Lish yu Shidai" (对话:历史与时代) [Dialog: History and the Era]. http://www.eduww.com/Article/200904/23710.html. Accessed December 12, 2015.

Zhang, Yaxuan (张亚璇), Jian Ning (简宁), and Jia Zhangke (贾樟柯). "Fangtan: Ba Jia Zhangke gao qingchu" (访谈:把贾樟柯彻底搞清楚) [Interview: Understanding Jia Zhangke]. http://cn.cl2000.com/film/dypx2.shtml. Accessed January 1, 2008.

CHAPTER 7

Conclusion: The Politics of Dignity and the Destiny of China's New Wave Cinema

It has been observed that visual culture in contemporary China is marked by a "hasty embrace of digitized simulacrum and the consumerist model," and "billboards, glamorous stars, and images of the nouveaux riches are dictating what people see and hear."[1] Within this milieu, through revealing "shifting classes, as well as gender and economic forces that increasingly drive human relations," Chinese New Wave cinema laudably shows, as critic Kin-Yan Szeto puts it, the "human consequences of China's reconfiguration of socioeconomic power, especially its impact on the vast working class."[2] This heightened desire for authenticity, as well as "recording and witnessing the twisted mindset, the drift of life experience, the loss of meaning, and the disintegration of the social fabric," seeks what scholar Ban Wang calls "truth against commercial technique, melodrama, and simulacrum."[3] On the other hand, Chinese film critics have also noted that its thematic concern merely shows "the humanistic search for the meaning of life, which is typical of young filmmakers and hardly revolutionary."[4] Consequently, as critic Ma Ning suggests, and as is also widely acknowledged, "the humanistic values so prevalent in underground films do not constitute a serious challenge to mainstream ideology."[5] Why is that so?

The so-called "mainstream ideology," from Ma Ning's point of view, probably refers to the dogmatic Marxist-Leninist orthodoxy, which, indeed, China's New Wave cinema does not openly criticize. Paul Pickowicz has arguably suggested that this is due to self-censorship.[6]

© The Author(s) 2018
X. Wang, *Ideology and Utopia in China's New Wave Cinema*, Chinese Literature and Culture in the World, https://doi.org/10.1007/978-3-319-91140-3_7

By all accounts, if China's New Wave cinema intends to denounce the state's lip-service to Marxist ideology, it should have exposed the incongruence between alleged socialist ideology and pro-capitalist reality; however, it has little interest in doing so. But what cannot be neglected is that, in reality, the mainstream, or dominant, political idea being asserted by the Chinese government at the present moment is not the socialist ideology that opposes oppression and exploitation; rather, it is the so-called Chinese value of "harmony." This concept is allegedly founded on "traditional" Confucian values; in actuality, it is but an incarnation of a sort of political pragmatism predicated upon the harsh censorship of dissident voices and violent suppression of protests from workers, peasants, and other citizens whose constitutional rights are inexorably violated and trampled. In terms of this ostensible sacred moral compass of harmony (also the typical ideology of the middle class, which yearns for a long, peaceful life) which often calls for the lower class's willing cooperation (in the name of the so-called socialist spirit of sacrifice) for its pro-capitalist reform agenda, China's New Wave cinema eagerly accepts and endorses this with its artistic orchestrations. However, it does so not in the name of socialism but, rather, in the spirit of humanism.

To attain this invaluable harmony, while the government resorts to censorship and suppression, the directors of Chinese New Wave cinema rely on the discourse of dignity. When responding to the reporter's inquiry, "Do you think there's any way to end the cycle of violence as presented in the movie (*A Touch of Sin*)?," Jia Zhangke's answer is: "I think the film serves to describe and observe these events because that forms a kind of necessary platform to change. In our current social reality in China, I think we need to have a deeper focus on respecting other people and respecting one another's freedom and pride."[7] In other words, to him, "the most extreme form of violence is to take away a person's pride or dignity with your violence."[8]

The English term "dignity" is derived from the Latin word *dignitas*, meaning "worthiness" in the early thirteenth century[9]; its modern usage, however, denotes respect and status. It is often used in discussions about ethical-moral and political issues to proclaim that a human being has inalienable rights to be respected and to receive proper treatment.[10] Thus, it could be taken as an inheritance of the Enlightenment concept of inherent, inalienable human rights.[11] In this light, "*human dignity* and *human rights* are two separate and interdependent concepts."[12]

In the contemporary era, human dignity is often applied in a negative way—namely, to criticize the unfair treatment of oppressed and vulnerable groups. In other words, the concept of human dignity in the modern era is often used in legal documents as the foundation and justification for human rights, and in the moral-philosophical arena as encapsulating rights, duties, and honor, and is defined negatively as against the humiliation of human worth.[13]

From this perspective, it is highly reasonable to witness its omnipresent existence in the New Wave cinema which concerns the outcasts and underprivileged in China who are the leftovers of globalization. This sincere concern for the downtrodden and unlucky—due to a humanist spirit, which essentially calls for a universal equity of brotherhood—accounts for its appeal.

Nevertheless, it is also noted that human dignity can be used as a linguistic symbol to "represent different outlooks, thereby justifying a concrete political agreement on a seemingly shared ground":

> The very fact that various worldviews and ideologies are strongly related to the concept of human dignity produces a paradoxical situation in that human dignity *as for itself* does not contain any concrete content or meaning. Because human dignity anchors different worldviews, it cannot represent any particular set of values or meaning that "naturally" stem out of it. There is no fixed and universal content that spouts out of human dignity and, hence, *its content and meanings are determined separately in each legal document in accordance with the political agreement achieved at that time.*[14]

In other words, as Doron Shultziner aptly notes, "the content of human dignity is a corollary of a political agreement and compromise set in each legal document by the cultural, political, constitutional and other conditions, which can evolve and change in the course of history."[15]

Since human dignity can be defined as "the particular cultural understandings of the inner moral worth of the human person and his or her proper political relations with society,"[16] we might consider the differences between the liberalist and the socialist concepts of dignity. It is widely acknowledged that "in liberal-democracies, human dignity is inseparably understood as granting all citizens equal rights without any sort of discrimination."[17] As Charles Taylor aptly summarizes, "with the move from honor to dignity has come a politics of universalism, emphasizing the equal dignity of all citizens, and the contents of this politics has been the equalization of rights and entitlements."[18] Accordingly, it brings out the politics of equal dignity and the politics of difference, the latter being the inalienable part of the former, demanding recognition of the unique distinctness of a certain group of community.

Thus the politics of recognition arrives on the scene, which, being "formulated in the 1990s, developed out of political movements centered upon such concepts as gender, sexuality, race, ethnicity and culture,"[19] becomes an indispensable component of the modern theory of justice contributing to contemporary identity politics. However, this politics of recognition is usually discussed merely from the cultural perspective; some scholars decline the inclusion of the issue of redistribution in the topic, because "recognition seems to promote differentiation," whereas "redistribution supposedly works to eliminate it."[20] However, as Nancy Fraser has pointed out, "economic inequality cannot be reduced to cultural misrecognition"; rather, for her, "injustice in the form of both misrecognition and maldistribution is detrimental to the extent that it inhibits participatory parity."[21] Thus, she proposes that, since recognition and distribution are both irreducible for justice, a radical restructuring of society is necessary, one attained by socialist transformative redistribution and cultural deconstruction or revolution.[22]

The major premise underlying these discussions is that the honor and dignity of the lower classes are not adequately respected; rather, they are disregarded, violated and trampled. By contrast, in the long process of China's socialist revolution, the innate moral goodness of the laboring people had been recognized ever since the time of the New Culture Movement (roughly between the mid-1910s and 1920s) by China's early socialist thinkers such as Chen Duxiu (1879–1942) and Li Dazhao (1889–1927). After the working-class state of the People's Republic was established in 1949, the workers enjoyed unprecedented dignity, honor, political-economic privileges and social welfare, proudly becoming the leading class as the socialist party had promised. In terms of both cultural recognition and economic redistribution, they reaped the benefits of the Maoist Revolution. As Wang Hui aptly summarizes, "In contrast to the classical liberal perspective which views equality only in terms of the rights of citizens and the right to vote in elections, socialism and socialist democracy hold that equality must be expanded into the economic realm because inequality within modern economies has already produced new hierarchical and hereditary systems, which invalidates the politics of dignity."[23] As he further perceptively remarks, this "demand for economic equality brings collectivities with a common goal and their distribution mechanisms into the politics of equal recognition, which conflicts with a view of rights centered purely on the individual."[24]

As Wang observes, the modern concept of dignity, closely tied to class and nation, arose with the reappearance of a hierarchical system after the decline of the aristocracy and its corresponding value of honor. After that, "the universalist politics of dignity and the political struggle for equal recognition" were witnessed in the "opposition and competition between the liberal democratic model and the socialist movement and its attempt to establish workers' state."[25] Studying the nineteenth-century Chartist movement in Britain, social historian Dorothy Thompson finds that this working-class movement, as an organized resistance from the lower orders fighting the capitalist mode of production and its social-political consequences, brought dignity to the disenfranchised.[26] Referring to Maoist China as an example, Wang points out that the dignity of the laboring class was safeguarded by several concrete institutions during the socialist period:

> Political justice in a workers' state was a universalist justice with the concept of class at its center. It included the leading role of the working class, the political foundation of the alliance between the workers and the farmers, the nation-state as the general representative, and an internationalism focused on the oppressed classes and the oppressed nations. Within this framework, the question of the dignity of the working class was the question of the liberation of classes and the universal liberation of humanity.[27]

The competition between the two models ended when socialism was seemingly defeated after 1989; consequently, cultural pluralism emerged out of the debate of the politics of difference or recognition, substituting the idea of class struggle and socialism versus capitalism to challenge the liberalist version of recognition and respect in the rhetoric of politics of difference. However, in recent years, the issue of economic inequality has again resurfaced, when financial crisis leads to polarization between the rich and poor, as well as deepened social divisions, which is instrumental to a reconsideration of the problematic of class politics.

Therefore, the problems of class and dignity are closely tied. As Wang convincingly argues, in China, "the failure of modern worker states and of the decline of class politics" has caused "the rupture of representativeness in domestic and international political relations," which is also witnessed by the fact that:

The concepts that structured the politics of dignity within twentieth-century China, such as class, the political party of a class and the associated political categories were long ago or are currently being replaced by the concepts of modernization centering on "development." The theory of the "end of history" seeks to finish the "history" organized by those categories. After the great changes of 1989–91, politics relating to the Chinese Revolution and the workers' state have even been regarded as standing in opposition to the politics of dignity.[28]

Therefore, as happened in the West, the discourse of dignity in China also rarely touched upon the political economy of the (shortage of) dignity in this age of semi-neoliberal reform—namely, the pro-capitalist exploitation and repression.

Unfortunately, this trend for de-politicization also engulfs China's New Wave cinema in this post-socialist era. While the directors are concerned with the destiny of the underprivileged and outcasts—in addition to the fact that many social-political problems are usually dealt with in their films in a similar way to personal issues, or are formulated to be an exploration of human nature, intended or not, with the effect of causing catharsis—these movies also often release the audience's anxiety brought about by the rapidly "transformative" era with its ruthless social-economic arrangements. One constant situation is that the relentless class struggle is transformed to be allegorically akin to a practice of self-immolation, or internecine fights among homogenous groups of people with a universal human nature. Meanwhile, the dire consequences of semi-neoliberal reform are merely understood to be the unfortunate aftermath of the lure of materialism. Thus, rather than composing a salient and poignant critique with a political edge, many of these features ultimately only become a nuanced melodrama behind the façade of what is commonly understood as an "art film."

In this regard, we need to further reflect further upon why directors only concern themselves with personal rights (thus, an individual-centered dignity) rather than the collective-oriented political-economic rights of the lower classes. It is well-known that the middle-class West cherishes the rights centered purely on the individual, and what we often hear nowadays in China's mainstream media. It is widely observed that "the post-socialist condition is fraught with experiences of fragmentation and anxiety in addition to the awakening of new desires and identities."[29] One of these desires is to get as rich as possible during the rising tide of globalization. This desire, to be sure, emerged as early as the 1980s when official policy encouraged the populace to rid itself of poverty. But the urge to become nouveaux riches reached a feverish level when the new round of reform and opening-up, with the tenet of "establishing the socialist market economy," launched itself with a fanfare which attracted unprecedented numbers of the rank and file. Therefore, one of the new characteristics of Chinese identity, which most social elites desire to acquire, is membership of the club of the so-called "middle class." The Sixth Generation is no exception.

Although they were penniless when they started their careers, after they made their names and achieved distinctions at the international film festivals, the cultural capital brought about economic privilege. In addition to continually obtaining handsome funds from transnational investors—after the government extended its olive branch to them in 2002 with the promise of allowing their films to be given public release—the great appeal of the vast domestic market converted and included most of these elites. The outcome is obvious; one critic is thus so skeptical of the self-marginalized position now that he contended, "this position is partly a strategy used by the filmmakers to gain publicity and increase their professional profile before joining the mainstream film industry."[30] Meanwhile, if, in regard to the ruling party, the "increasingly close alliance between capital and power has made the state's 'representation' of the rights and interests of labor increasingly hollow,"[31] then, in reference to these avant-garde "intellectuals", their self-proclaimed role as spokespersons of the people becomes unstable. Even their early banner of self-proclamation—"My camera doesn't lie!"—becomes a hollow slogan the validity of which is discredited. Since the middle class's (and even the new poor's) "concern for individual rights and related political reforms does not fundamentally conflict with the system of values of the newly emergent socioeconomic system,"[32] it is not surprising to find that the directors of China's New Wave cinema has moved "towards the new mainstream in terms [of] narrative, narration, and visual style" ever since the New Century.[33]

However, this is not totally their fault. Jameson has informed us that "ultimately, any discussion of globalization surely has to come to terms, one way or another, with the reality of capitalism itself."[34] However, Wang Hui also finds that while "China's economic policy and developmental trajectory are locked into the process of capitalist globalization, whose outcomes have included successive financial crises and growing social tensions and inequalities;" in China, "capitalist globalization is never viewed as a factor in the contradictions and conflicts of interest at the national level."[35] In this regard, the directors of China's New Wave cinema, just like the common populace, have yet to be sufficiently well-equipped to learn and cope with the capitalist reality.

On the other hand, Wang also contends that "the class phenomena" of contemporary Chinese society differs from the "class politics" of the past two centuries.[36] One of the differences is that the political consciousness of the Chinese working class is difficult to attain:

> the most striking fact is this: instead of being able to constitute themselves as an urban working class, members of this massive wage-earning workforce – 225 million by the end of 2008 in the official account, with 140 million as migrant workers…are not able to reproduce themselves as a "full proletarian" materially and culturally in the cities.[37]

Thus, Wang uses the term "work resistance" rather than "class struggle" to describe "the political character of the labor movement as it currently stands," and makes the following inquiry and judgment:

> to what extent does prominent movement centered on preserving legal rights (*weiquan*) amount to "class struggle," and to what extent does it amount to no more than a struggle to preserve the interests of urban residents? While class struggle is a movement that transforms society and the system of production, the *weiquan* movement is a struggle, which uses the legal framework of this system to defend individual rights.[38]

As a result, the resistance "fights for incremental improvement within the transitional system rather than overturning it entirely;" and "attempts to preserve legal rights have been ineffective or largely ineffective for those workers who have not received the protection of labor laws."[39] Furthermore, there is no vista of the alliance of the new workers and the new poor on the horizon to facilitate the emergence of a progressive social movement. As Wang Hui asserts:

> Even as contemporary media flourishes and the division between classes widens, it is difficult for the new workers and the "new poor" to achieve genuine social unity and political cooperation. Thus there seems to be little prospect of their social unity and cooperation producing a new politics.[40]

Nevertheless, we need to explore any opportunity to change the status quo which is unfavorable to the laboring class, one means of which would be to undertake a study of the "archeology of the future" to reactivate the socialist inheritance. Wang further elaborates:

> If we can say that at the heart of de-politicization is the subversion and weakening of political values, then the road to re-politicization must lead through a reconstruction of political values, an activation of our political space and political lives, and the destruction of the order of depoliticized politics and de-ideologized ideology.[41]

In this regard, we still see many opportunities. It has been pointed out that it is "not only the party's official socialist slogans per se, but also their re-appropriation by various Chinese social forces and the unfolding societal processes of subordinating both state and market to the social needs of the working people, [that] are what the struggle for socialism in China is about."[42] For instance, Wang argues, "reaffirming and defending the rights and interests outlined in the constitution of the socialist state is an effective path toward linking legal justice and political justice."[43]

In this light, the New Wave Cinema produced by the Sixth Generation filmmakers vanishes. This is not necessarily because it has accomplished its self-styled mission to successfully change the collective socialist theater to an individualistic (and essentially bourgeois, in my view) cinema—which is but its ideological fantasy. Rather, it is because Chinese society has almost completed its transfiguration after two decades of pro-capitalist, semi-neoliberal reform, which speaks to its historicity. In this regard, it is instrumental for us to recall the history of Italian neorealism, which rapidly declined in the early 1950s due to the gradual rises in income levels, which meant the themes of neorealism such as poverty and despair seemingly lost their contemporary relevance. By contrast, many Italians began favoring the optimism shown in American movies at that time. The post-war Italian government also disliked the films that were made for, in a nation anxious to pursue prosperity and change, the vision of the neorealist cinema was seen to be demoralizing. Consequently, Italian cinema in the 1950s shifted from the neorealist focal point of humanitarian concerns to a more humanist-oriented focus. Rather, cinema was concerned with the frailty of the human condition (such as alienation from society and failure to communicate), which took place in the subsequent decade. All of these events can be compared to the fortunes of China's New Wave Cinema, as China also experienced dramatic economic growth, since the 1990s, which contributed to the fanfare of the discourse of the so-called "Rise of China."

When the Conclusion to this inquiry—a preliminary study—was nearly complete, the editor sent me some cover designs for me to peruse. I was a little surprised to find that one of them is the logo of the Hong Kong Film Festival Award, which has little to do with Chinese New Wave cinema. However, after careful consideration, I finally decide to make it my final choice. There are several reasons for this selection. First, many Chinese Sixth Generation directors, early in their professional careers, had sent their "underground," "independent" films to Hong Kong to solicit various awards within the international filmic circle, so as to raise sponsorship for their next production. Some of them did achieve their financial support there and received their first pot of gold accordingly—Jia Zhangke being the most prominent among them. They were not the first group to do so, however. Fifth Generation directors such as Zhang Yimou and Chen Kaige had been their pioneers. In the meantime, Hong Kong cinema has always provided a reference and a model for these two generations of auteurs. To win an award or receive acclaim at the Hong Kong Film Festival is always a dream for them. Second, although the image of the goddess reminds us of the Statue of Liberty of the United States, it is more reminiscent of the statue of the Goddess of Democracy in Tiananmen Square in 1989. This statue was erected by the students, articulating their hope that China would become more democratic. China's Sixth Generation auteurs are from exactly that 1989 generation. They could also be called the post-1989 generation, for most of them experienced their intellectually formative years during the 1980s, and graduated from college and initiated their professional careers after the student movement was suppressed in 1989. Consequently, the ideas for Western-style liberty and democracy which were popular in the "high culture fever" of the 1980s took root in their minds. Though little trace of this desire has appeared in their cinematic works, the fashionable trend of repudiating Marxist thoughts and its methodology of class analysis apparently continues to have an effect upon their intellectual world, which then set limits on their cinematic work. Third, this image of a Goddess holding a star (like a moon) in her hand also recalls the traditional Chinese legendary character Chang'e, the Chinese goddess of the moon. The subject of several legends in Chinese mythology, she generally symbolizes the will to immortality, liberty and beauty; nevertheless, she is also often believed to be lonely and narcissistic. Also, in this sculpture, we witness an idealistic gesture of pursuing her ideal above ordinary people's understanding and beyond their political-economic stakes, which shows a sort of elitism that the directors of China's New Cinema more or less share.

Indeed, China's New Wave cinema's humanitarian concern regarding the underclasses in its early period rapidly shifted to a humanist ethos of making inquiry of human nature, which looks little different from the official rendition of the underprivileged. In fact, since becoming elites themselves, and since the convergence of their social-political ideas with the authoritarian regime, most of the directors of the New Wave cinema have themselves unabashedly embraced commercial culture and proudly walked into mainstream cinema, although some of them still more or less wish to entertain the dream of adding a few elements of "art film" into their productions.

However, since the politics of dignity in China nowadays frequently comes across the politics of recognition of the laboring class, which is struggling for its inalienable political-economic rights, the class consciousness of the subaltern is correspondingly experiencing fast growth, even though it is still waiting for political (re-)education. Therefore, while the destiny of the New Wave cinema is sealed by the limited horizon of the auteurs (and ultimately over-determined by epochal transformation), their utopian impulse, as expressed in their work, still calls for the sublation of the humanitarian spirit of the latecomers.

NOTES

1. Ban Wang, "In Search of Real Images in China: Realism in the Age of Spectacle," 498–499.
2. Kin-Yan Szeto, "A Moist Heart," 106.
3. Ban Wang, "Epic Narrative, Authenticity, and the Memory of Realism," 211–212.
4. Shixian Huang, "Diliudai," 25. Quoted from Chen Mo and Zhiwei Xiao, "Chinese Underground Films: Critical Views from China," 149.
5. Ning Ma, "Zhongguo dianying keneng cunzai de kunhuo," 64. Quoted from Chen Mo and Zhiwei Xiao, "Chinese Underground Films: Critical Views from China," 152.

6. Paul G. Pickowicz, "Social and Political Dynamics of Underground Filmmaking in China," 16.
7. Hubert Vigilla, "The Director and Star of A Touch of Sin Discuss the Changing Face of China."
8. Ibid.
9. Douglas Harper, "Dignity."
10. As Doron Shultziner informs us, "the meanings of human dignity are socially constructed in accordance with particular cultural and historical contexts." Doron Shultziner, "Human Dignity—Functions and Meanings," 1.
11. It is also observed that in the U.N. documents, "human dignity is regarded as a supreme value that not only stands separated from human rights but also supercedes them. Human rights are derived from human dignity, while the latter encompasses the essential characteristics of human beings." Two conventions of the United Nations reveal the affinity between the two concepts: "recognition of the inherent dignity and of the equal and inalienable rights of all members of the human family is the foundation of freedom, justice and peace in the world. Recognizing that these rights derive from the inherent dignity of the human person." *United Nations Covenant on Economic, Social and Cultural Rights*, adopted by GA Res. 2200A (XXI) of 16 December 1966; *United Nations Covenant on Civil and Political Rights*, adopted by GA Res. 2200A of 16 December 1966, *Preamble* (emphasis added). Quoted from Doron Shultziner, "Human Dignity—Functions and Meanings," 2.
12. Doron Shultziner, "Human Dignity—Functions and Meanings," 1.
13. Ibid.
14. Ibid., 5.
15. Ibid.
16. Rhoda Howard, "Dignity, Community, and Human Rights," 83.
17. Doron Shultziner, "Human Dignity—Functions and Meanings," 17.
18. Charles Taylor, "The Politics of Recognition," 37.
19. Paddy McQueen, "Social and Political Recognition."
20. Ibid.
21. Ibid. See Nancy Fraser, *Justice Interruptus*, 19.
22. See Nancy Fraser, "Rethinking Recognition" (2000); and "Recognition Without Ethics?" (2001).
23. Hui Wang, "Two Kinds of New Poor and Their Future," 182–183.
24. Ibid., 183.
25. Ibid.
26. Dorothy Thompson, *The Dignity of Chartism*.
27. Ibid., 221.
28. Ibid., 181.

29. Jason McGrath, *Postsocialist Modernity*, 2.
30. See Xiong Ying, "Tianjiang daren: diliudai de jiyu yu wenti," 126–127. Quoted fom Chen Mo and Zhiwei Xiao, "Chinese Underground Films: Critical Views from China," 153.
31. Hui Wang, "Two Kinds of New Poor and Their Future," 207.
32. Ibid., 193.
33. Yingjin Zhang, "Rebel without a Cause?" 73.
34. Fredric Jameson, "Globalization and Political Strategy," 60.
35. Hui Wang, "Depoliticized Politics, From East to West," 43.
36. Hui Wang, "Two Kinds of New Poor and Their Future," 181.
37. Yuezhi Zhao, "The Challenge of China," 565–566.
38. Hui Wang, "Two Kinds of New Poor and Their Future," 197.
39. Ibid. Wang further observes that, "Within the new context, attempting to pursue political justice while at the same time avoiding the question of the workers' collective economic struggle, as does the *weiquan* movement to protect legal rights, is an empty, unrealistic dream. If we cannot expand the search for legal justice into an effort to fundamentally change this model of development—that is, if we cannot seriously discuss the relationship between legal justice and political justice—then we cannot fundamentally change the predicament of the workers." Ibid., 210.
40. Ibid., 193.
41. Hui Wang, "Depoliticized Politics, Multiple Components of Hegemony, and Multiple Components of Hegemony and the Eclipse of the Sixties," 700.
42. Yuezhi Zhao, *Communication in China: Political Economy, Power, and Conflict*, 343.
43. Hui Wang, "Two Kinds of New Poor and Their Future," 210.

References

Chen, Mo, and Xiao, Zhiwei. "Chinese Underground Films: Critical Views from China." In Paul Pickowicz, and Yingjin Zhang (eds.), *From Underground to Independent: Alternative Film Culture in Contemporary China*, pp. 143–160. Lanham, MD: Rowman & Littlefield, 2006.
Fraser, Nancy. *Justice Interruptus: Rethinking Key Concepts of a Post-socialist Age*. London and New York: Routledge, 1997.
Fraser, Nancy. "Rethinking Recognition." *New Left Review* 3 (2000): 107–120.
Fraser, Nancy. "Recognition Without Ethics?" *Theory Culture & Society* 18 (2–3) (2001): 21–42.
Harper, Douglas. "Dignity." Online Etymology Dictionary. http://www.etymonline.com/index.php?term=dignity&allowed_in_frame=0. Accessed February 2, 2016.

Howard, Rhoda. "Dignity, Community, and Human Rights." In A.A. An-Na'im (ed.), *Human Rights in Cross-Cultural Perspective: A Request for Consensus.* Philadelphia: University of Pennsylvania Press, 1992.

Huang, Shixian (黄式宪). "Qingchun dubai: qianweixing yu dazhongxing— Zhongguo dianying xinshengdai jiqi xinzuo *Chaoji chengshi*" sumiao (青春独白:前卫性与大众性-中国电影新生代及其新作《超级城市》素描) [Monologues of the Youth: Avant-gardism and Mass Appeal—A Sketch of the Newborn Generation Film *Super City*]. *Dianying shuangzhoukan* (电影双周刊) [*Films Biweekly*] 7 (1988): 70–72.

Jameson, Fredric. "Globalization and Political Strategy." *New Left Review* 4 (2000): 49–68.

Ma, Ning (马宁). "Zhongguo dianying keneng cunzai de kunhuo" (中国电影可能存在的困惑) [Some Possible Confusions for Chinese Cinema]. *Dianying yishu* (电影艺术) [*Film Art*] 1 (2002): 62–67.

McGrath, Jason. *Postsocialist Modernity: Chinese Cinema, Literature, and Criticism in the Market Age.* Stanford, CA: Stanford University Press, 2008.

McQueen, Paddy. "Social and Political Recognition." In *Internet Encyclopedia of Philosophy.* http://www.iep.utm.edu/recog_sp/. Accessed March 17, 2016.

Pickowicz, Paul G. "Social and Political Dynamics of Underground Filmmaking in China." In Paul G. Pickowicz, and Yingjin Zhang (eds.), *From Underground to Independent: Alternative Film Culture in Contemporary China*, pp. 1–22. New York: Rowman & Littlefield, 2006.

Shultziner, Doron. "Human Dignity—Functions and Meanings." *Global Jurist* 3 (3) (2003): 1–21.

Szeto, Kin-Yan. "A Moist Heart: Love, Politics and China's Neoliberal Transition in the Films of Jia Zhangke." *Visual Anthropology* 22 (2009): 95–109.

Taylor, Charles. "The Politics of Recognition." In A. Gutmann (ed.), *Multiculturalism and "the Politics of Recognition."* Princeton, NJ: Princeton University Press, 1992.

Thompson, Dorothy. *The Dignity of Chartism.* London: Verso Books, 2015.

Vigilla, Hubert. "The Director and Star of A Touch of Sin Discuss the Changing Face of China." October 9, 2013. http://www.flixist.com/interview-jia-zhangke-zhao-tao-a-touch-of-sin–216577.phtml. Accessed January 15, 2016.

Wang, Ban. "Epic Narrative, Authenticity, and the Memory of Realism: Reflections on Jia Zhangke's *Platform*." In Ching Kwan Lee, and Guobin Yang (eds.), *Re-envisioning the Chinese Revolution: The Politics and Poetics of Collective Memories in Reform China*, pp. 193–216. Washington, DC: Woodrow Wilson Center Press, 2007.

Wang, Ban. "In Search of Real Images in China: Realism in the Age of Spectacle." *Journal of Contemporary China* 17 (56) (2008): 497–512.

Wang, Hui. "Two Kinds of New Poor and Their Future." In Saul Thomas (ed.), *China's Twentieth Century: Revolution, Retreat, and the Road to Equality*, pp. 176–189. London and New York: Verso, 2016.

Wang, Hui. "Depoliticized Politics: From East to West." *New Left Review* 41 (September–October 2006a): 29–45.

Wang, Hui, "Depoliticized Politics, Multiple Components of Hegemony, and Multiple Components of Hegemony and the Eclipse of the Sixties." *Inter-Asia Cultural Studies* 7 (4) (2006b): 683–700.

Ying, Xiong (应雄). "Tianjiang daren: diliudai de jiyu yu wenti" (天降大任: 第六代的机遇与问题) [An Immense Responsibility: Opportunities and Problems Faced by the Sixth Generation]. *Beijing dianying xueyuan xuebao* (北京电影学院学报) [*Journal of the Beijing Film Academy*] 1 (1995): 126–127.

Zhang, Yingjin. "Rebel Without a Cause? China's New Urban Generation and Postsocialist Filmmaking." *Cinema, Space, and Polylocality in a Globalizing China*, pp. 49–80. Honolulu: University of Hawaii Press, 2010.

Zhao, Yuezhi. *Communication in China: Political Economy, Power, and Conflict*. Lanham, MD: Rowman & Littlefield, 2008.

Zhao, Yuezhi. "The Challenge of China: Contribution to a Transcultural Political Economy of Communication for the Twenty-First Century." In Janet Wasko, Graham Murdock, and Helena Sousa (eds.), *The Handbook of Political Economy of Communications*, pp. 562–563. Hoboken, NJ: Wiley-Blackwell, 2011.

FILMOGRAPHY

1993 *Beijing Bastards* (*Beijing zazhong*).
1994 *In the Heat of the Sun* (*Yangguyang canlan de rizi*).
1995 *Weekend Lover* (*Zhoumo qingren*).
2002 *Blind Shaft* (*Mangjing*).
2003 *Green Tea* (*Lücha*).
2004 *Pirated Copy* (*Manyan*).
2004 *The World* (*Shijie*).
2006 *Summer Palace* (*Yiheyuan*).
2006 *The Contract* (*Zuqi*).
2008 *24 City* (*Ershishichengji*).
2012 *A Touch of Sin* (*Tianzhuding*).
2012 *Eleven Flowers* (*Wo 11*).

© The Editor(s) (if applicable) and The Author(s) 2018   259
X. Wang, *Ideology and Utopia in China's New Wave
Cinema*, Chinese Literature and Culture in the World,
https://doi.org/10.1007/978-3-319-91140-3

INDEX

© The Editor(s) (if applicable) and The Author(s) 2018   261
X. Wang, *Ideology and Utopia in China's New Wave*
Cinema, Chinese Literature and Culture in the World,
https://doi.org/10.1007/978-3-319-91140-3